Perspectives on Development and Population Growth in the Third World

Perspectives on Development and Population Growth in the Third World

Ozzie G. Simmons

Fordham University
The Bronx, New York

PLENUM PRESS • NEW YORK AND LONDON

Library of Congress Cataloging in Publication Data

Simmons, Ozzie G.
    Perspectives on development and population growth in the Third World /
Ozzie G. Simmons.
        p.   cm.
    Bibliography: p.
    Includes index
    ISBN 0-306-42941-1
    1. Developing countries—Population. 2. Developing countries—Economic
policy. 3. Economic development. I. Title.
HB884.S56   1988   88-19866
338.9′009172′4—dc19   CIP

© 1988 Plenum Press, New York
A Division of Plenum Publishing Corporation
233 Spring Street, New York, N.Y. 10013

Printed in the United States of America

To my wife Charlotte

Foreword

Until the early to mid-1970s, social scientists in the fields of population and development were largely going their own ways. Demographers relied almost exclusively on demographic transition theory as their paradigm for understanding the role of development in population change and fertility decline. Conversely, most development economists and other specialists were certainly aware of the constraints placed upon development objectives by population growth. However, the main development theories paid little attention to population and the implications of population growth for development. Indeed it was not until after the World Population Conference in Bucharest in 1974 that the interaction of population and development became a serious and purposive theme for social scientific study. Accordingly, since about the mid-1970s, an extensive literature in the field of population and development has been generated. And in 1975, under the auspices of The Population Council, the journal *Population and Development Review* was founded, a journal which in the past decade has developed into the premier publication in the world for work in this area. But our understanding of development as it refers to change in Third World countries remained fragmented. Moreover, our understanding of the linkages and interactions between population and development was very limited.

It is in this regard that Ozzie Simmons's *Perspectives on Development and Population Growth in the Third World* will certainly have an impact. This extraordinarily important book endeavors to review past and current thinking in the fields of population and development. Professor Simmons is all too aware that even today there is yet no commonly accepted conceptual framework for us to use to understand better the relationships between development policy and population growth. But, he notes, available knowledge does point to recurrent and important linkages, and these in turn are useful departure points for the conceptual and empirical work that remains to be done. And it is in the last chapter of his book that Simmons identifies the tasks that still confront theory and research in the field of population and development.

But the contributions of this superb book go considerably beyond the relevant and important discussions in the last chapter. Professor Simmons guides us through a maze of definitions of development and then articulates the historical context within which development perspectives may be viewed. He presents and assesses the various perspectives that have dominated development thinking, and considers specifically problems of and prospects for equity-oriented development policies. Demographic transition theory, as well as alternative frameworks for understanding population and fertility change, is next considered. Then he analyzes a number of relevant development sectors (natural resources, health, the employment of women, and education) that influence and are influenced by population growth and change.

As already noted, in the final chapter, Simmons reviews and highlights the tasks comprising the research agenda in the field of population and development. These tasks are set forth following a fine review of the various positions assumed by scholars in recent years about the effects of population growth on development. He notes that if the view that population growth is detrimental to development is to continue to be accorded credence, then there is an urgent need for careful and focused empirical research and study on the nature of the interactions between population growth and both economic and social development. This is especially important given the increments of population still in store for the world, i.e., population momentum, as well as the gains in development that have yet to be attained in Third World countries.

In my estimation, two particularly noteworthy points about Simmons's book are his arguments calling for (1) an articulation of quantitative and qualitative analyses, and (2) the investigation of development and demographic variables among the different strata in a country. With respect to the first point, he claims justifiably that if research were designed to collect national- and community-level data on the one hand, and individual- and household-level on the other, the findings would have the potential of substantial application for policy recommendations. Regarding the second, he stresses the importance of investigating relationships among the different occupational, socioeconomic, and cultural groups within a country. Simmons notes that a combined research methodology employing quantitative and qualitative procedures would enable the investigator, for instance, to focus on how changes in incomes and welfare affect reproductive behavior among different groups in the population based on social class, residence, kinship, occupation, ethnicity, and religion. He tells us that research could be designed to test ongoing or projected experimental and innovative program interventions so as to determine more precisely their demographic impacts.

Without doubt our understanding of the interaction and relationship between population and development will be significantly enhanced by a careful reading of Simmons's excellent book. He reviews and synthesizes for demographers the basic features of development economics and for development economists he provides a fine overview of the knowledge base of demography. But, moreover, he attempts to do in his book what no scholar in the past has been able to do successfully: to identify, discuss, and synthesize the linkages and intersections between development and population. In my opinion, he more than accomplishes this laudable task.

DUDLEY L. POSTON, JR.

University of Texas
Austin, Texas

Preface

For a number of years, I left academia and worked in Latin America and subsequently in Southeast Asia in Ford Foundation programs to help strengthen human and institutional resources in those regions in the fields of population research and training, encompassing the relevant social sciences as well as the biomedical sciences. During most of that period, "population and development" served mainly as a slogan for those persons and agencies engaged in international population assistance who wanted to disseminate the message that rapid population growth was impeding economic and social development in the Third World. Not much more than a decade ago, scholars began to consider carefully the complex and difficult questions involved in assessing the implications for processes of development of the determinants and consequences of population growth. A great deal has been published since then on population and development.

When I returned to academia in the early 1980s, I had an unparalleled opportunity to read widely in the literature on both development and population change. Had I known when I worked abroad what I learned from this reading, I might not have had the courage to undertake that work. A number of journal articles and edited collections have made valuable contributions to our understanding of the enormously complex interrelationships between population and development. This book attempts to bring together in one discussion a review of the relevant bodies of literature and a systematic treatment of the principal questions and issues that need to be addressed in this field, as well as to provide a historical perspective on how they have been addressed.

This book is intended for scholars and their students in the several social science disciplines who are concerned with the issues of population and development. But a wider audience is envisaged, namely, those who are part of the "international development assistance community." This group includes not only the representatives of donor governments and multilateral agencies but also, particularly, the policymakers and development planners in the developing countries who serve as the managers of development assistance funds and perform a strategic role in the achievement of development objectives. Thirteen years ago, Lyle Saunders and I wrote about the need for the "policy analyst," a social scientist who could engage in population policy research and who could assume the role of change agent for the government officials in the developing countries who are responsible for public policy intervention relevant to the issues of population and development. Population policy units have since been established in the national planning organizations of a substantial number of developing countries, but as this book shows, much remains to be done in the coordination of development and of population policies.

By inviting me to serve as Distinguished Visiting Professor of Sociology with no specific obligations beyond those I imposed on myself, Fordham University provided me with the time to undertake the reading required for this enterprise and to write the original draft. I am particularly grateful to John J. Macisco, Jr., my long-time colleague and friend, for his helpful criticism, not only of the original manuscript but also of the revised version. His participation extended to teaching jointly with me a course on population and development. This acknowledgment of his assistance cannot begin to repay the debt I owe him.

OZZIE G. SIMMONS

River Vale, New Jersey

Contents

Introduction | 1

Scholars in the fields of development and of population largely went their separate ways until relatively recent years. Explicit and systematic consideration of economic development processes and issues in the Third World began essentially after World War II, although some of the ideas central to development thinking have been around for a long time. Concern with population growth was also mainly a post–World War II phenomenon (with the important earlier exception of the Malthus controversies), but population growth did not engage worldwide attention until the mid-1960s. Attention to the issues raised by the *interaction* of population and development emerged in the 1970s and coalesced as a focus at the World Population Conference in Bucharest in 1974.

Until the mid-1970s, references in the development literature to the links between development issues and population change were sparse indeed. As early as 1970, a few development economists, such as Myrdal (1970), were calling attention to the severe constraints that rapid population growth was imposing on development objectives and urging that the less-developed countries (LDCs) needed to initiate national family planning programs (which, in fact, some LDCs, particularly in Asia, had already proceeded to do). This message was an important one, to be sure, but it did little to highlight the need for understanding the interrelationships between population growth and development. Two of the pioneer works of the 1970s that were early advocates of equity-oriented approaches to development (Chenery, Ahluwalia, Bell, Duloy, and Jolly, 1974; International Labour Office, 1977) mention population only in passing and have little to say about the implications of population growth for these development approaches. This omission has been shared by Third World statesmen. Neither the "Declaration of a New International Economic Order" nor its associated "Program of Action," adopted at the Sixth Special Session of the United Nations in April 1974, contains any explicit reference to population as a factor in international economic relations or in national development. Though Haq (1976) wrote about the "population burden" on development, he took the position that the solution lay not in family planning programs but in promoting development, thus reflecting one side of the lengthy debate (which continues in some quarters) between the two extreme positions that either family planning programs or development programs are the "correct" solution to the population problem (Teitelbaum, 1974).

Population variables, then, were accorded minimal importance in economic and social development planning, just as population studies did not reflect much of the change that was occurring in perceptions of development. It was only in the mid-1970s that population and development began to move beyond serving as a slogan at international conferences and that scholars in both fields began to address some of the complex issues raised by the interrelationships between the two. This beginning is best marked, perhaps, by the founding of The Population Council's journal, *Population and Development Review*, in 1975, and the publication of the comprehensive survey paper of Cassen (1976).[1] Since then, an enormous volume of literature and discussion, both scientific and nonscientific, has been generated in the fields of population and development.

This book offers a selective consideration of some of the models that have been dominant in the literature on development and on population growth. It constitutes an attempt to assess past and current thinking in both the development and the population field in the interest of identifying the tasks for both theory and research to enlarge the current knowledge base relating to the determinants and consequences of population growth in the Third World.

Despite the amount of work that has been done, this knowledge base still yields only a very broad understanding of the links between development policies and perspectives and population growth. There is as yet no generally accepted conceptual framework for explaining the conditions, correlates, causes, and consequences of population change in the LDCs, and within which to view relationships between development policy and processes and population growth. Nevertheless, as this discussion will indicate, the knowledge base that has been generated does point to recurrent significant links, at least at the aggregate level. These links provide useful departure points for the conceptual and empirical work that still needs to be done to clarify these relationships at national and subnational levels to arrive at an understanding of them that can be operationally useful for development planning and policy-making.

The remainder of this chapter takes up the matter of definitions of development and provides the historical context for a consideration of development perspectives. Chapters 2 and 3 focus on those components of the development literature that are most relevant for an identification of the links between development perspectives and strategies and population growth. Chapter 2 portrays a series of perspectives that were successively dominant in development thinking and assesses their limitations. Chapter 3 considers problems and issues relevant to the prospects for implementation of equity-oriented development policies.

Chapter 4 begins with a consideration of demographic-transition theory as the most important paradigm that has dominated demographic thinking in "explaining" the role of development in reducing fertility, then examines the close ties of this theory to the modernization model as a "mainstream" development perspective, and concludes with a specification of the interrelationships among equity-oriented development approaches, poverty, and population growth. Chapter 5 focuses on other conceptual frameworks concerned with fertility and a range of development factors. This chapter constitutes a selective overview that highlights the contributions and limitations of this body of literature.

Chapters 6 and 7 present analyses of a series of key development sectors that affect and are affected by population change. The sectors investigated are natural resources; health, nutrition, and food; the status and employment of women; and education. Although the several sectors are treated separately, they are so treated with the important qualification that they do not operate independently and can be understood and interpreted only in the larger context in which they interact.

Chapter 8 summarizes the discussions of the interrelationships between population and development, including the "new population debate" on the consequences of population growth; of the connections between equity-oriented development and fertility reduction; and of the present state of international population assistance. On the basis of the conclusions to these discussions, the tasks that still confront theory and research in the field of population and development are identified. Finally, the requirements for the coordination of population policy analysis and development planning are specified.[2]

DEFINITIONS

Definitions of "development," as it refers to processes of change in the LDCs, are many and diverse. Definitions have focused on increased production or consumption and more recently have embraced distribution of goods and services. Any brief (or unidisciplinary) formulation is likely to be of dubious value, because development is essentially a multidimensional process involving important changes in a society's economic, political, and social sectors, as well as in cultural beliefs and practices. Moreover, if definitions are not to be hopelessly parochial or ethnocentric, which unfortunately has too often been the case, they must consistently address the questions of development by whom, for whom, and for what, and how it is to be achieved.

Reflecting increasing awareness of the complexities of the development process, the earlier simplistic and specialized definitions that held sway until the early 1970s have given way to more holistic definitions, and at least some economists have been in the vanguard of these attempts. Myrdal (1974:84), for example, defined development as "the movement upward of the entire social system," which embraces both economic and noneconomic factors.

Some writers have stressed the quality of life as the principal criterion of development, as "the provision of a decent life not for some but for all" (Cassen, 1976:821), as "helping men to live and to have life more abundantly" (R. M. Miller, 1974:87–88), or "as the perceived improvement in the quality of life, even where this means fewer goods and services" (Pitt, 1976b:8–9).

Seers (1979a) recommended moving away from the customary identification of development with economic growth and instead proposed to address such questions as whether positive changes are occurring in a country's development with regard to poverty, unemployment, and inequality. To the extent that such changes can be identified, that country is experiencing development. Seers goes on to discuss the serious conceptual and measurement problems in the use of these development indicators. Goulet (1971:x), an ethical theorist, advocates a broad definition of development that poses even more difficult problems of measurement, namely, "the ascent of all men and societies in their total humanity."

Brookfield (1975:xi–xii), a geographer, shares the values embodied in many of these definitions, but is unhappy with the presumed linearity of most definitions. Although he asserts that he is not willing to offer a definition of development because his entire book constitutes an approach toward a definition of development, he proceeds to provide one anyway, it being that "development is the whole process of change (positive and negative) brought about by the creation and expansion of an interdependent world system." This is a relatively unusual view, one with which few policy-makers or development practitioners are likely to be comfortable, but it does dispense with the linear assumptions that equates development with progress.

Like those of the term "development," definitions of "Third World" are many and diverse, so much so as to indicate that the term is of limited use. Since the mid-1970s, the development literature has been employing a loose designation of four "worlds": the capitalist and socialist worlds, a third world of developing countries, and a fourth consisting of the poorest and most powerless countries (Chilcote, 1984). The World Bank divides the developing countries into "low-income economies," with 1983 gross national product (GNP) per person of less than $400, and "middle-income economies," with 1983 GNP per person of $400 or more (International Bank for Reconstruction and Development, 1985:xi). Although they pose difficulties, the terms "Third World" and "LDCs" are used interchangeably in this book.[3]

For the reasons stated at the outset of this section, it seems profitable not to dwell further here on definitions of development, but to move on to providing some historical context for consideration of the main views in development thought. It may be pointed out, however, that the improvement of human welfare is the central theme running through most of the definitions cited here. It follows, then, that a prior condition is that of strengthening the capacity of individuals, communities, organizations, and governments to create and maintain access to the necessary resources for the improvement of human welfare and to use these resources. This is a fundamental criterion of development.

HISTORICAL CONTEXT

Development economics, which has constituted the starting point for contemporary thinking about development, is a relatively new branch of economics that emerged largely after World War II (Streeten, 1979). Some of the ideas that have become central to development thinking, however, have been around for a long time. The perception of poverty afflicting large groups of a society as unacceptable and not inevitable goes back to the 18th century, while the view of development as the realization of economic potential and the idea of economic and social progress as the way of the world have a much longer history (Brookfield, 1975).

Most classic and neoclassic economic thought, however, from Adam Smith through John Maynard Keynes, has proved to have little relevance for development economics. The neoclassic economists' notion of "perfect competition" is central to traditional economic theory. It assumes that all prices, wages, interest rates, and other economic components are determined by the free play of the forces of supply and demand and that each of the millions of consumers and thousands of producers is so small in relation to total demand that they cannot individually influence to any extent the market prices and quantities of goods, services, and resources bought and sold. This model is based essentially on Adam Smith's idea of the "invisible hand" of capitalism, which maintains that if all pursue their own self-interest, they will be promoting the interests of society as a whole. As Todaro (1977a:11) pointed out, this model has little relevance to the facts of economic life in either the developed countries (DCs) or the LDCs, and "the so-called 'invisible hand' often acts not to promote the general welfare . . . but to lift up those who are already well-off while pushing down that vast majority . . . which is striving to free itself from poverty, malnutrition and illiteracy."

As late as the 1920s, economic theory was still dominated by the principles of laissez-faire, and it took the cyclical downturns in production and unemployment that culminated in the American stock market crash in 1929 and the ensuing Great Depression of the 1930s to make it clear that it was necessary for government to intervene in economic affairs to reduce unemployment and reactivate investment, a realization that finally eroded the credibility of laissez-faire. Enter, then, Keynes, with his concept of competitive equilibrium as controlled by the determinants of supply and demand for national output, a model that provided a clear justification for government intervention. For example, if unemployment is due to a deficient aggregate demand for national output, then government can increase such demand by, say, massive public works, support to private enterprise, and/or lowering taxes, thereby accelerating economic activity and consequently fostering higher levels of employment. On the other hand, when demand exceeds output capacity so that inflation ensues, government can reduce its spending and increase taxes so as to depress consumer demand and thus slow price rises (Brookfield, 1975).

The Keynesian model was eagerly embraced, since it seemed to present a viable alternative to socialism, permitting capitalism to survive in partnership with the state. Manipulating aggregate supply and demand curves by general government monetary and fiscal policies no longer appears to be very effective, however, since the model cannot help governments deal with a combination of inflation *and* high unemployment. If this macrotheory has dubious relevance for the economic situation in the DCs, it is even less relevant, as Todaro (1977a:12) observed, "for the underdeveloped countries whose institutions and economic systems do not even approximate to those of the developed nations, now or in the past." Although claimed to have the status of a "general" theory, the Keynesian model was in fact specific to the time and place of its formulation—the special European and American circumstances of the 1930s.

Although Keynes and his predecessors were not concerned with the economies of the developing countries, his successors did try to translate equilibrium theory into a theory of growth, which was to provide prescriptions for economic growth in the LDCs that dominated the drive, after World War II, to develop the Third World. Keynes himself was not directly responsible for the application of his model to the thinking that went into economic planning in the LDCs, but his influence was clearly important (Brookfield, 1975).

As noted earlier, development economics is largely a post-World War II phenomenon. Although there were some critics early on, the mainstream thinking was dominated by a relatively simple paradigm: If the poor countries were to solve their social and economic problems, they needed "development" such as had occurred in the DCs, which could be measured by per capita income growth. Economic growth was equated with development, which could be accelerated with the help of trade and aid and investment of private capital from the DCs. Distribution was not regarded as an issue, since the priority was accorded to economic growth. Inequality was regrettable but necessary to generate savings and provide incentives. It was assumed that income could be redistributed later; indeed, it was thought that this redistribution would happen automatically through a "trickle-down" effect.[4] This neoclassic growth paradigm, although no longer central to theory in development economics, still persists in some quarters because it has served a wide variety of political and ideological interests. As Seers (1979a:25) has noted, it has provided justification for aid policies aimed at containing Soviet Communism, it has been employed by international assistance agencies as an "objective" basis for project evaluation, and it "has not been fundamentally unacceptable to economic modernisers across a broad political spectrum, including Marxists as well as members of the Chicago school."

When the large-scale effort at development of the Third World began in the 1950s, economists in the DCs and those they trained from the Third World had virtually no experience in national development planning. They did have at hand, however, the experience of the rapid postwar reconstruction of the economies of the industrial countries of Western Europe, supported by Marshall Plan aid. Neoclassic models, which they regarded as responsible for this success, were considered just as appropriate for investment planning to generate growth of national income in the LDCs. In retrospect, many writers have lamented that the problem of economic development was taken up in the wake of the successful postwar reconstruction in Western Europe, which led to unfounded optimism about what could be done in the LDCs on the assumption that the problems of Third World development could be solved by employing the same kind of planning strategy that had worked in Europe. A. O. Hirschman (1979:xvii) maintained, however, that this turned out to be a fruitful error: "Had the size and toughness of the problem been correctly visualized from the outset, the considerable intellectual and political mobilization around it would most likely not have occurred and we would be even farther away from an acceptable world."[5]

The view that prevailed during the 1950s and 1960s, then, was that if economic growth were only fast enough, the "trickle-down" effects would solve the poverty and income distribution problem—that is, when the problem was thought about at all. The best way to attack poverty was indirectly, by supporting growth that would have the effect, after a time, of benefiting the poor, and thus the goals of development could be narrowly defined with reference to GNP and its growth.

The GNP of the LDCs grew at an average rate of 3.4% a year during the period 1950–1975 (Morawetz, 1977; Warren, 1979). This rate was faster than either the LDCs or the DCs had grown in any comparable period before 1950 and exceeded all expectations. To be sure, this average growth rate concealed wide differences in performance among LDCs. Per capita income in some countries grew at an average annual rate of 4.2% or better and in others at between 3 and 4%. But in the large, poor countries of South Asia and many countries in Africa, with a total of 1.1 billion people, per capita income grew by less than 2% a year between 1950 and 1975. Despite the impressive LDC record of GNP growth in the 1960s, which has been called the First Development Decade, development in the Third World, instead of being viewed as a great success, was instead, as Higgins (1977:99–100) has noted, "regarded as a miserable failure. . . . Even countries with quite respectable rates of growth of national income did not enjoy 'development' in the sense of wide and deep improvements in welfare for the masses of the population. On the contrary, unemployment grew, inflation accelerated . . . there were more children out of school than in school, health targets were not attained, and inequality of income distribution became worse than ever." Given this dismal picture, the prevailing development paradigm came under increasing attack after the mid-1960s, and this deterioration was severely exacerbated by the "oil crisis" of the early 1970s.

What went wrong? In retrospect, it is clear that there were many errors in development thinking and policy. Streeten (1979) lists some of them: Industrialization and infrastructure were accorded priority, but capital investment turned out to account for only a relatively small portion of growth, which was, as indicated above, not synonymous with development. Centralized government planning dominated development policies and strategies, so that the need for mobilization and involvement of local labor went unrecognized. There was a prevalent belief that high average growth rates of production would lead, if only indirectly, to reductions in poverty. The rate of population growth and the problems generated by it were seriously underestimated. The goals of development were focused almost exclusively on growth of GNP. The Third World was viewed monolithically as an area with common problems, but the differences within some LDCs were at least as great as those between them and other LDCs. To this list could be added, among others, the ethnocentric notion that DC models could be easily applied to solve LDC problems, the effects of urban bias at the expense of the rural sector, the vagaries of foreign aid, the frequent introduction of advanced technologies that treated labor as a scarce factor in generally labor-surplus economies, the frequent lack of political will in the LDCs to initiate changes that might offend their elites, and, of course, the huge diversion of economic resources into expensive armaments. A number of these factors are considered in the subsequent discussion.

The development field, perhaps more than most other areas of human effort, has been notably subject to shifts in fads and fashions. During the past three decades, a variety of ideas have held center stage in the mainstream of development thought. Perhaps this diversity is to be expected in a field in which there have been many disappointments, in which problems of development seem to persist as intractable whatever strategy is devised, and in which development theorists and practitioners seem to become excited about particular factors to the neglect of others that may be equally important. What the development field does have in common with other areas of human effort is the seeming inability to build a stock of cumulative wisdom on the basis of lessons learned. Indeed, the rapidity with which different prescriptions for development come into vogue attests to this lack of cumulativeness.

Haq (1976), for example, identified a series of ideas that were accorded priority at different times between 1948 and 1975, only to give way to others. From 1948 to 1955, import substitution was heralded as the key to development, but from 1960 to 1965, import substitution was discredited and export expansion was advocated. In the late 1960s, industrialization came to be regarded as an illusion, and rapid agricultural growth was touted. By the mid-1970s, GNP growth began to lose favor as the development indicator, and concern with distribution became prominent. In a similar vein, Ghai and Alfthan (1977:1) provided a list of strategies that at different times were perceived as "decisive solutions to development problems," which include capital accumulation; availability of foreign exchange; industrialization, first of the import-substitution variety and then export-oriented; rural development; population control; human resource development; employment-oriented strategies; and redistribution with growth. And they said they were mentioning only the star contenders. Streeten (1979) spoke of cycles in development fashions and cited many of the same changes in emphasis identified by Haq and by Ghai and Alfthan.

Whatever may have been the variety of shifts and swings in development objectives over the past 35 years, the one that is clearly most prominent is the perception that maximization of GNP per capita is too narrow an objective and that other objectives, concerned with equity and the reduction of poverty, such as improving income distribution, creating greater employment opportunities, and satisfying "basic needs," must be taken into account as well. Some writers regard this change as just another fashion in a fashion-prone field, but Morawetz (1977:7) disagrees. He argues that the "discovery" of equity-oriented objectives is in fact a rediscovery of ideas that were central in the development literature just after World War II. Consequently, he said, "the recent heightened concern with eradication of poverty is not likely . . . to be just another fad. On the contrary, in the long term it is the narrow preoccupation of the late 1950s and the 1960s with growth in average per capita income that, although it had its reasons and even its benefits, may turn out to be the passing fashion."

With this brief historical sketch to be kept in mind, the discussion now moves on to an overview of the major perspectives that have influenced development thought over the last three and a half decades. The most noteworthy dimension of the changes that have occurred is the shift from the earlier exclusive focus on GNP per capita growth as the objective of development to the inclusion of equity for the poor, in addition to economic growth, as an integral part of the objectives of broad-based development.

NOTES

[1]An important collection concerned with the consequences of rapid population growth for economic development was published in 1971 (National Academy of Sciences, 1971), and between 1974 and 1976, other works on issues of population and development appeared. Among the more notable of these publications are King, Cuca, Gulhati, Hossain, Stern, Visaria, Zachariah, and Zafros (1974), McGreevey and Birdsall (1974), Robinson (1975), Coale (1976), and Ridker (1976).

[2]This book is concerned with fertility only as a major component of population dynamics.

It should be noted that internal migration, its determinants and consequences, and their links to national development strategy constitute a problem area perhaps equal in importance to that of fertility. It is a reasonable proposition that the goals of development strategy in a country ultimately determine the geographic distribution of the population and changes in that distribution. If the principal goals include making the best use of natural and human resources where they are to be found and reducing the disparities in access to the benefits of development both between social classes and between the rural and urban sectors, then it will be necessary to implement policy measures aimed at eliminating the urban bias and rural neglect that characterize so many LDCs.

[3]The World Bank includes 35 "developing countries" in the group of low–income economies. China and India are classified as low-income economies, but are considered separately from the others by virtue of their size and other characteristics. The other main group, the middle-income economies, includes 59 developing countries. The World Bank employs this particular economic distinction between two major groups of LDCs, but of course there is much greater diversity among these countries, in cultural heritage, historical experience, and economic patterns, masked by such broad terms as "developing" and "Third World." For an enlightening discussion of the political, economic, and cultural influences that have figured in the emergence of models of the Third World, see Worsley (1984).

[4]Streeten contends that the early discussions by economists about development were characterized by the proliferation of ideas, criticisms, and qualifications, which contrasts sharply with the monolithic view that a single paradigm existed. This view, says Streeten (1979:25), "is an optical illusion created by looking back from later vantage points." For some other views on development theory, see Papanek (1968), Uphoff and Ilchman (1972), Ranis (1977), Lehmann (1979), and Ohlin (1979).

[5]This is a later application of Hirschman's "Principle of the Hiding Hand," which he formulated in the process of accounting for the undertaking of development projects that would not have been initiated if the project managers had known initially how complex the task would turn out to be (A. O. Hirschman, 1967).

Perspectives on Development

MODERNIZATION MODEL

In the euphoria and optimism that characterized the immediate post–World War II period, confidence in the inevitability of progress had a critical influence on views about how development of the Third World ought to proceed. In this situation, the idea of "modernization" emerged as the model to which development efforts should be oriented, a model that in the 1950s and 1960s dominated conceptualizations of the development process not only in economics, but also in sociology, anthropology, psychology, and political science, to the extent that these latter disciplines paid attention to the development field (no easy task, it may be added, in view of the primacy given to economic development and thus to economists).[1] The concept's origins were diffuse, deriving from the ideas of Durkheim, Weber, Marx, and Parsons, among others, about social, cultural, and economic change. The model yielded a particular view of change that is essentially dualistic, namely, tradition and modernity seen as opposing forces, the latter increasing at the expense of the former. The content of modernity is given (with some differences depending on particular disciplinary formulations) by the experience of those societies that have achieved it, namely, the societies of Western Europe and North America, which combine industrial economies with representative democracy (Bernstein, 1979). In the words of Eisenstadt (1966:1), ". . . modernization is the process of change towards those types of social, economic and political systems that have developed in Western Europe and North America . . . and then have spread to other European countries and . . . to the South American, Asian and African continents."

The model was extensively criticized for its ethnocentric, deterministic, and linear characteristics, and indeed for the blithe overlooking of the empirical reality of what was going on in the less-developed countries (LDCs). Nevertheless, it held center stage for a time because it is a

13

comforting notion about how to get from here to there in a world of otherwise confusing uncertainty. It is no longer securely ensconced in mainstream thinking, but as Goldthorpe (1984:135) observes, "The modernization school continues to have many adherents, especially in the United States."

European and North American economists certainly found appealing the idea that the historical experience of the developed countries (DCs) in transforming their economies from poor agricultural subsistence societies to "modern" industrial giants had important lessons for the LDCs. Chirot (1985:193–194) observes, however, "that the account [by proponents of modernization] of the rise of the West given here is so situational, so bound by the context of a given time, that it offers no lessons for the present. . . . The past is not a guide to the future, or to the creation of a general theory of human behavior." These "lessons" from history were reinforced by the evidence the economists had at hand, as noted earlier, from the case of the postwar reconstruction of Western Europe as to what massive injections of capital could do.

It is not surprising, therefore, that W. W. Rostow's doctrine of the stages of economic growth, first published in 1960, dominated the popular development thinking of the 1960s and early 1970s. Rostow's work is virtually the pure case of subjection to the traditional–modern dichotomy. Although Rostow (1971) began his treatise with some mild qualifications to the effect that his stages of growth are an arbitrary and limited way of looking at the sequence of modern history, he quickly brushed these qualifications aside and entered on the heady business of contending that the stages of growth were designed to grapple with a substantial range of issues. As Rostow (*ibid.*:4ff.) saw it, development is a linear path along which all countries travel through a series of five stages: the traditional society, the preconditions for takeoff, the takeoff, the drive to maturity, and the age of high mass consumption. Further, ". . . the central fact about the traditional society was that a ceiling existed on the level of attainable output per head. The ceiling resulted from the fact that the potentialities which flow from modern science and technology were either not available or not regularly and systematically applied." The preconditions stage "embraces societies in the process of transition," a transition that is initiated "not endogenously but from some external intrusion by more advanced societies . . . [which] shocked the traditional society and began or hastened its undoing." During the takeoff stage, "the rate of effective investment and savings may rise from, say, 5 percent of the national income to 10 percent or more," and a "new class of entrepreneurs expands; and it directs the enlarging flows of investment in the private sector." During the drive to maturity, some

10–20% of the national income is steadily invested and modern technology expands throughout the economy. Finally, as societies achieve maturity, there is high consumption of durables, diffusion of services on a mass basis, and, if other societies follow the example of the DCs, allocation of resources to the welfare state and social security.

The subtitle of Rostow's book is *A Non-Communist Manifesto,* and the final chapter compares the stages-of-growth schema with Marxism, of course not to the latter's advantage. Indeed, Rostow refers to Communism as a "disease of the transition," so it is not surprising that he was severely attacked by Marxist critics. He comes under heavy fire from other economists as well, however, including Myrdal, Kuznets, T. W. Schultz, and Hirschman, among others. Streeten (1979:39) makes the acerbic comment that the book "veers between the tautologically trivial and the historically false" and observes (*ibid.*:26) that "the linear view begged a host of questions about the nature, causes and objectives of development." Despite its rejection in some academic circles, the Rostow model had a powerful grip on the imagination of policy-makers, planners, and other development practitioners.

A brief review of the influence of the modernization model on other social science disciplines is appropriate. Although the writings of social scientists in disciplines other than economics had only a mild impact on development thinking among policy-makers and planners, compared with Rostow's work, much of these writings were compatible with and supportive of the stage theory in economics. In sociology, the Parsonian set of pattern-variables, conceived theoretically as a limited set of choices presented to the "actor" as an effect of the social structure, was used by Hoselitz to construct two ideal types of society (J. G. Taylor, 1979). One side of the pattern-variable choices was viewed as characterizing traditional societies, the other side modern societies. Thus, the modern type combined universalism, functional specificity, achievement-orientation, and collectivity-orientation. The traditional type combined particularism, diffuseness, ascription, and self-orientation.[2]

In anthropology, Redfield's earlier concept of a "folk–urban continuum" between primitive, peasant, and urban communities was superseded by Steward's theory of multilinear evolution, and more recently, Nash (1977:21) proposed the following broad and clearly linear definition: "Modernity is the social, cultural, and psychological framework which facilitates the application of tested knowledge to all phases and branches of production. Modernization is the process of transformation toward the establishment and institutionalization of the framework of modernity."

In political science, political modernity was equated with representative democracy. The best-known and most influential proponent of the identification of modernization with Western democracy was Gabriel Almond. As D. C. O'Brien (1979:53) puts it:

> It can be no great surprise to learn that "rational, analytical, empirical" secularization has reached its fullest expression in the "civic" political cultures of Great Britain and the United States. The idealized version of modernity has an American face, and Almond's well articulated model may perhaps serve as another reminder of the potential propaganda value of political classifications drawn in terms of ideal type polarities. This ideal type is in effect the end of history, the terminal station at which the passengers to modernization can finally get out and stretch their legs.

In psychology, a principal advocate of the modernization model has been McClelland (1977:65–66), who has repeatedly emphasized as key elements in modernization the "need for achievement or a concern for efficiency," "a capacity for disciplined hard work," and "an openness to change and a general knowledge of what is going on in the world." According to McClelland, development cannot be realized in the Third World unless these "psychological factors" are inculcated in its inhabitants.

As exemplified by some of these statements, the modernization model constitutes a mirror image of Western society, in which the virtues of sustained economic growth, democracy, efficency, and "rationality" are to be emulated by the LDCs if they want to become "developed." Goldthorpe (1984:134) says that ". . . modernization seems to mean becoming more like the United States. . . . It seems plain that we have here not just a social science theory or set of explanatory ideas helping us to understand what is happening in the world, but also a set of evaluative criteria by which to judge the policies and performance of Third World countries and their governments."

Leaving aside the question of whether this version of the "good life" is worth emulation by the people of the LDCs, a major constraint imposed by the model is its teleological nature. It is a process that is constituted by the view of its destination, modernity, and can lead only to circular reasoning rather than to a conception of development as an empirically observable process of change and growth within a variety of societal contexts. As Bernstein (1979:83) observes, the model "is incapable of producing any knowledge of the object it poses other than that given by its definition. . . . It is condemned to the closed circle of an ideological discourse from which it cannot break out."

The modernization model has further doleful consequences because it carries with it the assumption that modernity has a monopoly on "rationality" and that tradition is an opposing force, the obstacle that modernization must overcome if it is to arrive at its destination. This view is essentially a historical one that constitutes a stereotype of traditional society (primarily peasant society) as an unchanging equilibrium and obscures, among other things, the fact that many prominent characteristics of so-called "traditional" societies emerged during the 19th century as a result of the widespread social, political, and economic changes following colonialism (Hutton and Cohen, 1975). Thus, there is need to ascertain the extent to which the social, economic, and political patterns that characterize LDCs are in fact traditional and derive from endogenous sources and the extent to which they are a consequence of nontraditional and exogenous sources. In any case, as Levine (1986:337) maintains: ". . . the whole conceptual construct that places rationality and tradition in opposition seems to be open to doubt insofar as it presumes that tradition is irrational. Societies should be understood whole, and the behavior of their members should be understood in relation to that whole, not in relation to some other scale." It may be noted that the view of traditional beliefs and practices as obstacles strengthens the justification for their replacement by the "modern" qualities for which McClelland, for example, makes such a fervent plea. Just as the modernization perspective leads away from systematic empirical observation, so the view of traditionalism as obstacle leads to the glossing over of first-hand observation of the variety of actual situations in which different peasant groups find themselves—observation that is necessary to achieve an understanding of why they behave as they do.

Acknowledging that the earlier development models were replete with biases and oversimplification, Myrdal (1970:26ff.) maintains that the modernization ideals must continue to be employed as instrumental value premises in guiding research and development planning in the LDCs, since rapid strides toward realization of these ideals must be made to avoid "actual impoverishment with increasing misery for the masses." He contends that orientation to these value premises does not necessarily have to be limited to formulations in Western terms, because these values determine only the point of view from which reality is studied. The point of view, however, does not determine what facts and factual relationships are brought within the scope of observation and analysis. Indeed, ". . . economic study must be comprehensive enough to be adequate to reality, and . . . this reality is very different in the underdeveloped countries from what it is in the developed countries." He goes on to say, however, that traditional values, which are static and therefore cannot be employed in determining goals for development planning, will have to be replaced where they constitute inhibitions and obstacles to such planning. Thus, Myrdal does not escape the trap of the dichotomy of tradition and modernity, despite his claim that he is not bound by Western biases.

In dichotomous thinking, it is not easy to avoid the notion that movement is from "lower" to "higher" levels in societal change. For example, "dualism" is a concept that has received a great deal of attention from social scientists working in the development field. It is a fact of life in the LDCs that their societies are organized in two parts, one situated largely in the urban areas, the other in the rural. They differ, sometimes dramatically, in levels of income, power, technology, and so on. This dualism characterizes both international relations between developed and developing countries and domestic relations within countries. When viewed through the lens of the modernization model, the concept of the "dual society" neatly categorizes the poor countries in the traditional (or backward) sector and the rich countries in the modern (or advanced) sector. And within the LDCs, the potential for economic, social, cultural, and psychological change is perceived as located in the modern sector, around which the traditional sector is seen as forming a hinterland largely resisting the introduction of modern ways of life. Again, the polar concepts of modernity and tradition obscure what in fact may be going on in the way of symbiotic and other kinds of interaction between the two parts of the country that may be important for all the society's members but is not amenable to interpretation with respect to modern vs. traditional (Bernstein, 1971, 1979; Griffin, 1969).

For Singer (1975), a development economist who has written extensively on the subject, the concept of dualism embraces four key elements: (1) Different sets of conditions, of which some are "superior" and others "inferior," can coexist in a given space at the same time. Examples are the coexistence of modern and traditional methods of production in urban and rural sectors, of wealthy, educated elites with masses of illiterate poor people, and of powerful and wealthy industrialized nations with weak, impoverished peasant societies in the international economy. (2) This coexistence is chronic and not merely transitional. (3) The degrees of superiority or inferiority show no signs of rapidly diminishing; they may be constant or even increasing. (4) The interrelationships between the "superior" and "inferior" elements, if interrelationships exist, are such that the superior element does little to pull up the inferior element or may even serve to pull it down.

Singer regards this fourfold characterization of dualism as equally descriptive of the international situation and of the intranational situation within LDCs. It does describe the contemporary situation in both international and national settings, but the dominant focus is on traditional (read "inferior") vs. modern (read "superior")—a polarization that permits no assessment of what may be the actual and potential relative contributions of the two sectors to each other and to the process of development in Third World countries. Exploitation by the dominant sector may be the most compelling feature of the dual society and economy, but other elements involved in the dynamics of the interrelationships cannot be systematically identified as long as the governing assumption is unilinear change emanating from the dominant, or urban, sector. The urban–industrial bias, which is considered later, is certainly a reflection of this assumption.

By no means have all the leading social scientists who have worked in the development field succumbed to the beguilement of the modernization model, but those proponents of the model cited herein have been given primary attention because they constituted the "mainstream" position. It may be noted that opposing views by social scientists from a range of disciplines are cited in this section.[3]

UNDERDEVELOPMENT AND DEPENDENCY

Beginning in the 1950s, and partly in response to the growing disenchantment with linear views of development, there came to popularity another view in which the international system of rich country–poor country relationships creates and maintains the underdevelopment or dependency of the poor countries. The coexistence of rich countries (the "center"), whether they are deliberately exploitative or unintentionally neglectful, and poor countries (the "periphery") renders the efforts of the poor countries to choose their own style of development more difficult, if not impossible (Streeten, 1979). In the LDCs, the groups who have wealth, high social status, and political power constitute ruling elites who perpetuate the international system of inequality.

The most voluminous and sophisticated body of thought advocating this view emerged in Latin America.[4] One source of the views on underdevelopment (a term ordinarily used, as it is here, interchangeably with dependency) was the work of the United Nations Economic Commission for Latin America (ECLA), established in Santiago, Chile, just after World War II.[5] The ECLA's position was based on the belief that conventional economic theory as pursued in the DCs was inadequate for dealing with problems of underdevelopment. The study of underdevelopment called for a "structuralist" approach, namely, an appreciation of different historical situations and national settings. The ECLA argument was that conventional economic theory, with its emphasis on the theory of prices and general equilibrium, failed to recognize the existence of the different structures (P. J. O'Brien, 1975). According to the ECLA view of "center–periphery" relations, technical progress was concentrated at the center, which had the effect there of diminishing the share of primary inputs in the value of end products. This led to a progressive deterioration in the "terms of trade" for the primary producers, so that a given unit of manufactured imports was costing the periphery countries increasing measures of primary exports. The gain from increased primary production was therefore appropriated in the economies of the center countries. Consequently, the primary producers experienced balance-of-payments problems, which had inflationary effects (Brookfield, 1975).

The ECLA therefore proposed that Latin America industrialize, and with high protective barriers to assist infant industries. This strategy became known as "import-substitution industrialization" because it mainly involved setting up local industries that could satisfy demand previously met by imports. It was assumed that this substitution would lessen the demand for imports and thus help the balance of payments, but events did not follow this course. By the 1960s, it was clear that import–substitution industrialization had not diminished dependence, income distribution appeared to be growing more unequal, and national policies for industrialization were being weakened by the inroads of multinational corporations and foreign investors. All this contravention of the initial assumption led to a growing perception of the problems of Latin American societies as "dependent" rather than merely "peripheral," and the concept of dependency was advanced as an explanation of these problems. As P. J. O'Brien (1975:11) has noted, "There are . . . a number of different traditions within the theory of dependency: one clearly stems from the ECLA structuralist perspective. . . . Another stems from a Marxist perspective, particularly that perspective which broke with the stultifying dogmatism of the Stalinist heritage."

The Brazilian economist Celso Furtado is prominently associated with the ECLA structuralist perspective. As an ECLA economist, he at first strongly favored industrialization, but eventually he rejected this approach to focus on the dependent situation of the Latin American economies. Writing in 1965, he saw a vicious interaction between a wedge of industrial economy in the Latin American countries linked both in interests and behavior to its external patrons and an untransformed internal structure the existence of which enabled both local and foreign capitalists to maintain high profit levels by relying on an army of the unemployed (as described by Brookfield, 1975). In later writing, Furtado (1977:256–257) said: "Among the most relevant points emerging from the list of topics being debated in the region . . . are . . .

re-entry of the regional economies into the expanding lines of the international economy . . . reshaping of economic relations with the United States . . . [and] reshaping of relations with the big international consortia. . . ."

Deriving from the Marxist perspective, the basic hypothesis of the concept of dependency is that development and underdevelopment are partial and interdependent structures of one global system. In the view of Dos Santos (1976:76), the interdependent relationship among national economies or between them and the world economy "becomes a dependent relationship when some countries can expand through self-impulsion while others, being in a dependent position, can only expand as a reflection of the expansion of the dominant countries, which may have positive or negative effects on their immediate development." This statement summarizes the central thesis of dependency.

Perhaps the best-known (because his work has been available in English) proponent of the notion that the development process itself is the independent variable in creating underdevelopment is Andre Gunder Frank.[6] In particular, he is noted for his slogan "the development of underdevelopment." Frank (1969:4–5) vigorously attacked the stage theory of development and maintained that "neither the past nor the present of the underdeveloped countries resembles in any important respect the past of the now developed countries." Valenzuela and Valenzuela (1981:45) put this rather more concretely: "The interdependent nature of the world capitalist system and the qualitative transformations in that system over time make it inconceivable to think that individual nations on the periphery could somehow replicate the evolutionary experience of the now developed nations." A. G. Frank (1969) described a world system in which the "metropoles" tend to develop and the "satellites" to underdevelop, an assumption from which he derived three principal hypotheses: (1) In contrast to the development of the world metropolis, which is no one's satellite, the development of the national and other subordinate geopolitical entities is limited by their satellite status; (2) satellites of a given metropolis experience their greatest economic development and especially their most classic capitalist industrial development if and when their ties to that metropolis are weakest; and (3) the regions that are the most underdeveloped and feudal-seeming today are the ones that had the closest ties to the metropolis in the past.

Frank's ideas assume a kind of rigidity of structure that prohibits all possibility of internal transformation. Indeed, Frank (ibid.:78) perceives that the only alternatives are "capitalist underdevelopment" or "socialist revolution": "If the developed countries refuse development, development theory, or development policy to the underdeveloped countries, then the people of these countries will have to develop them by themselves." And he concludes (*ibid.*:408–409) that "the Latin American intellectual and Marxist will have to decide whether he will remain inside pursuing reformism, or outside with the people making the revolution."

There is at least a third perspective in Latin American thinking on dependency, one that seems to straddle the ECLA structuralist and the Marxist perspectives. A leading exponent of this view is the Brazilian sociologist Fernando Cardoso. He and his colleagues (Cardoso and Faletto, 1979) are interested in development primarily as a social process. They emphasize that dependency is not an external variable but part of a system of social relations between different social classes within the same context of dependency. They do not agree with Frank's dependency model, which they characterize as one that emphasizes that technical progress and financial control of the results of international expansion are concentrated in a few capitalist centers that will go on exploiting and preserving the dependence and underdevelopment of the periphery. In contrast to this view, Cardoso and Faletto believe that it is possible to have a "dependent development" that has structural dynamism rather than stagnation, a dynamism that stems in part from the multinational corporations, which have a role to play in this process—under conditions controlled by the LDCs to be sure—that could lead to important reforms in the traditional patterns of underdevelopment. Again, unlike Frank, they do not see the only options as either remaining mired in underdevelopment or making the revolution. Cardoso and Faletto (*ibid.*:xxiv) do observe, however, that "it is not realistic to imagine that capitalist development will solve basic problems for the majority of the population. In the end, what has to be discussed as an alternative is not the consolidation of the state and the fulfillment of 'autonomous capitalism,' but how to supersede them. The important question, then, is how to construct paths toward socialism."

As P. J. O'Brien (1975:23–24) observes, the actual mechanisms of dependency are seldom spelled out in detail: "Everything is connected to everything else, but how and why, often remains obscure. . . . The failure to enumerate and analyse the essential characteristics of dependency leads to confusion when it comes to policy. . . . The main policy advocated is that of changing the internal structure to obtain national development." Frank makes a clarion call for revolution, while Cardoso seems to be viewing socialism as the road to achieving national development, although not necessarily as a precondition. Furtado is perhaps more directly linked to the reformist ECLA tradition that wants national development without the class struggle and independence without revolution. In his most recent book, A. G. Frank (1980) laments that the revolution seems further away then ever, and he is ready to call down a plague on all their houses, whether the development ideologies come from the right or the left.

This discussion now moves on to a consideration of the limitations of both the modernization and the dependency perspective. Whatever may be the limitations of the latter, however, it has in any case made a basic point of substantial importance, namely, that the "interplay between the internal Latin American structures and international structures is the critical starting point for an understanding of the process of development in Latin America" (P. J. O'Brien, 1975:25).

MODERNIZATION AND DEPENDENCY: THE LIMITATIONS

The dependency perspective has provided a useful function in undermining the strong influence of the modernization model on development studies, but is largely subject to the same limitations already noted in the case of that model. Taking the two perspectives, for present purposes, as represented by Rostow and Frank, the former maintaining that development can be speeded up by promoting international capitalism and the latter contending that underdevelopment is caused by it, they can best be understood as aspects of competing ideologies rather than faithful depictions of reality. Both perspectives derive from Western ethnocentric views of the world and therefore, as Van Den Bergh (1979) has observed, have little patience with attempts to build on the enormous diversity and richness of cultural traditions in Asia, Africa, and Latin America. It is not uncommon for "theories" to be enshrined and to mask or distort empirical reality. The role of both these perspectives in development thought reflects this tendency. To take an illustration from another field, Coles (1986a,b) was very much aware of this tendency. In undertaking his empirical research on the moral and political life of children, he took care neither to let the preconceived ideas and constructs of psychoanalytic theory get in the way of direct observation of reality nor, even more counterproductively, to "confirm" psychoanalytic theory by a selective "reading" of reality.

The dependency perspective replicates the circularity of the modernization model and is similarly couched in a series of conceptual polarities: developed–underdeveloped, metropole–satellite, domination–dependence, center–periphery, and so on (Bernstein, 1979). Like modernization, underdevelopment is perceived as a unitary process with uniform causes and uniform effects. Again like modernization, the underdevelopment or dependency perspective employs a unilinear social determinism to arrive at the desirable end state. In the case of modernization, indigenous development will be achieved by the replacement of the traditional society through international capitalism, while the dependency perspective asserts that this capitalist penetration constitutes the barrier to genuine development, which can come to fruition only if the penetration is removed. Just as tradition is the obstacle to be overcome if modernization is to triumph, so the penetration of international capitalism constitutes the obstacle to be removed if indigenous economic and social development is to occur in the countries of the Third World. The dependency thesis is thus an inversion of the modernization thesis.

Both perspectives, then, share a unilinear view of stages of development. According to Brookfield (1975:80), the link between the two is Marx himself; proponents of both perspectives are indebted to his interpretation of the historical sequence from medievalism to capitalism, and "the difference between [them] therefore concerns essentially the meaning of modernity and the present trend of events, whether it is toward an American-model capitalist democracy, or toward the replacement of capitalism by socialism. Equal ingenuity with the task of interpretation is demonstrated on both sides." Consider, for example, the view of a Russian social scientist writing about development (Dreyer, 1976:294):

> Cultural change in Third World countries depends directly on the social restructuring of society: the more profound and consistent the changes are in the interests of the people, the more successful is cultural development, which actively influences ethnic psychology, promotes the break-up of traditional links within a society with many survivals of old modes of production, and the formation of social forces capable of revolutionary strides.

This linear view of progress in development is shared by adherents of modernization. The difference, of course, is that this view is oriented toward the goal of socialist development rather than that of capitalist development.

Seers (1979b) contends that Marxist economists and those of the Chicago School (the group of economists at the University of Chicago of whom Milton Friedman is the most widely known representative) share a common and important core of neoclassicist basic doctrine, since the origins of both their doctrines can be found in the work of Adam Smith and Ricardo, early in the Industrial Revolution. He points out that there are also important differences, which, of course, are related mainly to desirable end states, but he asserts that the common points are numerous and fundamental.

The earlier faith in development as measured by modernization no longer dominates development thinking, but as noted earlier, the model still has its proponents. Faced with the real problems of achieving development and the new problems in their own countries, the DCs have become increasingly receptive, particularly among the academicians of development, to indictments of their own social and cultural values. As Van Den Bergh (1979:48) put it, people in the DCs who thought they had "arrived" and had achieved the end stage of development "are now once more beginning to see their own states as developing countries." The dependency perspective, on the other hand, although it has facilitated the shift in focus to the interaction between the internal economic and social situations in the LDCs and the international system, also appears, at least in the Frankean version, to have serious limitations for generating viable development strategies.[7]

These sobering experiences have given new impetus to a search for development perspectives that will not be so closely tied to competing ideologies and limited by dichotomous thinking, perspectives that can embrace a variety of development alternatives for the LDCs by discarding the lens of ethnocentrism. It is understandable that most of the work thus far has focused on the relations between the DCs and LDCs. What is needed in the future is a greater concern with comparative study of different countries and regions in the Third World that will bring development thinking closer to the reality of the diversity of situations in the LDCs.

This discussion now turns to a consideration of other views and issues that have become prominent in development thought. It was remarked earlier that the most prominent shift in development objectives during the past 35 years was the perception that the exclusive pursuit of economic growth was too narrow an objective and that account must be taken of other objectives related to poverty reduction and oriented to equity—improving income distribution, increasing employment, and satisfying "basic needs." By the late 1960s, Dudley Seers and other development specialists were insisting that these objectives were the essence of the meaning of development; in doing so, they were in fact rediscovering issues prominent in the literature on economic development just after World War II. What they rediscovered was that production objectives could not be separated from those of distribution—production as such could not be put ahead of its intended purposes and beneficiaries.

REDISTRIBUTION WITH GROWTH

In the early 1970s, staff of the World Bank and of the Institute of Development Studies at the University of Sussex undertook a study of the relationships between growth and distribution. The study resulted in a report (Chenery et al., 1974) that propounded as its main theme that distributional objectives should be treated as an integral part of development and growth strategy and advocated "redistribution with growth." The argument can be summarized as follows: In the early stages of development, the distribution of income becomes more concentrated. Increases in output come disproportionately from relatively small modern sectors of primary production and industry, which absorb a high proportion of total investment and have relatively high rates of productivity growth. This pattern of concentrated economic growth is perpetuated by limited access to land, credit, education, and modern-sector employment. It is often reinforced, unintentionally or otherwise, by a government's fiscal and trade policies as well as by the distribution of public expenditures. As growth continues, its benefits are more widely spread, but the obstacles just mentioned limit the share received by the poor. The poor are prevented from sharing equitably in a general increase in output by a number of specific disabilities that can be summed up as lack of physical and human capital and lack of access to resources. Policies designed to offset these handicaps must take account of the particular socioeconomic characteristics of given target groups. Although growth tends initially to be concentrated in a few sectors of the economy, with little effect on major poverty groups, a number of countries (Taiwan,[8] South Korea, Sri Lanka, and Tanzania being most frequently cited) have devised policies for offsetting this tendency so that the benefits of growth can be shared more equally (Chenery et al., 1974:xiv–xv).

In the view of the Chenery group, the design of a poverty-oriented strategy requires the selection of a mix of policy instruments that can reach the target groups that have been identified, namely, small farmers, landless laborers and submarginal farmers, and the urban underemployed and unemployed. They advocate maximum use of market instruments, but since these instruments will not often be sufficient for the purpose, they also focus on a range of direct measures, such as land reform, the distribution of education and other public services, and measures to redistribute assets toward the poverty groups. This approach needs to be adapted to the different characteristics of the rural and urban poverty groups. The rural strategy focuses on increasing the productivity of the small farmer and the self-employed through better access to land, water, credit markets, and other facilities. The urban poor require a more diversified strategy. To begin with, the modern sector must be restructured to make it more responsive to the opportunity costs of labor and capital, which implies a shift to more labor-intensive products and policies. Even with optimal policies, however, the modern sector cannot provide employment for the bulk of the rapidly growing urban labor force, so that a second range of policies must be designed to reach the self-employed and to make small-scale producers more efficient. This direct approach has much in common with the direct approach to rural poverty problems by focusing on improved access to inputs, the redirection of public investment, and the removal of discrimination against small producers.

The Chenery group emphasizes that this approach to poverty-focused planning implies, not the abandonment of economic growth as an objective, but rather redistribution of the benefits of growth. Ahluwalia and Chenery (1974) contend that their group's analysis of the relationships between distribution and growth leads to a basic change in the terms in which development objectives are formulated. The allocation of investment cannot be separated from the distribution of its product—they are different dimensions of a single development strategy. In addition, attention must be paid to the allocation of investment among the capital stocks of different socioeconomic groups. The need to direct public investment to support incomes of poverty groups by building up their ownership of and access to physical and human resources is a common theme that runs through the book. Without some increase in such ownership and access by the poor, their per capita income will grow more slowly than that of higher-income groups, at least for a considerable period. Some redirection of the investment of the economy toward the poverty groups can modify this process substantially over one or two decades: "If it is provided in an appropriate mix of education, public facilities, access to credit, land reform, and so forth, investment in the poor can produce benefits in the form of higher productivity and wages in the organized sectors as well as greater output for the self-employed poor (*ibid.*:47)."

The Chenery group acknowledges that the political problems of implementing redistribution with growth are likely to be formidable in many LDCs. C. L. G. Bell (1974:71) observes that those countries that are dominated by entrenched elites are not likely to give anything to their poor majorities unless pressured by armed force, while other countries have attacked the causes of poverty in far more direct and radical ways than those proposed in the Chenery report. But he goes on to say that this still leaves many countries "for which the strategy is at least plausible, even though in some of them the likelihood that it will be adopted is remote. In such cases, the key factor is the emergence of a coalition of interests able to grasp power which sees some advantage in implementing a redistributive strategy, despite the fact that some sections of it stand to lose relatively thereby."

One of Chenery's associates (Rao, 1974) indicates awareness of the complexity of the problems of rural and urban poverty, the great diversity in the LDCs of the relative proportions of the populations in urban and rural areas, and the paucity of reliable information about income distribution, the economic characteristics of the poor, and the actual nature and extent of underemployment and unemployment among both rural and urban populations. Given the serious data deficiencies, the comment of Seers (1979b:6) on the naïve belief of many economists "in the collection of guesses and hypotheses—together with a few facts— called 'growth rates' in Africa, Asia, and Latin America" is relevant here. Another of Chenery's colleagues (Jolly, 1974) takes up the issue of international dimensions and emphasizes that action on the international front must be part and parcel of action domestically if there is to be any effective shift to give greater attention to poverty–focused policies. Chenery and Duloy (1974) state that the formulation of a general distribution theory for the LDCs is not likely in the near future and that the main contribution of their discussion is to cast doubt on the usefulness of separating the analysis of income distribution from the study of economic growth. They call for a research agenda, but contend that better policy-making for redistribution can go forward even on the basis of present knowledge.

The issue of redistribution with growth has become the subject of a voluminous literature.[9] Much of it is pessimistic. Rothstein (1976:601), for example, believes that redistribution policies make eminently good sense. They are obviously justified on purely humanitarian grounds, but they may also exert a beneficial impact on birth control, on the productivity of the labor force, and on incentives to save and to invest—and thus ultimately on the rate of economic growth itself. But, like Bell, he regards it unlikely that the ruling elites in the LDCs would embrace policies of redistribution for a number of reasons, such as "the sacrifices demanded from the elite in terms of their own opportunities to amass wealth, the loss of ties with an external world that serves as a point of reference for many elites, continued fascination with the status aspects of economic growth, [and] potential political threats from newly powerful interests."

Morawetz (1977:41), however, is more concerned with whether a policy of redistribution with growth itself has any validity and concludes that what is required is redistribution *before* growth.[10] He says that the "historical evidence suggests that it simply may not be possible to 'grow first and redistribute later,' because the structure of growth may largely fix the pattern of distribution." If more equitable income distribution is to be the objective, then the way to achieve it, he suggests, is "by land reform, mass education, and whatever other means are available, rather than leaving it until after growth has taken place." Adelman (1979:165) carries this a little further and argues that, for equity-oriented development, "the slogan should be: redistribute first—improve productivity later."

It remained for the conclusion to be reached that the Chenery group's work on redistribution with growth constituted an attempt to find a common ground between what was left of economic growth theories, on one hand, and poverty-eradication goals, on the other, without the need for major—and potentially revolutionary—changes in the socioeconomic structures of the LDCs. According to Garcia-Bouza (1980:9), the "basic-needs" approach, to be considered presently, dismissed "this optimistic view and stressed the fact that the marginal redistribution (i.e., the distribution of a part of the additional income generated by economic growth) is insufficient to solve the problem of widespread unemployment and mass poverty." Whatever its realistic limitations with regard to redistribution, it should be noted that the Chenery study made a significant contribution in highlighting the need to view production and distribution as integrally related and to focus on equity through reduction of poverty.

In this chronicle of changing views of development strategies, a report by the Dag Hammarskjöld Foundation, which appeared soon after the publication of Chenery's work, merits at least brief attention for its close linking of equity-oriented development with country-specific societal values and with direct popular participation in the formulation and implementation of development strategies. In July 1975, a special issue of *Development Dialogue*, the journal of the Dag Hammarskjöld Foundation, was published with the title *What Now: Another Development*. The publication of this report, which was prepared as an independent contribution to the Seventh Session of the United Nations General Assembly, comprised the first phase of the 1975 Dag Hammarskjöld Project on Development and International Cooperation. The report, subsequently incorporated into a book (Nerfin, 1977), outlines the basic features of "another development," which was viewed as required in all societies, whether developed or developing, centrally planned or market-dominated, and at a high or a low level of productivity.

As summarized by Nerfin (*ibid.*:10–11), another development would be: "need-oriented," satisfying the basic needs of the world's poor majorities; "endogenous," deriving from the values of each society and eschewing linear universal models; "self-reliant," requiring each society to rely primarily on its own strength and resources at the local level, although self-reliance also needs to be exercised collectively at national and international levels; "ecologically sound," using rationally local and global natural resources with equitable access to these resources by all; and "based on structural transformations," to occur in social relations, economic activities, and power structure "so as to realize the conditions of self-management and participation in decision-making by all those affected by it." According to Nerfin: "These five points are organically linked. Taken in isolation from each other, they would not bring about the desired result. For development is seen as a whole, as an integral, cultural process, as the development of every man and woman and the whole of man and woman. Another development means liberation."

As for the Third World, two parallel strategies are recommended (as cited in Minhas, 1979:85): "One is the reallocation of resources to meet basic needs, to reduce inequality internally and dependence externally and to increase the scope and depth of participation in decision making. The other is raising the level of productive forces in accordance with the objectives of another development."

This global manifesto, inspired by egalitarian and humanitarian values, proposes a development perspective and strategy that in fact calls for a worldwide conversion or change of heart, embracing all the groups that have a share of power along with the groups that have been powerless. For the present, at least, "another development" remains a manifesto, a conceptual statement that has little likelihood of being implemented in its totality, as its advocates claim it must be. It constitutes, however, an important departure point for further debate and action-oriented, focused research. Its basic propositions are likely to remain a prominent part of equity-oriented perspectives in the ongoing development dialogue. Like the "basic-needs approach," to which the discussion now turns, "another development" called for the adoption of a new development strategy. Its output has remained relatively small, however, compared with the volume of literature generated by "basic needs."[11]

BASIC-NEEDS APPROACH

For some development specialists, the emergence of a "basic-needs approach" in the mid-1970s was seen as the culmination of 25 years of development thought. In this view, a basic-needs approach constituted a development strategy that embraced all the previous strategies that were concerned with reduction of poverty and increase of equity, not only those reflected in Chenery's work on redistribution with growth, which has been considered in this discussion, but also other strategies and approaches not explicitly treated here, such as creation of employment opportunities, integration of rural development and expansion of agricultural output, and improvement of human resources and capital. The basic-needs approach did have links to these several strategies, particularly the concern with making the poor more productive, but its distinctive contribution is that it brought to center stage, as a complement to these earlier approaches, a concern with meeting the consumption needs of the poor majorities in the Third World, in health, education, nutrition, housing, water supply, and sanitation, not only through provision of public services in these sectors but also through ensuring opportunities for individuals and communities to obtain direct access to resources for the formulation and implementation of policies oriented to the satisfaction of their basic needs.

Major impetus for the adoption of a basic-needs approach came from a recommendation by the World Employment Conference of the International Labour Office in 1976. The recommendation appears in a report prepared by International Labour Office staff for the conference and subsequently published (International Labour Office, 1977), which outlines in some detail the national and international strategies required for the implementation of the basic-needs approach. In the intervening years, a great deal of literature on basic needs has been generated. Only four years after the International Labour Office report appeared, Garcia-Bouza (1980) published a bibliography of over 300 pages on basic needs. Until recently, the basic-needs perspective has occupied a prominent place on the agenda of international meetings. Just as Chenery and his associates published a "landmark" book on redistribution with growth, so Streeten and his colleagues prepared another such "landmark" book on basic needs (Streeten, Burki, Haq, Hicks, and Stewart, 1981). It should be noted that both books were published for the World Bank and written by economists who were either employed by the bank or have served the bank as consultants.

In the International Labour Office formulation, basic needs include two elements: (1) certain minimum requirements of a family for private consumption—adequate food, shelter, and clothing; and (2) essential services provided by and for the community at large, such as safe drinking water, sanitation, public transport, and health and educational facilities. The report goes on to say that the satisfaction of an absolute level of basic needs as thus defined should be placed within the broader frame-work of the fulfillment of basic human rights, which not only are ends in themselves but also contribute to the attainment of other goals (International Labour Office, 1977). There are many lists of needs in the literature. Cassen (1978a), for example, limits his list to the "core" basic needs of food, health, education, and shelter, while Streeten *et al.* (1981) consider "essential basic needs" in six areas: "nutrition, primary education, health, sanitation, water supply, and housing and related infrastructure. This list is merely illustrative, not exhaustive, and all needs do not have the same status" (*ibid.*:92).

Although the number and nature of needs on a list may vary, and the precise content and strategy for implementation must be left for the countries and groups that may adopt a basic-needs approach to formulate, there is no question that however needs are defined, large portions of the populations of many LDCs are in want of them. Estimates by the World Bank in 1980 that the number of people in LDCs living in absolute poverty was around 780 million (and this excluded China and other centrally planned economies) probably have not changed much (International Bank for Reconstruction and Development, 1980a).[12] A more recent source (World Bank, 1985a) indicates the likelihood that per capita consumption has continued to decline, at least in Latin America and sub-Saharan Africa.

Increased employment and income for the poor are central to the basic-needs perspective. As Cassen (1978a:4) pointed out, "A Basic-Needs strategy is not primarily a welfare, 'handout' approach, but one founded on the generation of productive employment." As indicated earlier, the heavy reliance on rapid industrialization that dominated development perspectives in the 1950s and 1960s and was intended to generate employment and maximize the rate of growth of income proved to be misplaced. Substantial industrial progress was achieved in the LDCs, but it would have had to be much greater to absorb even the rapidly growing urban labor force, let alone the labor force in agriculture, which in many LDCs constitutes around 75% of the total labor force. An International Labour Office report (Sheehan and Hopkins, 1979) analyzed basic-needs performance (i.e., the performance of a country in satisfying the basic needs of its population) in 135 countries, including 83 LDCs, for the period 1960–1970. The principal conclusion of the report is that not only was the gap between rich and poor countries in basic-needs performance very wide but also in most LDCs only very slow progress was being made toward closing that gap.

Myrdal (1970), among others, pointed out early on that the main problem of poverty in the LDCs is not unemployment, as it is understood in the DCs. Rather, it is long hours of labor at insufficiently productive and inadequately remunerated work. In particular, these conditions have prevailed for women, especially rural women, who have performed difficult and essential labor that was unpaid and thus not counted in statistics on employment. The issue is not one of simply increasing employment, but of more fully utilizing labor for greater productivity, for which better nutrition, health, and education are required, in addition to being desirable in their own right. Streeten *et al.* (1981) maintain that in poor countries, better nutrition, health, and education can be very productive in developing human resources, and these sectors are among the major ones embraced by the basic-needs approach.

Although most of the literature has been focused on the problems of meeting the economic and physical dimensions of basic needs, some efforts have been made to place the basic-needs strategy within the broader framework of attaining human freedom and other factors that contribute to people's sense of identity, achievement, and satisfaction. Indeed, Streeten *et al.* (1981:34) affirm that nonmaterial needs are a critical component of a basic–needs approach, since they are "important conditions for meeting material needs. They include the needs for self-determination, self-reliance, and security, for the participation of workers and citizens in the decision-making that affects them, for national and cultural identity, and for a sense of purpose in life and work."[13] Even in limiting problems of definition of basic needs to material needs, Cassen (1978a) indicated that the definition of a "minimum standard" could not be done by an outsider on any objective or universal basis, so that precise definition must be left to those involved in the implementation of the approach. How much more difficult, then, is the task of defining the content of nonmaterial needs? Ghai and Alfthan (1977) suggested that the dilemma be resolved by making a statement on fundamental human rights and freedoms an integral part of any formulation of a basic-needs strategy.

Just as setting a "minimum standard" for defining the precise content of basic needs on a universal basis is so arbitrary as to be virtually meaningless, so attempts at global estimates of the costs of meeting the basic needs of the poor are likely to be closer to fantasy than to reality. In one attempt to estimate the rough order of magnitude of "shortfalls" being suffered by the poor in the LDCs, and limiting core basic needs to food, safe drinking water, and shelter, Streeten and Burki (1978) find that the number of people with deficiencies in any of these three core basic needs ranges from 500 to 800 million. An attempt to estimate resource requirements for meeting these shortfalls (*ibid.*) yielded a rough order of magnitude for the annual cost of meeting basic needs in the poorer countries of $30–40 billion, which is 12–16% of their estimated average gross national product (GNP) for the period 1980–2000, 80–105% of their gross domestic investment, and 85–110% of their government resources. Clearly, costs of this magnitude, if a global basic-needs program were to be implemented over a period of two decades, would require substantial transfers from the DCs in the form of concessional assistance. Streeten and Burki (1978:418) conclude "that development assistance would have to undergo a radical transformation in both scope and quality if a substantial step were to be made towards meeting basic needs by the year 2000." Streeten *et al.* (1981) maintain that although only a part of the development assistance received by the poorest countries is devoted to meeting basic needs, it would be a mistake to redirect a greater share of current assistance to basic-needs programs because doing so would be neither politically desirable nor technically possible. Middle-income countries that receive assistance also have poverty problems, and the commitments and expectations now current cannot be simply discarded. Consequently, they propose (*ibid.*) that the international community make substantial additional contributions to basic-needs programs in the poorest countries, which would supplement the formidable domestic efforts required on the part of the LDCs and current available international assistance to implement these programs.

The role of international assistance in Third World development merits special treatment and is considered subsequently, but a few observations in relation to basic needs are in order here. The International Labour Office (1977) report called for important reforms in official development assistance policies, particularly as they applied to the poorest countries, in the direction of greater flexibility, less project orientation, a higher proportion of grants, easier credit terms, and longer-term commitments. In the way of needed reforms, Streeten *et al.* (1981:178–179) emphasize that votes in the international agencies should be distributed so as to ensure fair representation for the LDCs, that members of international secretariats "must transcend narrowly national loyalties and be sensitive to the social and cultural issues in developing countries," and that "narrow technocracy and an excessive politicization of issues will have to be avoided." Since 1976, some of the bilateral donors and multilateral agencies, particularly the World Bank, have been increasingly directing their attention to support for basic-needs activities. Robert S. McNamara, in his World Bank speeches (International Bank for Reconstruction and Development, 1981a), for example, gave increasing emphasis to basic needs beginning in 1976 (although as early as 1971, he was expressing concern about problems of poverty, inequality, and unemployment), when he called for "the meeting of the basic human needs of the absolute poor in both the poorest and the middle-income countries . . . by the end of the century" (ibid.:359), through his last speech in 1980 (see also International Bank for Reconstruction and Development, 1975). Indeed, these many calls for support of basic needs indicated that the donors were finally recognizing that development assistance had failed to reach those who needed it most. Although the use of the term "basic needs" has become somewhat attenuated recently, as is noted presently, the focus of this approach on equity and on core needs is still in the forefront of attention, particularly on the part of the World Bank. McNamara's successor, Clausen (1985a), (who has now in turn been succeeded by Conable), continued to accord highest priorities in bank assistance, as attested in a recent speech, to problems of nutrition, health, education, water supply, population, agricultural productivity, and natural resource management among the poor majorities of the poorest countries. Nevertheless, in the same speech, Clausen noted (ibid.:9) that "the growth of official development assistance has fallen below even minimal expectations" and predicted (ibid.:23) that "for the poorest countries, the outlook for an increase in concessional flows is bleak."

The difficulties of setting a minimum standard for defining the precise content of basic needs on a universal basis and of making global estimates of the costs of meeting basic needs are substantial, but the problems of measurement of basic needs, of finding a "suitable yardstick," are even more formidable (Grant, 1977; Khan, 1977; Streeten et al., 1981). Dell (1978:12–14), for example, points out that even in the case of food consumption, for which it should be easiest to set a quantitative target, the setting of an absolute standard for minimum intake would be essentially arbitrary, since knowledge of human requirements for most nutrients is quite limited. He concludes that "the scientific, statistical and analytical foundations for a basic needs strategy are extraordinarily weak even in the sector where they should presumably be strongest— namely, that of food consumption—while in other sectors they are nonexistent."

Hicks and Streeten (1979), in a search for a "basic-needs yardstick," maintain that growth of GNP per capita and related concepts by themselves are not adequate indicators of development, so that the reduction of poverty and the satisfaction of basic needs are goals that should appear in a measure of development. In seeking ways of designing better measures of development, they consider modifications of GNP per capita, social indicators and associated systems of accounts, and composite indices of development. In Streeten et al. (1981), this work is carried a little further. They identify a series of "core indicators" for each of the basic-needs sectors and consider the possibility of narrowing this range to one or two indicators that correlate highly with basic-needs satisfaction. These indicators would supplement, rather than replace, GNP per capita as a measure of reduction of poverty. Whatever its limitations, GNP remains an important indicator, with some modifications, because economic growth continues to be one of the essential conditions of the reduction of poverty.

It appears that the search for valid yardsticks may be a long one. For the present, at least, perhaps the matter has to rest with the position of Cassen (1978a:17) that "a government which made a determined effort to improve employment prospects, health, nutrition, education and housing would deserve well of its citizens, even if it never defined the levels to be attained or counted the numbers of the deprived. Of course, depending on countries' planning capacity, a degree of counting and costing (not to mention delivering) may be necessary and desirable."

A major criticism of the basic-needs approach that appeared from many quarters, not least from LDC officials, was that vigorous pursuit of this approach would impair the rate of economic growth, i.e., that the consumption and welfare required to satisfy basic needs would be at the expense of the savings, productive investment, and incentives to work deemed necessary to fuel the engine of economic growth. In the argument about basic needs vs. economic growth, Sri Lanka was offered as an example of a country that went too far down the welfare path at the expense of growth and strengthening of its productive capacity. But in an International Labour Office study of the relationship in Sri Lanka between the pursuit of basic-needs policies and a slow rate of economic growth, Richards and Gooneratne (1980:172) conclude that the negative effects of such policies on growth can be easily exaggerated. They go on to say: "Furthermore those policies also have positive effects which are not generally specified. . . . For Sri Lanka we are not optimistic that with greater investment resources at hand they would have been fruitfully spent. Correspondingly we feel that the operation of welfare programmes was a reflection of the over-all social and political situation in Sri Lanka and not an aberration from it."

Taiwan and South Korea are the most frequently cited examples of countries that managed to maintain both above-average growth rates and above-average improvement in basic needs. In the case of Taiwan, Ranis (1978) made a strong argument for growth strategy oriented to rural development as a means of approaching equity. Specifically, he accounted for Taiwan's success as the result of, among other factors, land reform, early concern with increasing agricultural productivity, development of nonfarm rural enterprises, and a shift from import substitution to export of labor-intensive products. For South Korea, Rao (1978) argued that employment was the most important factor in that country's success in combining rapid growth with improved equity.

With regard to investment and basic needs, Streeten *et al.* (1981) looked at this relationship in ten LDCs and concluded that there is no evidence that implementing a basic-needs approach is consistently associated with low investment ratios. They found that five countries, Taiwan, South Korea, the Philippines, Paraguay, and Thailand, had good basic-needs performance and also had above-average investment ratios, while five others, Sri Lanka, Cuba, Jamaica, Colombia, and Uruguay, also did well at basic-needs performance, but had only average investment ratios.

As already indicated, the satisfaction of basic needs depends not only on the provision of government services but also on generation of productive employment and greater income for the poor so that they can pay their share. Moreover, the basic-needs approach calls for a search for low-cost solutions to problems of food, health, education, and shelter through reallocation of current patterns of expenditure in favor of the poor. Relevant here is the mobilization of community action to contribute, among other matters, to the financing of public services.

There have been a number of claims (Cassen, 1978a; Sewell, Gwatkin, Howe, Kallab, Mathieson, McLaughlin, and Streeten, 1980; Streeten *et al.*, 1981) that the emphasis in the basic-needs approach on the development of human resources could yield some important tradeoffs to offset whatever might be the initial consequences for growth by virtue of meeting basic needs, but there is little research as yet to document how important these tradeoffs might be, in addition, of course, to the substantial value they hold in their own right. For example, better nutrition, health, and education may strengthen incentives to work and enhance the productivity of labor. And in this connection, it should be noted that some advocates of the basic-needs approach called for improvements in the social and economic position of women that could be crucial in the thrust to meet basic needs. As one writer put it (Ahooja-Patel, 1977:83): "The development of the poor world has become the object of a number of economic theories. But in all this . . . the best minds of the day have successfully omitted any reference to the place of women in the development process." The human and economic costs of this neglect are particularly high in many areas of the Third World, especially in rural areas.

The concern with achieving equity for the poor through satisfaction of basic needs is an understandable response to the fact that aggregate economic growth, even though its rate had been dramatically high in the

LDCs for a quarter century, had done very little for the poor majorities of Third World countries. For some of the principal advocates of the basic-needs approach, even though rapid rates of economic growth continued to be regarded as an essential part of a basic-needs strategy, the preferred locus for such growth apparently shifted from industrialization to rural development, which was accorded major emphasis as central to the implementation of basic-needs programs. It is likely that this shift helped to account in part for some attenuation, in the last few years, in the prominence of the basic-needs approach as the central perspective in the development debate. LDC officials, as well as some members of the international development assistance community, continued to fear that pursuit of a basic-needs approach oriented primarily to rural development would be at the expense of economic growth, which to a large extent they continued to equate primarily with industrial development (A. Singh, 1979).

Actually, much of the literature has seemed to suggest that priority for successful implementation of basic-needs objectives should go to the rural rather than the industrial sector in development strategies (Dell, 1978). The International Labour Office (1977) report, for example, stressed the need for a rapid rate of economic growth as an essential part of a basic-needs strategy, but the principal requirements listed for implementation of the strategy made no mention of industrial development.

In an analysis of the relationships among poverty, economic growth, and development including case studies of six LDCs, Fields (1980:241) cautiously argued that a "distributionally oriented development program that integrates the poor into the mainstream of the economy may *cause* a higher growth rate, other things being equal. Obversely, a development strategy aimed at a limited segment of the economy may result in a lower growth rate than could be achieved given that country's resource endowment." But he says that this argument is far from proven, given the limits of current knowledge, and that research on the economic, social, and political dynamics of growth should be given the highest priority.

Paul Streeten, probably the staunchest and most eloquent advocate of the basic-needs approach, has consistently maintained that there is no conflict between economic growth and satisfaction of basic needs. Indeed, early on, Streeten (1975:1) viewed industrialization as necessary for both economic growth and the effective realization of broad-based development objectives and contended that "to rise above poverty, industrialization is necessary." The important qualification, however, is that rapid economic growth, especially industrial growth, must be compatible with basic-needs objectives. When this compatibility is attained, then "industrialization as the servant of development regains its proper place in the strategy. Industry should produce the simple products and consumer goods required by the people, the majority of whom live in the countryside" (ibid.:2–3). More recently, Streeten et al. (1981) argued that meeting basic needs can be an effective means of improving the quality of human resources, which in turn contributes to economic growth, and a higher rate of growth augments the resources available for meeting basic needs. They concluded (ibid.:108): "Growth by itself . . . does not guarantee the satisfaction of basic needs. A distinctive feature of the basic needs approach is that policies must be implemented to ensure a rising and properly distributed supply of goods, both private and public, if basic needs are to be met."

A. Singh (1979) argued not only that there is no conflict between the basic-needs approach and accelerated industrialization but also that there is in fact a close interdependence between the two. It seems clear that to meet the basic needs of the poor in the Third World on a sustainable basis, it is essential to raise the rate of economic growth in the LDCs. At the same time, since the rate of growth of demand is likely in the future to be an increasingly important constraint, among others, a basic-needs approach could positively help foster industrial development, especially given the present state of the world economy. This position has hardly received universal acceptance, however, judging by the frequency with which arguments about whether there is a conflict between economic growth and basic needs have appeared in the literature.[14] Indeed, Streeten and his colleagues still found it necessary to devote a chapter to this issue in their book in 1981.

It is important to note that the principal source of proposals for a basic-needs approach has been the DCs and the international agencies (as has been the case for some other equity-oriented strategies such as redistribution with growth) rather than the LDCs themselves, although some LDCs were concerned with problems of poverty reduction long before the declaration in 1976 by the International Labour Office World Employment Conference. Such declarations, according to Wolfe (1979:10), "while they are presented as demands of the dispossessed majority of the world's people, they are, to a much greater extent than the accompanying demands for economic equality between nation-states, the brain children of circles of intellectuals and reformers meeting in differing combinations in one forum after another." The term "basic needs" has elicited a variety of negative as well as positive reactions in both the DCs and the LDCs (Haq, 1981). According to Garcia-Bouza (1980:45), there is a "widespread perception—especially in non-developed countries—of the basic-needs approach as either a 'second best' development strategy, excluding poor countries from the benefits of industrialisation and economic modernisation, or as a ploy to thwart the legitimate efforts of Third World countries to modify in their favour the structure of international exchanges."

Whatever may be the factual basis for the negative perceptions regarding basic needs, there is no question that the prominent position this approach assumed in the development debate served to reinforce substantially the concern with alleviation of poverty; with certain critical consumption needs in such core sectors as nutrition, health, and education; and with provision of opportunities for individuals and communities to gain direct access to resources and to participate in development efforts.

CONCLUDING OBSERVATIONS

The development thinking of the 1950s and 1960s was dominated by linear views in which the pursuit of economic growth driven by the engine of industrialization was seen as the key to development. By the early 1970s, there was growing awareness not only that this strategy was not yielding the intended effects for Third World economies but also that the poor majorities were being excluded from whatever benefits were reaped through economic growth. Consequently, it became clear that distribution had to become an integral part of development objectives along with economic growth. Development policies became equity-oriented rather than exclusively growth-oriented, and the subsequent emergence of the basic-needs approach reflected the importance attached to consumption and the strengthening of human capital, in addition to production and distribution, as essential to the realization of the objectives of broad-based development.

Some advocates of the basic-needs approach appeared to regard it as the central component of a comprehensive development strategy that would not only accord absolute priority to meeting the basic needs of the poor but also provide the grand design for national development as a whole. As noted, however, little attention was paid in the International Labour Office formulation to industrial development and little was said about the need for fundamental social and structural change if equity was to be achieved. For these and other reasons, some development specialists denied that the basic-needs approach could lay claim to constituting a comprehensive development strategy. Dell (1978), for example, maintained that even if a country had egalitarian goals, it might not necessarily wish to accord overriding priority to achieving certain absolute targets for consumption, but instead might prefer to limit current and short-term consumption so as to permit a more rapid rate of growth and structural transformation. He conceded that the advocates of basic needs had made a contribution to the development dialogue by emphasizing the importance of equitable distribution of the benefits of development, but argued that they claimed too much in according it the status of a comprehensive development strategy.

In reacting to the neglect of the poor sustained by the exclusive focus on economic growth, it may be, as World Bank staff put it (International Bank for Reconstruction and Development, 1985:98), that some advocates of basic needs created an artificial dichotomy in which economic growth and the alleviation of poverty were seen as mutually exclusive, when in fact they are interdependent. Thus, the issue is "not one of equity versus growth, but rather the nature of growth. Supporters of this 'growth with equity' approach have emphasized the need for a mixture of efforts, some aimed directly at the problems and constraints faced by the poor, others aimed at increasing growth and output and improving economic policies, which directly or indirectly benefit the poor." Substituting a "growth with equity" approach for a basic-needs approach does have the virtue of allaying the concern with a conflict between economic growth and basic needs that has persisted in the reactions to the basic-needs approach.

Equity-oriented development may no longer go by the label of "basic needs," but the essential objectives of this approach continue to constitute a critical component of development policies and strategies. As indicated in the earlier quotation from a 1985 speech by the World Bank's former president, A. W. Clausen, the bank continues to accord high priority to the alleviation of poverty through support in areas that have been central to the basic-needs approach, particularly health, nutrition, education, and agricultural productivity, a priority that is also reflected in two recent bank reports (World Bank, 1985a; International Bank for Reconstruction and Development, 1985). Moreover, as indicated in the latter report (*ibid.*:98), this concern is not limited to World Bank assistance. Bank staff observe that most donors have been encouraged in their support for aid programs by the fact that aid funds "seek to address the basic long-term problems faced by the poor." The heritage of the basic-needs approach is also reflected in the functional definition of income now being advanced by some development economists, a definition that includes, in addition to economic returns, such specific components as basic schooling, improved health care, improved nutrition, and other resources for the creation of human capital (Kocher, 1984).

NOTES

[1]See Worsley (1984) for one account of "modernization" in social science theory.

[2]For a large-scale sociological study oriented to the modernization model, see the report by Inkeles and Smith (1974) of their findings on modernization in six developing countries.

[3]Other critics of the modernization model are, for example, Apthorpe (1976) and Hutton and Cohen (1975) in sociology, Nafziger (1979) in economics, Uphoff and Ilchman (1972) in political economy, and Pitt (1976a,b) in anthropology.

[4]For a view of dependency from one of the Communist countries, see the work of Szentes (1977, 1980), a Hungarian economist. Griffin (1969) has made a detailed study of underdevelopment in Latin America. Kahl (1976) has reviewed the work of three leading Latin American sociologists who have worked on dependency: Germani, Gonzalez Casanova, and Cardoso.

[5]See Cardoso (1979) for an assessment of the ECLA contribution. See also a statement by Raul Prebisch (1979), the father of ECLA economics, of his position.

[6]Valenzuela and Valenzuela (1981) point out that Frank is often thought of as the most important exponent of the dependency view because his work was available in English, but that in fact he presented oversimplified versions of the contributions of the Latin American writers that unintentionally distorted those contributions.

[7]Although their assessment of the modernization perspective is close to the one presented here, Valenzuela and Valenzuela (1981:53) take a different position regarding dependency. They say: "The dependency perspective . . . in the long run . . . should provide a set of propositions capable of providing a real test for the assumption that the evolution of international structural linkages over time have conditioned development."

[8]Although Taiwan is listed as a country here and subsequently, it should be noted that the Taiwanese think of themselves as constituting a province of the Republic of China and the mainland Chinese regard Taiwan as a province of the People's Republic of China.

[9]For a case study of an effort at redistribution in one of the few countries in which this has been attempted, namely, Tanzania, see Green (1977). See also Apthorpe (1979) and Stavenhagen (1975).

[10]Weeks (1975:101) makes a similar point: "Experience in rich countries indicates clearly that redistributive steps that leave the ownership of property unchanged have little or no long-term impact. If there are economic laws, a fundamental one is that wealth generates income, and if it is desired to generate a different pattern of income flows, it is necessary to alter the path of wealth-holding."

[11]On "another development," see Cardoso (1977) and Wolfe (1977, 1979).

[12]The *proportion* of people in absolute poverty in LDCs as a group is estimated to have fallen during the 1960s and 1970s (although probably not in sub-Saharan Africa in the 1970s). But because population has grown, the *number* of people in absolute poverty has increased (International Bank for Reconstruction and Development, 1980a). Poverty and lack of equity are by no means exclusively Third World problems. According to Edsall (1984:206), "In 1982 the number of people living [in the United States] below the govern-

ment's official poverty line . . . rose to 34.5 million, or 15 per cent of the population . . . a full percentage point above the 1981 level and the highest rate since 1965."
[13]In a report on a tour of six Latin American countries to assess the value of development
projects concerned with "cultural investment" rather than the more usual objective of
improving material well-being, Ariel Dorfman (1984:24), the Chilean poet and novelist,
said: ". . . the real advance consists in having made some people feel more human. . . .
How do you measure the amount of dignity that people accumulate? . . . With what
machines do you evaluate someone's rediscovered identity, the power that they now
feel to set their own goals and not merely take what others are willing to hand down?
With what graphs would you chart the curves of increased memory, increased self-
reliance, increased group solidarity, increased critical awareness?"
[14]Hicks (1984) has reviewed the literature on this issue.

Equity-Oriented Development

Problems and Prospects

Although there may be terminological differences, as well as conceptual differences, regarding development approaches, current development thinking, at least on the part of the international development assistance community, is oriented to the promotion of equity in national development strategies. Such strategies would be designed to help both the poor and the society as a whole achieve their development objectives, whatever each less-developed country (LDC) decides its specific objectives should be. The prospects for adoption of equity-oriented development policies by Third World governments vary widely. The range includes such variations as the following: regimes that have no concern with reduction of poverty, but employ their concentrated power to benefit only the ruling elite; regimes that may be open to adoption of equity-oriented programs, but in which resistance by vested interest groups will have to be overcome by coalitions of reformist groups; and regimes that can be said to have already done well in promoting equity, on the basis of such indicators as life expectancy and literacy rates, as well as increases in income per capita. In this chapter, consideration is given to a series of factors that are relevant, historically and currently, to the prospects for implementation of equity-oriented development policies.

URBAN BIAS

Generally, about two thirds of the population in the LDCs live and work in rural areas and gain their livelihood from agriculture as farmers and farm workers, and these groups include the vast majority of the world's poorest people (Minhas, 1979; International Bank for Reconstruction and Development, 1982; Schutjer and Stokes, 1984). Thus, a major effort for the implementation of equity-oriented strategies will have to be made in the rural areas. Proponents of all the poverty-focused development perspectives have accorded great emphasis to rural development. Obtaining access to income and power by the rural poor looms large.

Urban bias in development perspectives and practice was essentially a reflection of the modernization model, an integral part of the dogma that industrialization was the engine of economic growth and that rural people had to be shifted out of agriculture, the "traditional" sector, into industry, or "modern" sector, as the principal path to progress. By the early 1970s, however, there was a growing realization that with a few notable exceptions, industrialization had not become the engine capable of pulling whole societies into the good life; reality was not conforming to theory.

According to the conventional wisdom, policy in the LDCs advocated leaving farming alone, allowing it few resources, taxing it heavily if possible, and obtaining its products cheaply to finance industrial development, which had top priority. When it became clear in the late 1960s that agriculture cannot be neglected if it is to provide workers, materials, markets, and savings to industry, policy shifted, in many LDCs, to advocating allocation of substantial resources to those parts of agriculture, mainly large farms, that could supply industry with raw materials and industrial workers with food. This policy was still permeated by urban bias, because the farm sector was allocated resources not mainly to improve the economic well-being of the rural sector, but to feed industrial growth. As Lipton (1977:20) put it, "Development of the rural sector is advocated, but not for the people who live and work there." When it became evident that concentration of resources on big farmers would neither relieve the needs of the rural poor (in part because big farmers use little labor per acre) nor use the resources very productively, and that any approximation to a balance between rural and urban sectors seemed as far off as ever, there began to emerge in the mid-1970s, at least within the international development assistance community, a consensus for according priority to the role of agriculture and to increasing the incomes of the poor. But Lipton (ibid.:17–18) contended that "so long as the elite's interests, background and sympathies remain predominantly urban, the countryside may get the 'priority' but the city will get the resources." Writing in 1981 about the consensus for a new strategy emphasizing rural development, Todaro and Stilkind (1981:8) concluded that "to date . . . the commitment to this strategy has not been strong enough to significantly change the urbanization–industrialization policies of past decades."

Nevertheless, the call for according first priority to acceleration of

growth in the agricultural sector, for which Mellor (1976) made an eloquent plea in the mid-1970s, has by now certainly been heeded. Just as
industrialization dominated development strategies from the 1950s into
the 1970s, so is agriculture now the watchword of development (Kristof,
1985; see also Fei and Ranis, 1984). It may be noted, however, that this
shift comes at a time when prices for export of agricultural commodities,
in both the developed countries (DCs) and the LDCs, are at their lowest
levels in years. Indeed, there is currently a worldwide surplus of food,
i.e., of the principal grains such as corn, wheat, and rice (Schneider,
1986). Grain harvests, in both the DCs and the LDCs, have been increasing dramatically due primarily to advances in knowledge of plant genet-
ics. Ironically, this worldwide surplus of food does not mean that problems of hunger in the LDCs, particularly in Africa, have been solved.
Nor does it mean that the core needs of the poor majorities, as defined in
the last chapter, are any closer to being met now that agriculture has
priority than they were when industrialization was thought to be the
key to development. Issues of food supply are considered subsequently
in relation to population growth. Suffice it to say here that hunger and
malnutrition continue to plague many millions of people, most of whom
are to be found in the LDCs. Despite the abundance of food, they continue to suffer hunger because of inadequate incomes, inefficient distribution of food, and political turmoil and internecine struggles in various regions of the world.

Neither has urban bias done all that much for the cities. Concomitant with the push for industrialization came rapid urbanization. The
movement of people and resources from the country to the city was
expected to provide the cheap labor and forced savings to stimulate
urban industrialization. The movement certainly occurred, but the results were rather different than expected. There has been massive migration of people from rural to urban areas, and such migration continues even though many of the larger cities in the Third World have
essentially ceased trying to do more than provide minimal services in
health, housing, sanitation, transportation, and other areas for these
huge populations (Todaro and Stilkind, 1981). Although in 1970 there
were almost 30 million more people living in cities in the DCs than in the
LDCs, by 1985 there was not only a reversal but also at least 300 million
more people living in urban areas in the LDCs than in the DCs, and by
the year 2000 there will be almost twice as many urban residents in the
LDCs as in the DCs (Salas, 1986). As Salas (*ibid.*:13) says, "The blessings
of cities are mixed. . . . As always, the numbers of the poor grow fastest
and suffer most. And while cities grow, the rural base on which they
depend may be eaten away."

Writing in the early 1970s, Schumacher (1975) argued strongly against massive urbanization and the use of high-cost technology in industry and advocated instead the dispersal of industry into the countryside by creating millions of new workplaces that would employ, in his term, "intermediate technology." Schumacher's idea that "small is beautiful" captured the interest of many and has perhaps had some influence on rural development strategy even though no one has rushed to implement his particular proposals. The disincentives to agricultural growth imposed by urban bias effectively discouraged not only rural nonfarm development of the kind proposed by Schumacher and others but also small-farm agricultural development. Writing about development in an Indonesian village, Keyfitz (1985:716) concludes: "What it [the village] needs . . . is small industry—clothing, ceramics, furniture—that is no small part of the immediately feasible rise in the standard of living. . . . If village development is to occur fast enough to prevent an unbalanced growth of the biggest cities, someone needs to determine what fraction of its talented youth the village ought to be holding and what measures should be taken to encourage those young people to exercise their talents in the village."

The need for land reform is often cited as a critical component of equity-focused development strategies, and there are a number of studies that suggest that redistribution of land in larger farms into smaller ones would in many cases significantly increase output and employment, and therefore equity.[1] In an extensive study of agrarian structure and productivity in a number of LDCs, R. A. Berry and Cline (1979) conclude that the small-farm sector makes better use of its available land than does the large-farm sector, largely through applying higher levels of labor inputs (family labor) per unit of land. The central policy conclusion of their analysis is that land redistribution into family farms is an attractive policy instrument for raising production and for improving rural employment and equality of income distribution. They maintain that this policy of land redistribution merits consideration not only in Latin American countries with enormous landed estates but also in the land-scarce countries of Asia.

Although Lipton (1977) devotes most of his book to examining the deleterious consequences of urban bias for the rural poor, he by no means advocates the substitution of rural bias for urban bias.[2] He is for industrialization, but maintains that poverty is a barrier to rapid and general industrialization and that a developed mass agriculture is needed before widespread successful development can occur in other sectors. Lipton does, however, neglect the symbiotic aspects of urban–rural relationships. As indicated earlier, the modernization model generates the dichotomy of modern vs. traditional, in which "modern" is equated with "urban" and "traditional" with "rural," a polarization that obscures, among other matters, what may be the actual and potential relative contributions of the two sectors to each other and to the process of development in the LDCs. In reality, there may well be symbiotic and other kinds of interactions going on between the rural and urban sectors of a country that may be important for all the members of that society. As Salas (1986:14) has observed: "The concept of urban and rural population should not lead us to think of them as opposites whose interests are diametrically opposed. Social research has shown a kaleidoscope of rural–urban contacts . . . with infinite variations."

The current emphasis on agricultural development will not by itself, of course, pave the way to implementation of equity-oriented development policies. The fact that the rural poor's share of income and power in the majority of the LDCs is still as small as ever, and may in some instances have actually decreased, speaks for itself. Changing this situation will require delicate and intricate maneuvering. LDC governments and their policy–makers may engage in impressive rhetoric about the need and intention to make such changes, but undertaking them will require action that will be perceived as harmful to their interests by a variety of established power groups in the rural as well as the urban sector. Lipton (1977) offers a number of suggestions concerning how support can be mobilized and opposition reconciled or weakened on the part of the interest groups that would be affected, including trade–union leaders, businessmen, and politicians and planners. Similarly, Todaro and Stilkind (1981) suggest a series of short-term and long-term policies to foster rural development and counter rapid urbanization. The political and other constraints that confront the implementation of equity-oriented development are formidable and are considered in the next section.

POLITICAL AND OTHER CONSTRAINTS AND STRUCTURAL CHANGE

Much has been written in the development literature about the need for equitable distribution of the benefits of development (and this discussion is no exception), but little about how the DCs and LDCs alike might generate the political will and determination to initiate and implement the requisite changes to obtain that equitable distribution. Nor has the increase in expressions of concern for the poorest groups in the poorest countries been matched by a parallel increase in the number of programs in the LDCs effectively aimed at that poverty through policy measures.

As indicated earlier, the historical evidence suggests that it may not be possible to maximize economic growth first and redistribute assets later because the structure of growth may largely fix the pattern of distribution. The assumption that the fruits of economic growth would automatically "trickle down" has not been borne out by the experience of most LDCs, because there is unequal access to the opportunities of producing, or obtaining the income from, incremental gross national product (GNP). It is the richer groups that have privileged access and are likely to appropriate the increased GNP, producing even sharper disparities in income distribution, at least up to medium-income levels (Singer and Ansari, 1982). These considerations strongly imply that poverty is structural and should be regarded as a product of a social system that reflects differences in access of various groups to sources of economic and political power. Given a structural definition of poverty, it follows that development policies and strategies aimed at the effective reduction of poverty require structural change for their implementation, i.e., changes in the patterns, or structures, of possession and use of resources that can elicit, channel, and transform resources most appropriately to meet the needs of people more fully.

Analyses of what has happened to absolute poverty in the LDCs over recent decades (Morawetz, 1977; Streeten, 1978; Streeten *et al.*, 1981; International Bank for Reconstruction and Development, 1982, 1986; Population Reference Bureau, 1987) have yielded these indications: Some countries experienced rapid economic growth and noteworthy decreases in the numbers of the poor, such as China, Hong Kong, Singapore, South Korea, and Taiwan. These countries, with a combined population of 1,131,900,000, constitute about one third of the population in the LDCs. In a second group, which includes about 750 million people, there was rapid or moderate economic growth, but increasing inequality. This category includes, among others, countries such as Argentina, Brazil, Malaysia, Mexico, and the Philippines. A third group of countries, which experienced slow economic growth together with increasing impoverishment, includes Bangladesh, the poorer African countries, and perhaps (the evidence for these countries being disputed) India, Indonesia, and Pakistan.

A wide variety of explanations for the persistence of poverty have been offered. Development policies obviously play a part, but the social and political structures, the cultural traditions, the extent of formation of human capital, the distribution of assets, and the extent of foreign trade all influence the relationship between economic growth and poverty.

The empirical basis for assessing the relative importance of each of these components is thin indeed. If these are the critical components, however, then the remedy would appear to be structural change, for which there have been increasing calls in the development literature, some of which have been cited earlier in this discussion.[3] Griffin and Khan (1978:303) bluntly concluded that "both micro- and macro-economic tinkering are almost certain to fail. The remedy lies in structural change, in changing the distribution of productive wealth (and consequently the distribution of economic power) and in increasing the participation of the poor in decision-making (and consequently enabling them to exercise political power)."

If an equity-oriented development strategy is to be effectively implemented in an LDC, the most critical prerequisite may be a major restructuring of political and economic power relationships. Nevertheless, as indicated in the discussion of redistribution with growth, the political, social, economic, and administrative constraints on attempting this restructuring in one fell swoop in most LDCs are likely to render such an attempt an exercise in futility. In coping with the constraints, it will be necessary to take into systematic account the size, organization, and strength of the various interest groups and coalitions that stand to gain or lose from proposed equity-oriented policies and the resulting changes in social and economic status and political power. With regard to the concern for increasing the poor people's share of income and power, Lipton (1977), as indicated earlier, offered a number of suggestions about how support can be mobilized and opposition reconciled or weakened on the part of the interest groups who would be affected, including trade-union leaders, businessmen, and politicians and planners. Similarly, Ilchman and Uphoff (1975) examined the political and administrative implications of a wide variety of policies to help the poor that were recommended by an International Labour Office employment mission to Kenya and identified the likely supporters and opponents of these policies. In this vein, C. L. G. Bell (1974:72) noted that "as the rich do not constitute a class with identical interests, potential disputes among them provide other bases for political alignments, in which the poor may have enough representation to press their cause effectively."

Incremental approaches, rather than all-out attacks, seem to be the most realistic way to proceed in countries in which the constraints are severe.[4] There are some countries dominated by entrenched elites who will relinquish nothing to the poor unless they are forced by revolution, while others are already engaged in attacking the causes of poverty (*ibid.*) It may be noted that among the latter are countries with regimes covering a wide political spectrum, including, among others, China, Costa Rica, Israel, Japan, Singapore, South Korea, Sri Lanka, and Tai- wan (Streeten *et al.*, 1981). Between those who will relinquish nothing and those already committed are many LDCs, perhaps the majority, in which the political decision to allow the poor to share power with groups that are already powerful seems at least possible through refor- mist tactics and tradeoffs, as suggested by C. L. G. Bell (1974) and the others cited. In pursuing strategies of power-sharing, the discussion of urban bias showed that it would be misguided to view development as requiring a choice between favoring either the urban or the rural sector. Rather, broad-based development requires a restructuring of a country's distribution of economic and political power as a whole.

Even if the political prerequisites for the implementation of equity- oriented development strategies are met, there are a number of opera- tional issues that must also be considered. As Morawetz (1977) has observed, there is a voluminous literature available on how to foster economic growth and on what policies have been tried and what conse- quences have ensued. But there is little reliable knowledge about what kinds of attempts at redistribution of land and other assets have worked, including why they have worked, much less any documentation of the necessary and sufficient conditions for the success of particular types of redistribution and their relationship to economic growth.

No conclusive answers to these questions are available, nor is much known about a number of other operational issues, some of which were touched on in the discussion of basic needs. Among these issues are: the extent of domestic and external resources required for meeting the basic needs of a very large and growing number of people in the LDCs, the designing of public services to maximize their benefits for the poor, and the designing of social change and of institutions that would allow the poor not only to make their needs known but also to involve themselves in helping to create and maintain the services they need.[5] It is to the last of these issues that this discussion now turns.

POPULAR PARTICIPATION AND COMMUNITY-LEVEL ACTION

Mobilizing programs of popular participation and community-level action is a critical area for attention if equity-oriented development strat- egies are going to work. Accordingly, there has been much emphasis on "growth from below" at the village level as the place where develop- ment must be based and motivated.[6] The International Labour Office (1977:66) report that initially proposed the basic-needs approach gave high priority to "mass participation in the development process by the poverty groups." And in another International Labour Office report (Ghai and Alfthan, 1977), it was maintained that the scope, content, and priorities of basic needs must be determined by the people who are to be the recipients. This emphasis on popular participation as a prerequisite for implementation of an equity-oriented approach was underlined by Cassen (1978a:6) in a pragmatic way: "One may well generalize and say that the cost—even the affordability—and the effectiveness of Basic Needs provision will depend in many situations on the extent to which community work can be mobilised." And Saunders (1979:8) makes the point that community mobilization may be one effective way of overcoming political constraints, since "non-governmental local organizations can sometimes provide a mechanism for challenging entrenched social structures and for gaining more equitable access to resources and services."

Popular participation and community-level action constitute a complex area for development efforts. Much more needs to be known about how the commitment of local people can be mobilized and their participation secured and strengthened, as well as how local programs can be incorporated into national development efforts and linked effectively to larger networks of resources and economic relationships. There is only a thin knowledge base about who the poor are, where they live, the ways in which different types of rural groups gain their livelihood, and the principal constraints imposed on improving their well-being. Even in the poorest communities in the poorest countries, there are gradations of poverty, and an understanding of these differences is essential for any analysis of poverty or for any effective development intervention (Castro, Hakansson, and Brokensha, 1981). Most policy measures designed to further rural development have not done much to facilitate or encourage popular participation. Indeed, such measures as the Green Revolution and the injection of mechanization and capital-intensive technology, as well as the top-down management methods employed to implement rural development projects, have generally enhanced the interests of the rural elites of large farmers, merchants, and middlemen, rather than those of the mass of peasant farmers, landless laborers, and migrant seasonal workers. Chenery et al. (1974), in advocating "redistribution with growth," stressed the need to adapt their approach to the different characteristics of the several rural and urban poverty groups. Rural and urban development strategies need to be designed specifically to create the capacity for these groups, through access to the appropriate assets and resources and opportunities, to learn to help themselves and each other and to participate in the planning and decision–making that have important implications for their lives and their livelihood (C. L. G. Bell and Duloy, 1974).

There are no easy answers as to what particular mix of ingredients—such as land reform, administrative "decentralization," technical and financial assistance, cooperatives, and collective farming—should be incorporated in the design of development strategies. No single development strategy is appropriate, of course, for all social, cultural, and economic settings. But as Stavenhagen (1977:65) stated, "Planners and policymakers . . . often emphasize one strategy or one objective above all others (land distribution, or rural resettlement, or the 'green revolution,' or the creation of family farms, etc.), and a country's scarce resources will go mainly into one channel. In rural development planning it is necessary to consider various objectives . . . and clearly to order them according to priorities. . . . Peasants are rarely consulted when development priorities are set; they should be."

Administrative problems loom large. Actually, the effects of development plans and policies on the rural economies of most LDCs have been limited to date. The reason is in part that the rural areas are large and unevenly accessible and in part that governments usually lack the administrative capacity and locally based organization required to implement genuine social and economic change in the rural sector (Robinson, 1980). Rural development cannot easily be centrally planned. The issue of what form of decentralization is necessary for effective implementation of rural development strategies is assuming an important place on the agenda of the development dialogue. Griffin (1981) observed that the shift of thinking in favor of agriculture and the mobilization of local human and material resources has been accompanied by a reduced emphasis on national planning. This shift has also led to a growing awareness of the need to devise an administrative structure that would permit regional decentralization, local autonomy in making decisions of primary concern to the locality, and greater local responsibility for designing and implementing development programs. Griffin (ibid.:225) goes on to say: "Such changes . . . are not just technical or administrative; they are political. . . . It is conceivable, even likely in many countries, that power at the local level is even more concentrated, more elitist and applied more ruthlessly against the poor than at the centre. Thus greater decentralization does not necessarily imply greater democracy let alone 'power to the people.'"

Cassen (1978b), in his study of India, echoes this last theme when he observes that life in the village is not cooperative but competitive. The rich appropriate both externally supplied and internal resources and benefit most from subsidized irrigation and credit. Cassen (*ibid.*:339) goes on to say: "They lend not to enrich but to impoverish their fellows and to enhance their own estates. If all the inhabitants of the village were to cooperate for their mutual advancement, many of them other than those in the very poorest villages could solve most of their own problems."

Helping rural groups and communities to organize themselves to plan their own programs for access to and management of resources and to identify the specific kinds of help they need from government and other outside sources for implementing these plans and programs constitutes an imposing task. And the preconditions for enabling the rural poor to undertake these tasks, as indicated, are no less imposing. Building capacity for community action through a bottom-up process, linking this capacity to larger networks of resources and bureaucratic structures to enable the poor to control their own destinies, and overcoming the constraints imposed by urban and rural power groups pose a formidable agenda. Accomplishing all these objectives will call for the imaginative and flexible use of a wide array of established as well as new forms of social organization, including community-level and intermediary private organizations, churches, cooperatives, and so on. As Ohlin (1978:25) stated: "The search for alternatives to 'trickle-down' strategies of development is going on all over the Third World, and its importance is obviously far-reaching. It is not only an attempt to revitalize and stimulate production and consumption but amounts to a redefinition of development in terms of human fulfillment."

Within the international development community (i.e., the national and international agencies involved with development issues), there is a widespread assumption that the poverty groups who are to be mobilized for popular participation are eager to change their situation. It is understandable that development specialists tend to project their own values and aspirations on social groups for whom they feel empathy. As Wolfe (1977) points out, however, if the specialists assume a mass following that is nonexistent, or only superficially interested, or in fact preoccupied with questions that fall outside the concerns of the specialists, this lack of reciprocal enthusiasm can lead to feelings of defeat and disillusionment. There are, however, examples from around the developing world of oppressed groups that have successfully assumed control over their own destinies and development strategies in the face of substantial odds. Goulet (1979), for example, reports four such case studies from Guinea-Bissau, Sri Lanka, Ahmedabad (India), and Bolivia, and Hollnsteiner (1979) presents several from the Philippines. A particularly dramatic case is that of the farmers of Gujarat, India, who overcame exploitation and gained a measure of prosperity through their own efforts at organizing successful dairy cooperatives.[7]

RESPONSES FROM THE THIRD WORLD

As noted earlier, the principal source of proposals for equity-oriented development perspectives—such as redistribution with growth, another development, and basic needs—has been the international development assistance community, rather than the LDCs themselves.[8] This is not to say that the governments of the DCs have more concern for the poor in the LDCs than do their own governments. A number of LDCs were formulating plans and strategies for coping with problems of poverty for some time before these proposals emerged in the mid-1970s. The notion of "self-reliance" and proposals for a new international economic order are primarily Third World initiatives. They constitute separate but not unrelated views and have been regarded by many LDC officials and planners as essential ingredients of approaches to development.

The concept of self-reliance has been around for some time, but it received new emphasis in the wake of the "energy crisis" of the early 1970s, which brought into bold relief the cost of the economic and technological dependence of most LDCs and the dramatic changes in the international economy that affected the DCs as well (Mansour, 1979). A statement by a group of Third World officials and social scientists (Overseas Development Council Communique, 1974:53) referred to the energy crisis and called for the LDCs to become self-reliant, "to fashion their economic policies according to the needs, problems, and experience of their own economies," and observed that the emphasis on the domestic determination of development priorities was becoming increasingly widespread in the LDCs.

Haq (1976), who wrote extensively on self-reliance, contended that the concept was not clearly defined in the Western literature. Self-reliance has been confused with a movement toward autarchy and interpreted narrowly with reference to the issue of the vicissitudes of a country's external trade relations. Haq views it as a comprehensive philosophy of life and identifies four principal elements in the concept: (1) No consumer products should be imported that cannot be afforded by the vast majority of the population with their current income. (2) There should be maximum use of indigenous resources and technology along the lines of popular participation as just described and with emphasis on labor-intensive practices. (3) The amount of foreign assistance sought by the LDCs should be calibrated against the country's needs for fostering economic growth and implementing development strategies, not as the maximum amount that the country can negotiate. (4) There is also the implication that there must be a deliberate delinking of the Third World from its past dependent relationships with the DCs, particularly in the case of those LDCs that have been so intimately linked with their former colonial masters—politically, economically, and socially—that even minor crises in the mother countries can result in substantial upheavals in the LDCs that can impose major constraints on self-reliant national development. These elements are consistent with the objectives of equity-oriented development. Indeed, broad-based development programs that do not consistently depend on the self-reliance of countries and mobilize both public and private resources for self-help are likely to become simply large-scale charity or welfare programs for the poor (Streeten *et al.*, 1981). The concept of self-reliance has many connotations, economic, political, and psychological, but it usually does include, in most of its variations, the theme of control of the economy in national hands, diversification of foreign ties, designing of trade arrangements to reduce dependence on a single country or product, and reduced dependence on foreign investment and external assistance (Morawetz, 1977).

Pursuing the goal of self-reliance, as the concept is described by Haq and other writers, would require, among other things, reducing dependence not only on food imports but also on other imported necessities, such as oil and its products and capital equipment and expertise. It would also require reducing the importation of luxury items that serve the desires of the elite groups as well as limiting the local production of such items if the program is to meet Haq's criterion, namely, that no consumption goods should be introduced that cannot be afforded by the masses with their current income.

Policies would be needed to change ways of life at given income levels toward greater austerity, using taxation and price policies, persuasive advertising propaganda, and perhaps even rationing, all of which may be potentially threatening to the stability of current regimes. In many countries, self-reliance would also require increasing national ownership and control, especially of subsoil assets, and improving capacity for negotiating with multinational corporations (Seers, 1979a). This is not to say that export revenues should not be used for acquiring goods and services from abroad, but that such revenues should be used to import foreign products when they facilitate technological liberation and economic dependence rather than to pay for sophisticated armaments and high technology for imitative industrialization. Minhas

(1979:89) puts it bluntly: "Unless the poor countries are able to get rid of the elitist and imitative thrust of their strategies of development and modernization, the growth of exports as such would not assure self-reliant development."

Like basic-needs and other equity-focused perspectives, the concept of self-reliance—with its emphasis on selective disengagement from DC ties and the need for fundamental economic and social change toward the austerity of a "bicycle culture"—poses major challenges to powerful political alliances and commercial interests. Moreover, realization of its goals would also probably require, in many cases, curbing the power of multinational corporations in a variety of ways. To the extent, however, that self-reliance constitutes an indigenous response that reflects an attempt to deal with real and immediate problems, the reactions of elites may be tempered, not by social conscience, but by an appeal to their nationalistic sentiments, as Seers (1979a) suggests. Moves toward self-reliance could become cumulative. Increased cultural independence not only has direct economic effects but also strengthens the motivation of political leaders to make further reductions in dependence and weakens the internal opposition to such measures.

Moves toward self-reliance on the part of LDCs that differ widely in their types of political regimes have been stimulated by the LDCs' concern with the possible consequences of continually rising indebtedness and the successive shocks they are subjected to by the economic and political rivalries among the DCs. Nevertheless, the persisting crisis of the Third World's external debt threatens to make attempts at self-reliance an exercise in futility, an issue to be considered presently. It should be noted that although self-reliance may seem, for good reasons, critically important to some of the LDCs, it may make little material difference to the DCs whether the LDCs, excepting the few that possess important natural resources, attempt to limit their ties with the DCs. Attempts by the LDCs to lessen their dependence on and vulnerability to the vicissitudes of the world's economics and politics should nevertheless be encouraged by the DCs on altruistic grounds, to the extent that they can serve the interests of the LDCs, not to the selfish end of enabling the DCs to abdicate their responsibility for helping to promote the well-being of the poorer countries.

In view of the severe poverty in many LDCs, promoting self-reliance at levels that sacrifice economic growth could cause more problems than it would resolve, so that selection of an appropriate strategy of development is critically important. Choice of an industrialization strategy that will maximize national independence is one of the crucial policy tasks to be undertaken. Roemer (1981) examined a series of industrial strategies that either are often followed in practice or have received considerable currency in the development literature and measured them against the goal of reduced dependence. He concluded that on balance, a combination of export substitution (the promotion of diversified manufactured exports through outward-looking trade arrangements) and a basic-industry strategy (which emphasizes investments in the producer-goods sector to end dependence on raw-material exports) would seem to be the strongest contributors to reduced dependence. Finally, it may be noted that to the extent the LDCs can consistently give their first priority to enhancing the quality of their national institutions and the capabilities of their populations, they will be accordingly less susceptible to the ethnocentric and deterministic views of development that have masked the nature of their real problems.

The idea of collective self-reliance has also received some attention in the development dialogue. The argument for collective self-reliance is essentially that the LDCs will not be able to increase their bargaining power or attract the investments they desire without having to make costly concessions unless they manage to get together as have, say, the members of the European Economic Community. Moreover, networks for collective self-reliance could help to provide some insulation against at least the temporary disturbances in the DCs that tend to have a magnified impact on the LDCs (Haq, 1976). The most ambitious attempts at such cooperative arrangements have been the Andean Pact in South America and the Association of Southeast Asian Nations (ASEAN), which comprises Indonesia, Malaysia, the Philippines, Thailand, and Singapore.

According to Minhas (1979), although the notion of collective self-reliance has been around for some time, it is still somewhat amorphous and conceptually unclear. Some of the potential economic benefits from cooperative arrangements among the LDCs seem attractive indeed, but are not likely to be realized significantly unless a limited degree of political federation can be incorporated in such arrangements. The constraints imposed by the inviolability of sovereignty, however, are likely to limit the chances for success of Third World initiatives for collective self-reliance, at least in the near term. Nevertheless, the idea of building regional common markets continues to be attractive, judging by a recent initiative in Latin America taken by the leaders of Argentina and Brazil.[9]

It has been suggested (*ibid.*) that the causes of collective self-reliance could be advanced at least to some extent by identifying areas of technology and products in which technical assistance from some Third World countries, apart from that provided by the DCs, could be of benefit to those LDCs less endowed with expertise. This idea for developing multiple links among LDCs for cooperation in pooling resources, using regional specialists for exchange of experience and technical knowledge, and establishing or strengthening institutions or organizations for addressing common problems has been promoted and supported by several United Nations agencies under the rubric "Technical Co-operation among Developing Countries" (United Nations Fund for Population Activities, 1978).

The pursuit of self-reliance and collective self-reliance is, of course, severely hampered by the massive arms trade, in which the LDCs are major purchasers. Arms exports from the DCs grew by 241% in less than a decade, from $6.5 billion in 1970 to $15.7 billion in 1978. The main beneficiaries were the United States and the Soviet Union, each of which sold about 40% of the total export in 1978 (L. Taylor, 1981). In 1977, military spending by the LDCs was more than 1½ times that on education and health combined; the LDCs spent 5.9% of GNP on defense, but only 2.7% on education and 1.0% on health (International Bank for Reconstruction and Development, 1980a). The total value of arms deliveries to the LDCs in 1983 was $26.5 billion, with non-Communist countries responsible for $16.5 billion. The United States ranked first with $9.68 billion in deliveries, and the Soviet Union ranked second, with $7.8 billion (Biddle, 1983). Such large sums spent on arms clearly absorb much of the capital needed for economic and social development. Consider this statement by Perez de Cuellar, the Secretary General of the United Nations (as quoted in Nossiter, 1983): "As a national of a developing country, I am especially concerned at the grievous and senseless waste of resources on armaments which could be used to meet fundamental requirements in these countries. Armaments and development are in a competitive relationship for global resources." Arms imports account for a substantial proportion of the external indebtedness of the LDCs, an issue to which this discussion now turns.

The lack of parity in income and power that characterizes relationships between rich and poor countries is reflected in the concerns among LDCs for achieving greater equity among nations. Self-reliance, collective self-reliance, and demands for a new international economic order (the latter to be considered below) may be seen as strategies proposed by LDCs for coping with this lack of parity in international relations. Moreover, the concept of self-reliance, particularly as characterized by Haq, is also aimed at narrowing the income and power gaps between the rich and poor within many LDCs so that the goals of equity-oriented development can be pursued successfully.

One major barrier to the pursuit of these strategies and goals, however, is the massive external debt of the LDCs. It is beyond the scope of this book to consider in any detail the complex issues involved in the causes and consequences of Third World indebtedness, but the substantial negative impact of this indebtedness and of debt-servicing difficulties on prospects for broad-based economic and social development must at least be noted.

The "debt crisis" of the LDCs has received a great deal of attention in the news media, at least as much as the huge United States budget and trade deficits. Economic growth has slowed in most of the LDCs that are trying to cope with debt-servicing demands, as well as in many countries with less severe debt problems. In most of Africa, average per capita real incomes were about the same in 1984 as in 1970, and in many Latin American countries, these income levels are back to those of the mid-1970s (International Bank for Reconstruction and Development, 1985). World Bank staff (ibid.:1) contend that "dozens of countries have lost a decade or more of development." Szekely (1985:8) describes the problem of debt and development eloquently: ". . . the grand solutions that have been proposed seem increasingly futile. It is like trying to play chess by the traditional rules on a board where the squares are constantly changing. How can a nation make progress when a great share of its GNP, and sometimes its food supply, must be exported to pay interest on debts, even while its own people hunger?"

The medium- and long-term external debt of the LDCs has been increasing since at least 1970. Some LDCs were already saddled with high debt-service obligations in the 1970s (International Bank for Reconstruction and Development, 1980a). The amount of outstanding debt in 1970 was $68 billion and by 1984 had increased to $686 billion, an average rise of 16.7% a year (International Bank for Reconstruction and Development, 1985). Debt-service payments (i.e., interest and principal payments on outstanding debts) grew from $9.3 billion in 1970 to $100 billion in 1984, and interest payments, which were about one third of total debt service in 1970, increased to over one half in 1984 (ibid.). One dire consequence of this rapid growth in debt service, particularly in interest payments, is that an ever larger proportion of new borrowing has been spent to service outstanding debt, thus creating a trap of substantial proportions.

The two principal types of debt indicators are the debt–service ratio, i.e., interest and principal payments on long-term debt divided by exports of goods and services, which measures a country's capacity for making payments in foreign exchange, and the ratio of interest payments to GNP, which measures a country's capacity to generate real resources (International Bank for Reconstruction and Development, 1981b). Increases in these ratios are commensurate with the dramatic increases in outstanding debt and in debt-service and interest payments. The ratio of debt service to exports rose, for all LDCs, from 15% in 1970 to 20% in 1984, and the ratio of debt to GNP increased from 14% in 1970 to 34% in 1984 (International Bank for Reconstruction and Development, 1985).

There are notable differences among the LDCs in amounts of outstanding debt (International Bank for Reconstruction and Development, 1986). At the time of this writing, the largest debtors were Mexico, $69 billion; Brazil, $66.5 billion; and Argentina, $28.7 billion. In Asia, debt levels were lower, with South Korea's debt about $24.6 billion, Indonesia's about $22.9 billion, and India's about $22.4 billion. In Africa, the largest was Algeria, at $17.2 billion, followed by Egypt, about $15.8 billion, and Nigeria, about $11.8 billion. For most LDCs, the debt-to-GNP ratio has increased significantly over the years. In the poor countries of sub-Saharan Africa, World Bank staff (*ibid.*) note that debt-service obligations have risen to unsustainable levels. Although the absolute amounts of the external debts in these countries are small compared with the amounts indicated for the largest debtors, they are the highest among the LDCs in relation to income and exports.

The sharp rise in the external debt levels of the LDCs, and in their ratios of debt service to exports and of debt to GNP, was due primarily to increased lending by commercial banks. Over the past 15 years, there have been important changes in the composition of Third World debt as a consequence of a major shift from official to private financing in international capital (International Bank for Reconstruction and Development, 1985). There has been a substantial reduction in the share of net borrowing from bilateral official sources, a small increase in the share coming from multilateral agencies (like the World Bank and the regional development banks), and a dramatic increase in the proportion of loans from private sources, particularly commercial banks. These changes are mainly a consequence of what has been happening to the middle-income LDCs.[10] The share of their debt financed by official creditors constituted almost three quarters of their total debt by 1980. The composition of the debt of the low-income LDCs changed very little, however, since they continued to borrow mainly from the official and multilateral sources (International Bank for Reconstruction and Development, 1981b). The rise in borrowing from private banks together with higher interest rates has increased the burden of servicing debt. The terms on which the LDCs obtained medium- and long-term loans over the course of the 1970s changed notably because of the shift to private finance. Since loans from private creditors, the fastest-growing source, carried shorter maturities—an average of 8.2 years in 1983—the average maturity of the total external debt of the LDCs shortened from 20.4 years in 1970 to 14.2 years in 1982 (International Bank for Reconstruction and Development, 1985). Given these conditions, a number of LDCs have had to seek debt relief through a variety of negotiations for refinancing and rescheduling. The number of debt reschedulings has risen from an average of 5 a year in the period 1975–1980 to 31 in 1983 (*ibid.*).

The massive financial shocks and the slowdown in economic growth experienced by the LDCs have reinforced views in some of these countries that greater self–reliance should be sought by avoiding outward-oriented policies and by reducing their reliance on foreign capital. But World Bank staff (*ibid.*) argue that participating in the world economy provides substantial benefits, even though there may be some risks. They point out that inward-oriented LDCs grew less rapidly in the early 1980s and, over a longer period, much less rapidly than did those that were outward-oriented. As for foreign borrowing, they say that the greater the flexibility and efficiency a government has to diversify its exports to increase foreign exchange earnings, to implement austerity measures to curb domestic spending, and to institute other policy changes to strengthen long-term growth prospects, the more that government can afford to borrow. For many LDCs, these may be formidable conditions.

As would be expected, the emphasis of the creditors, both official and private, has been on encouraging LDCs to restore their "creditworthiness" so that bank lending may continue to flow and facilitate regaining the momentum of economic growth. This restoration will depend, of course, not only on policy reforms by the LDCs but also on the strength and stability of global economic growth (*ibid.*).

To help the LDCs reach this blessed state of credit-worthiness, the International Monetary Fund (IMF) has moved, on a country-by-country basis, into a key role in assembling economic "stabilization" programs, in which the country concerned agrees with the IMF on a program designed to reduce its balance-of-payments deficit to what it can finance through borrowing. For its part, the IMF undertakes to orchestrate an arrangement for rescheduling debt and obtaining new loans from the country's official and private creditors. In return, the country adopts the IMF recipe for economic reform, which usually includes severe cuts in government expenditures, a sharp devaluation of the national currency if it is overvalued, and, in some instances where relevant, the sale to the private sector of state-run business enterprises.

According to one World Bank official (World Bank, 1983), there are important limitations on this IMF assistance. These stabilization programs do not address the problem of how a country can not only borrow enough to meet its debt-service payments but also still have enough left over to get on with economic and social development. Moreover, the austerity measures required are politically difficult to introduce and maintain and are often resented as imposing tight external controls on the debtor country's economy. IMF financing is relatively short-term and consists of emergency measures that by themselves will not suffice. According to the World Bank official (*ibid.*:2): "A larger and longer-term response is needed . . . a large part of the debt . . . will have to be stretched out for perhaps 20 to 25 years. The size of the debt will remain the same, but the debt burden will be greatly reduced if borrowers did not have to roll over principal repayments at higher costs. Some of the debt might have to be restructured at concessional rates of interest, and some may have to be written off."

In any case, the IMF does have an important role to perform in getting a country's balance of payments back into equilibrium and in mobilizing its official and private creditors to help bring this state about. Beyond this help however, a variety of measures will have to be devised by both the DCs and the LDCs to offset the negative impact of external debt on development prospects over the longer term, for both economic growth and the alleviation of poverty.

In addressing effectively the debt problems the LDCs face, attention will have to be paid to the serious threat posed by protectionist pressures that are increasing not only in the United States and other DCs but also among the LDCs. For example, Japan, the United States, and the European Economic Community have restrictions on importing steel that affect not only one another's exports but also at least those of three of the largest LDC debtors, Brazil, South Korea, and Mexico. Import restrictions on sugar in these DCs hurt Latin America and the Philippines (International Bank for Reconstruction and Development, 1985). Fruit, vegetables, and beef also face substantial import barriers in the DCs (Clausen, 1984a).

If there is to be expansion in LDC exports, open access to DC markets is essential, since the economies of the DCs constitute almost two thirds of the world market for Third World exports. Increased protectionism in the DCs against LDC exports limits foreign currency earnings and thus the LDCs' capacity to import and to cope with their debt. Of course, the protectionist response in the DCs is understandable, there being 35 million unemployed in the industrial world for whom the benefits of "free trade" are questionable (World Bank, 1983). Nevertheless, the growth of protectionist measures will not only seriously jeopardize the prospects for the economic growth needed to sustain Third World development but also have adverse consequences for the DCs. Shrinking foreign markets due to the slowdown in economic growth in the LDCs will have to be faced by DC exporters, the banks will find it increasingly difficult to recover their loans, consumers will have to pay higher prices for imports from the LDCs, and all this will result in slower economic growth for the DCs as well as the LDCs (Clausen, 1984a).

In the array of responses from the Third World, one of the most notable has been in the area of international economic relations in the form of proposals for a "new international economic order" (NIEO). As indicated earlier, the term "Third World" is a gross oversimplification and is used mainly as a matter of convenience. In reality, of course, the range of differences among LDCs is very wide indeed. Not only are there major sociocultural and political differences among LDCs, but also they have experienced profound differences in rates of economic growth. At one extreme, economic development in such countries as South Korea, Taiwan, and Singapore has been dramatic, while among the poorest countries, including Bangladesh, Nepal, and a large number of African countries, economic growth has been negligible and in some cases even negative (Morawetz, 1977; Goldthorpe, 1984). In view of the differences among the LDCs in economic performance, political regimes, development approaches, and varying needs, it is remarkable that they were able, in the 1970s, to mobilize a substantial degree of unity around the issues of reforms in economic and political institutions and arrangements that the LDCs considered to be dominated by the DCs in ways that were discriminatory to the LDCs.

The success of the Organization of Petroleum Exporting Countries (OPEC) in 1973 gave substantial impetus to the LDCs' call for an NIEO, although this unity did not emerge overnight as a result of OPEC's actions, but evolved gradually over the preceding years. Third World disappointment over the years with development aid and with the failure of political independence to bring about economic independence set the stage for the call for an NIEO, but the dramatic advent of OPEC as a powerful arbiter in the world economy provided a special catalyst. The oil-importing LDCs were themselves adversely affected economically by the oil price increases, but this did not stop them from admiring OPEC's newfound power and from developing expectations that this power could somehow strengthen the influence of the rest of the Third World in effecting important changes in international economic and political relations. OPEC was seen as a model they could hope to emulate, but this hope was dissipated by increasing debt burdens, rising protectionism, sharp decreases in commodity prices, and slowdowns in economic growth, as just described.

The income gap between rich and poor countries, which has grown dramatically over the past 30 years, has been frequently used as the principal rationale in demands for an NIEO that would result in major transfers of wealth away from the rich countries (Seligson, 1984a). In 1950, the average per capita income (in 1980 dollars) of low-income countries was $164, while the per capita income of the DCs averaged $3841. By 1980, average income in the LDCs was only $245, but in the DCs it rose to $9648 (*ibid.*). This gap may symbolize for many the lack of equity in economic and political power as between DCs and LDCs, but as Morawetz (1984:11) points out, narrowing the gap does not make much sense as a development objective: "For the large majority of developing countries containing most of the developing world's population, the gap would never be closed, for their measured rate of growth per capita GNP has historically been slower than that of the OECD [Organisation for Economic Co-operation and Development] countries. Even among the fastest-growing developing countries, only eight would close the gap within 100 years, and only sixteen would close it within 1,000 years."

The term NIEO first appeared in a declaration that was produced at a special session of the United Nations General Assembly in 1974 and was subsequently followed by related declarations and statements by the LDCs in the late 1970s. In these declarations, which have been presented at meetings of the United Nations General Assembly and the United Nations Conference on Trade and Development (UNCTAD), the LDCs advocated the establishment of an NIEO that would include, among other things, nondiscriminatory treatment of their manufactured goods in DC markets, more stable prices for their commodities, renegotiation of their external public debt, rules of conduct for the activities of multinational corporations and greater access on more favorable terms to DC technology, greater participation in the management of the world monetary system, and a larger transfer of resources from the rich to the poor countries to decrease disparities in income (Sewell *et al.*, 1980; Streeten *et al.*, 1981; Bissell, 1983). These issues have become even more acute in the 1980s than they were in the 1970s. They were prominent in what has been called the dialogue between the "North" (the DCs) and the "South" (the LDCs), and whatever unity the LDCs were able to maintain in advocating these proposals was due in part to the fact that the differences between the LDCs and the DCs are greater than the differences among the LDCs. But the so-called North and South do not constitute homogeneous blocs any more than does the Third World. Streeten (1982:5–6) noted that ". . . there are rich and poor among the OECD countries, there are relations of dominance and dependence between developing countries, and even between regions within one country, there are biases and imperfections in the system of international relations that discriminate against members of the First World and there are important interest alignments that cut across national frontiers."

There have been many technical and political criticisms of the NIEO proposals in the literature (Cooper, 1979; Ford Foundation, 1982; Thompson, 1983), but they are outside the scope of this discussion. The links of these proposals to equity-oriented development are, however, of concern here. It seems likely that inequities and imbalances in the international economic order could constitute barriers to implementation of equity-oriented strategies within countries, but reforms through an NIEO would not, by themselves, guarantee that the governments of the LDCs would focus their efforts on reduction of poverty. Streeten (1982) contended that the best way to ensure that objectives of poverty reduction are achieved in the pursuit of an NIEO is not by tying resource transfers to an array of donor-imposed conditions, but by selecting and supporting governments explicitly committed to poverty-reduction programs, since it is not likely that the LDCs would suffer gladly the attachment of strict performance criteria or other specific conditions to resource transfers.

Efforts to achieve equity in international economic and political relations make full sense only if they are linked to efforts to achieve domestic equity. There is no assurance that achievement of NIEO reforms would bring about any long-term improvement in the well-being of the poor majorities in the LDCs. Rather, the result could well be the opposite, namely, strengthening the power of national elites at further cost to the poor. Structural changes in economic and political institutions at the international level are needed, but as discussed earlier, major restructuring in political and economic power relationships within the LDCs must also be pursued.

The optimism displayed by LDC officials in the 1970s that their proposals for an NIEO would be heeded by the DCs did not survive the events of the early 1980s. The serious economic problems experienced by the DCs eroded whatever interest they may have had earlier in the proposals for substantial resource transfers, and as one writer (Leff, 1983:260) has remarked about United States policy, "The main hope of pro-LDC officials in the U.S. government is now to prevent new barriers from being erected to restrict LDC exports, not to dismantle old ones." Finkle and Crane (1985) note that there have also been changes in the LDCs that have caused strategies to shift from the global strategy associated with an NIEO to bilateral or regional approaches in efforts to gain economic concessions from the DCs. They say (ibid.:4): "By 1984, changes in government or in the prevailing philosophies in many leading developing countries (including India, Mexico, Algeria, and China) were causing them to pursue more pragmatic and market-oriented development strategies." Finkle and Crane also point to the large LDC external debt as having the effect of making the LDCs "more cautious in their international political posture."

Nevertheless, the serious problems identified in the NIEO agenda of the 1970s still afflict international economic relations, and although the demands may be more muted, they are still being expressed by Third World leaders in a variety of United Nations forums (United Nations Fund for Population Activities, 1985; French, 1986). At least there is still a continuing dialogue about the substantial economic problems that confront both DCs and LDCs and need to be addressed systematically, such problems including trade barriers, capital flows to the LDCs, and development assistance to the low-income countries, among other issues (International Bank for Reconstruction and Development, 1985).[11]

Persuasive arguments (some of which have been cited earlier) have been advanced to the effect that there are no inherent conflicts between pursuing the goal of economic growth and that of reducing poverty, but the dichotomy between these two main strands of development perspectives persists. And the two strands tend to line up with the pursuit of international equity between the DCs and the LDCs (which somehow is linked with recapitulating for the LDCs the process of production and consumption characteristic of the DCs), on one hand, and the pursuit of equity and the reduction of poverty (linked with popular participation and the parsimonious use of resources to benefit the majority rather than the minority), on the other. Ideology holds sway, as always. The reality involves components of both strands, but this intertwining is not easy to perceive. It is to be hoped, however, that the recurring polarization will begin to merge with reality and that the stereotypes will lose out to a growing perception that the LDCs, and the DCs as well, need to maximize economic growth and equity both domestically and internationally if there is to be a world order at all.

MULTINATIONAL CORPORATIONS AND POVERTY-FOCUSED DEVELOPMENT

International organization for commercial purposes has a long history, beginning in medieval times with the charter companies. Direct investment by the DCs in the LDCs has been going on for most of this century. Unlike commercial bank lending, which provides only capital, direct investment brings not only capital but also technology and management expertise that can, according to World Bank staff (International Bank for Reconstruction and Development, 1985), increase the productivity of the capital.

The growth of the multinational corporation (MNC) over the past three decades and the strategic role it has come to perform in promoting world trade and development constitute a most dramatic phenomenon. That the MNCs have expanded by leaps and bounds in the postwar era may be the only point on which everyone agrees in the copious literature that has been generated on this topic. Much of this literature is polemical, taking one or the other of two extreme positions: that the MNCs are entirely benevolent or entirely malevolent. They are viewed, from these positions, as either stabilizing international relations or threatening the international economic and political order, as agents either of progress or of exploitation (Griffin, 1978).

The rest of the literature, to the extent that it is trying to shed some light amid all this heat, is devoted to identifying the pros and cons in relation to the particular economic and political context in which MNCs operate. Ranis (1976), for example, takes the position that the role of the MNC in development cannot be assessed independently of time and place and that such assessment must be related to the particular phase of a developing country's life cycle as well as to the type (e.g., size and resource endowment) of LDC in question. The predominant kinds of conflicts are those between the host and home governments and those between the MNCs and the governments of home or host countries.[12]

Much of the disagreement and controversy is generated, of course, by the complexities of the economics and politics of foreign investment, but is nourished by the severely inadequate data on the extent and nature of foreign investment (Bergsten, Horst, and Moran, 1978). In a detailed study of the MNCs, Lall and Streeten (1977) state that there are inherent problems in measuring foreign investment and, quite apart from the conceptual difficulties, great gaps in the statistics available on such investment from both investor and recipient countries. As for the conceptual difficulties, it should be noted that the MNC is not a monolithic organizational concept but in fact "a shorthand for a heterogeneous set of organizational forms ranging from wholly-owned subsidiaries, at one extreme, through various kinds of joint ventures, to licensing and management contracts, on the other" (Ranis, 1976:97).

Not so long ago, when the assumptions of neoclassic welfare economics still held sway (assumptions that are still persuasive in some quarters), the field of foreign private investment was seen as a competitive world of foreign investors acting as neutral agents of capital and technology transfer. Perceptions have shifted, and a prominent view now is that of a highly oligopolistic world of MNCs possessing great commercial and economic power and posing a challenge to national policy and economic independence (Lall and Streeten, 1977). Since the early 1960s, the fact that the MNCs have become increasingly involved in arrangements with the socialist and/or Communist countries indicates that the MNC is no longer the exclusive instrument of the Western industrial nations, but is looking for partners, whatever their ideology, that can offer stable and predictable conditions under which the MNC can operate with confidence and without threat of nationalization. This "transideological collaboration," as Wilczynski (1976) calls it, has become very extensive indeed. Moreover, a number of these socialist and Communist countries now also have MNCs that operate not only in their own countries but also in those of the West, with subsidiaries mushrooming in the best bourgeois tradition.

There is general consensus, at least among those writers not dominated by the ideological extremes, that assessing the favorable and unfavorable effects of MNCs on development in the Third World is severely constrained by the conceptual difficulties inherent in measuring foreign investment and by the pervasive lack of specific data about the nature of such investment in particular countries. Such studies as are available are only minimally comparable, since they use different methods, countries, and companies. Consequently, only a broad brush can be employed, and most observations are necessarily speculative.

At the core of the arguments in favor of the MNCs are the beliefs that the LDCs need the capital, the technology, the management expertise, and the international contacts and networks that the MNCs can presumably bring. The litany of their presumed negative effects is much longer, and in fact includes denials of some of the presumed benefits. In one list (Bergsten *et al.*, 1978), MNCs take out of LDCs more than they put in and thus can undermine balance-of-payments positions; they increase unemployment by using capital-intensive rather than labor-intensive techniques thought to be more appropriate for LDCs; they promote unequal income distribution because local high-income groups benefit through alliances with foreign investors; economic growth itself may be hampered, both short-term and long-term, because the MNCs drain away local capital and brain-power that could otherwise create strong local industries; they generate, through their advertising, consumption patterns inappropriate for poor countries; and they limit the LDCs' technological progress by conducting the bulk of their research and development in their home countries.[13]

Some of these effects could possibly be mitigated or even turned to advantage by particular policy measures that could be adopted by host governments. In the case of equity-oriented development programs, however, it seems likely that the oligopolistic nature of the growth of MNCs, and the fact that such growth is based on advanced technology and sophisticated marketing techniques supplemented by the economies of large-scale production, are incompatible with the objectives of such development programs regardless of what particular policy measures might be adopted by host governments (Griffin, 1978). Griffin (*ibid.*) makes the point that the adoption of a strategy of development such as basic needs requires a reallocation of resources toward the production of commodities needed by low-income groups, such as semi-processed foods, serviceable clothing, and inexpensive crockery, and the capital goods required to produce them, such as hand tools and simple power-driven equipment. It is unlikely that MNCs, accustomed to producing internationally standardized products in large volume with highly mechanized techniques, would have a competitive advantage in supplying these goods. Capital-intensive production on a small scale is usually inefficient and therefore costly. Consequently, the prices of such goods would generally be above international prices, thereby limiting further the expansion of the market and of employment.

Magdoff (1976) expresses even more acute doubts about the MNCs as a resource for attaining the objectives of broad-based development. He concedes that the MNCs have a great store of talent and experience that could be put to use in the poor countries that operate with a relatively primitive technology, and he notes that a few large corporations have been experimenting with the mass production of items that are especially adapted for wide use in the LDCs. As flexible as they may be, however, their ingenuity and enterprise are necessarily confined to producing and marketing items that meet their own profit objectives, and it is these objectives, however justifiable they may be in their own right, that stand in the way of responding to the needs of the poor majorities.

After World War II and until the early 1960s, MNCs were virtually the sole source of capital, technology, and managerial expertise for the LDCs. Their skills could be duplicated in the LDCs only with great loss in efficiency, if at all. And the tax subsidies offered by the LDCs were reinforced by tax deferrals in the home countries of the MNCs (Bergsten *et al.*, 1978). The enthusiastic receptivity that the MNCs enjoyed in those days has become somewhat qualified, but even today not many LDC governments are willing to forgo MNC investment. They continue to offer inducements to the MNCs, preferring immediate gains and the likelihood of postponed problems to postponed gains that may never materialize. For many LDC governments, the MNCs continue to be regarded as instruments of "modernization," relatively indispensable for economic growth (Apter, 1976; Leff, 1983).

Given these considerations, it is not surprising that the MNCs continue to play a powerful role in many LDCs. Even where they have become increasingly subject to local scrutiny and their relationships with host countries have been affected by growing political and economic tension, they still may have strong allies within the LDCs. The ruling elite of a poor country may, as Singer and Ansari (1982:212) say, "deliberately support a 'growth now, equality later' programme and be shortsighted enough not to recognize the nature of the two-way relationship between growth and equality. It will then permit the multinational to pursue policies that will accentuate economic inequalities." Singer and Ansari (*ibid.*) believe to be dim the outlook regarding the extent to which the government of a small LDC can realistically hope to influence the decisions of an MNC that has established a local subsidiary. Nevertheless, if private direct investment is to become a genuine agent of development, the bargaining power of the LDCs vis-à-vis the MNCs must be substantially increased. Given the organizational structure of the MNCs, the limited legal power that LDCs have over an MNC, and the staying power of the MNCs by virtue of the unified package they supply, LDC efforts to increase their bargaining power are subject to a formidable array of constraints. Lall and Streeten (1977) demonstrate how problematic and complex this bargaining process can be.

Whatever may be the gains LDCs can obtain from MNCs in the bargaining process, and whatever may be the resulting changes in the role MNCs can play in the direction of fostering development, the arguments presented above regarding the incompatibility between the inherent interests of MNCs and the objectives of equity-oriented development programs indicate that the contribution MNCs can make to the latter is likely to be, even under the best of conditions, marginally favorable. Unless the reduction of poverty assumes top priority for an LDC, with all other national economic interests subordinate to this priority, which seems highly improbable except in the rare case, MNCs are not likely to be rejected by the LDCs simply because they can make only a marginal contribution to equity-oriented development. Most LDCs continue to want the benefits they perceive the MNCs as bringing, such as technology, management expertise, and links to international networks. At the same time, some want sovereign control over the activities of the MNCs in their countries.

As indicated earlier, formulating rules of conduct for the activities of MNCs figured prominently in the proposals for an NIEO. While it is clearly in the interest of the LDCs to collaborate in the formulation of international codes of conduct, they can hardly leave the issue there. If they continue to find private direct investment attractive, they may have to enact policies to ensure that in their particular countries, MNCs are regulated to maximize the benefits they hope to extract from such investment. Policies will have to be based on careful assessment of the costs and benefits of the presence of MNCs and the implications of such assessment for the strategies the LDCs intend to follow in their pursuit of appropriate patterns of economic and social development.

Whatever these policies turn out to be, it is likely that they will focus, in many LDCs, on obtaining benefits primarily in the interest of the dominant political and economic elites rather than in the interest of the poor majorities. Thus, the policies regarding MNCs that are likely to be implemented by LDC governments would in many cases probably not pose significant challenges either to local elites or to the MNCs. Those that would, such as the strict control of entry of MNCs into an LDC, rigorous control of the technology the MNCs bring, and bans on luxury and high-technology products that are irrelevant to the consumption needs of the poor, will not be adopted by LDC host governments unless they have made or are prepared to make major commitments to poverty-reduction programs.

Most LDC governments are showing greater interest in controlling MNCs and strengthening their own bargaining position with regard to them. Lall and Streeten (1977) point out that the international climate for MNCs has changed greatly in recent years and that a variety of United Nations agencies are working on various aspects of the policy problems created by activities of MNCs (see also Gereffi, 1985). Moreover, the MNCs themselves have become more amenable to collaborating with some of the demands of the LDCs. Lall and Streeten (1977:224) conclude, however, that "unless there is a drastic change in the *internal* structures of the poor countries themselves, the undesirable effects we have analysed in this book will continue to be felt as these countries become more clearly integrated into the international structure of production and trade" [emphasis in original].

OFFICIAL DEVELOPMENT ASSISTANCE

"Official development assistance" (ODA), following the terminology of the Development Assistance Committee (DAC) of the Organisation for Economic Co-operation and Development (OECD), consists of funds made available by governments on concessional terms primarily to promote the economic development and well-being of the LDCs.[14] According to this definition, ODA (used herein interchangeably with "foreign aid") is that part of the total flow of resources from rich to poor countries that consists of loans on concessional terms, grants, and technical assistance provided for the express purpose of economic and social development of the LDCs. In this definition, aid for military or strictly political purposes would not be included, since it is not intended primarily to promote economic and social development. There are at least two other principal categories of resource transfers to the LDCs that would not be included in this definition of foreign aid, namely, other official flows, some of which may have a concessional element, and private flows, the principal forms of which are commercial bank lending and direct private investment, just considered. Grants are outright gifts, but loans, even those made by governments, would not be included in ODA, as defined here, if they are on commercial terms and for commercial purposes. Thus, ODA consists either of grants or of loans on "soft" or concessional terms.

Technical assistance is the other principal component of foreign aid and takes two main forms: (1) professional advisors, technicians, and other qualified people are sent from DCs to work for a time in LDCs, wholly or partly at the expense of the donors; and (2) people from the LDCs are trained at the expense of the donors, usually in the donors' home countries but sometimes in the LDCs and sometimes in third countries. In addition to the ODA provided by governments, foreign aid is provided by nongovernmental DC organizations, such as private foundations and relief organizations, but in dollar amounts such aid is modest compared with the size of ODA.

In keeping with the simple paradigm that dominated development thought after World War II, in which development was equated with economic growth and could be achieved by the LDCs to the extent that they became mirror images of Western society, the conventional wisdom of foreign aid focused on the transfer of resources from rich to poor countries, to be implemented mainly by the infusion of capital and of technical knowledge. In these terms, aid was seen as the quick fix that could bring about development in the near future. Much foreign aid, however, was dispensed for reasons that were rather less lofty than bringing development to the rest of the world. A good deal of aid was provided to compete with the Soviet bloc for the friendship of the LDCs, to achieve short-term political favors, to gain strategic advantages of one kind or another, or to promote exports from the donor country.

In the postwar period, there was little awareness of the need to distinguish among LDCs on the basis of their needs and potential and to design programs of aid appropriate to such differences. In particular, the current emphasis on equity-oriented development and special help for the low-income LDCs was still not in view. Consistent with the exclusive focus on economic growth, foreign aid was mainly directed to infrastructural and industrial projects and only incidentally concerned with investments in human capital, particularly with respect to the rural poor. National development planning was encouraged to focus on econometric models with relatively little attention to social and political goals. And technical assistance was approached mainly as a transfer of what the DCs knew (or thought they knew), rather than as help to find appropriate responses to LDC needs.

By 1960, the "development assistance community," consisting, as noted earlier, of the representatives of donor governments, multilateral agencies, and officials of recipient countries, was well on the way to becoming a world of its own, with its own specialist personnel, technical vocabulary, and issues and controversies. Foreign aid became a major activity with substantial resources allocated to it, and the governments of virtually all the rich industrial countries had become involved. The United Nations designated the 1960s the "Development Decade" (and later redesignated this period the "First Development Decade" when it became evident that "development" was not just around the corner), and in accordance with a United Nations resolution passed in December 1960, the DCs agreed to provide 1% of their GNP annually as aid to the LDCs. At about the same time, the DAC was established by the OECD to coordinate aid from the OECD countries. Outside the United Nations and the OECD, other international agencies were established after World War II. The Bretton Woods Conference in 1944 set up the IMF, to help countries stabilize their currencies, and the World Bank, which subsequently became the principal agency for multilateral aid to the LDCs. A number of donor countries set up special agencies to administer their bilateral aid programs, such as the United States Agency for International Development (USAID), the British Overseas Development Ministry, and the Ministry for Economic Cooperation in West Germany, and the Soviet Union also got into the aid business after 1956 (Goldthorpe, 1984).

As indicated, the notion of an international target for aid to the LDCs based on the available resources of the donor countries originally formed part of the proposals for the United Nations Development Decade of the 1960s. The original target, pegged at 1% of GNP, was later refined to distinguish foreign aid as defined here from other government financial flows made for commercial purposes and thus became a subtarget, within the overall target of 1%, of 0.7% of GNP in the flow of public government funds. The Pearson Commission (Pearson, Boyle, Campos, Dillon, Guth, Lewis, Marjolin, and Okita, 1969) recommended in 1969 that this target be achieved by no later than 1975. Only a few donor countries have achieved this target to date, but this failure did not discourage the Brandt Commission, issuing its report in 1980, from recommending that this target be achieved by 1985, with ODA to increase to 1% of GNP before the end of the century (Singer and Ansari, 1982). As will be seen, contributions of ODA continue to be measured as a percentage of donor GNP, but actual contributions to ODA are still receding from, rather than approaching, this target.

Much has been written about the rationale and purposes of foreign aid. The Pearson Commission report (Pearson *et al.*, 1969) posed the basic question as follows: If even the richest countries are burdened with heavy social and economic problems at home, why should the DCs attempt to help other countries? The commission's principal answer is the moral one: Those who have are morally obliged to share with those who have not because we all belong to a world community. But it is conceded that this rationale alone may not carry the day, so the appeal of "enlightened and constructive self-interest" is also invoked. Chenery (1979) points to a mixture of objectives that motivate foreign aid, the most important of which are the economic and social development of the recipient, the maintenance of political stability in countries having special ties to the donor, and export promotion.

Motives are indeed mixed, and debates as to whether the motives of donor governments are "selfish" or "unselfish" are unproductive. At one extreme is the moral case, as stated by the Pearson Commission, and at the other extreme are the motives of economic and political self-interest. Between these extremes is the other Pearson Commission argument of enlightened and constructive self-interest, and as stated in the report (Pearson *et al.*, 1969:9): "Who can now ask where his country will be in a few decades without asking where the world will be? If we wish that world to be secure and prosperous, we must show a common concern for the common problems of all peoples."

By the early 1970s, this concern for the economic and social development of the LDCs, which presumably had been the principal rationale for foreign aid from the beginning, began to overshadow the arguments that for two decades had loomed large in making the case for foreign aid, such as the Communist threat, the winning of friends and allies, the need for continued access to vital raw materials, and the economic benefits obtainable through increased trade. Beginning in the mid-1970s, as indicated in the discussion of basic needs, the givers of foreign aid increasingly emphasized, at least in their policy statements, the need to focus on problems of equity and of poverty reduction in the distribution of development assistance. The rhetoric was loud and clear, whether or not it was matched by practice, and professed concern with basic needs was the order of the day. In the United States, for example, it was reflected in USAID policy beginning in 1973 and was enshrined in the policy chapter of the Foreign Assistance Act in 1978 (Hough, 1982:59): "The Congress declares that the principal purpose of United States bilateral assistance is to help the poor majority of people in developing countries to participate in a process of equitable growth through productive work and to influence decisions that shape their lives, with the goal of increasing their incomes and their access to public services which will enable them to satisfy their basic needs and lead lives of decency, dignity, and hope." As indicated earlier, the speeches of Robert S. McNamara, former president of the World Bank, emphasized from the early 1970s on the problems of poverty, inequality, and unemployment, and from 1976 on his calls for meeting basic needs were expressed in a mounting crescendo (International Bank for Reconstruction and Development, 1981a).

The principal forms of aid are bilateral, i.e., aid given under an agreement between a single donor country and a recipient country, and multilateral, i.e., aid given by a group of countries working through an international agency. The most important of the latter are the World Bank and the United Nations and its specialized agencies. There are also regional development banks in Asia, Africa, the Middle East, and Latin America that provide multilateral assistance. In 1965, less than 6% of all ODA was multilateral. This proportion increased to 32% by 1977–1978, but then fell to 28% in 1982–1983 (International Bank for Reconstruction and Development, 1985). One major difference between bilateral and multilateral aid is in the criteria employed to allocate aid among different recipients. The allocation of bilateral aid has been influenced by political considerations and historical ties (which in fact is why most aid has been bilateral). Consequently, British aid has gone primarily to the Commonwealth countries, French aid to French-speaking Africa, United States aid to Latin America and to countries deemed strategically important in other parts of the world, and Russian aid to the few countries the U.S.S.R. has regarded as strategically important (Singer and Ansari, 1982).[15] Although multilateral aid has been on the increase, there was a shift in emphasis by the donors in the early 1980s back toward bilateral aid. Hough (1982:90) observed, at least for the United States, that "bilateralism is making somewhat of a comeback in Congress. As the world looks more unpredictable or unmanageable, the tendency is to favor the instruments over which one has greater control."

A common practice in bilateral ODA has been for the donor country to "tie" its aid to its own products. Thus, the recipient of the aid is required to purchase from the donor country whatever capital goods and services may be needed from external sources for the project in question. In 1979, about 55% of bilateral ODA was still tied (Goldthorpe, 1984), but this proportion went down to about 43% in 1982–1983. Nevertheless, nondevelopmental motives still influence bilateral aid programs, and World Bank staff believe that the proportion of tied aid may again be increasing, particularly by the use of mixed credits (International Bank for Reconstruction and Development, 1985). It is due to the increasing recognition of the importance of poverty-focused programs that practices have begun to change. In the past, most aid agencies preferred to limit their funding to physical investment and were reluctant to finance local and recurrent costs because of concern that projects to which an LDC did not make a substantial financial commitment might vanish after external aid stopped, but also because contributing to such costs would encourage consumption at the expense of investment. With the growing conviction, however, that development of human capital is also investment, as in education, family planning programs, and health and nutrition programs, the World Bank is now financing local and recurrent costs, and in 1979 the OECD's DAC adopted new guidelines on financing such costs that recognized that basic human development programs were particularly suitable for these kinds of financing (International Bank for Reconstruction and Development, 1980a). As World Bank staff have observed (International Bank for Reconstruction and Development, 1985:98), there was increasing awareness that the "development of human capital was a critical factor in the promotion of development."

In 1965, total ODA from the member nations of the OECD was $6.48 billion, while in 1984, total ODA was estimated at $28.5 billion. The largest contributions have come from the United States, a total of slightly more than $4 billion in 1965 and an estimated $8.7 billion in 1984. On the basis of estimated 1984 contributions, the next largest contributors are Japan, with $4.3 billion, France, with $3.8 billion, and West Germany, with slightly less than $2.8 billion (*ibid.*). After OPEC moved into the provision of ODA, its total contribution rose dramatically from $450 million in 1972 to $4.2 billion in 1974 to a peak of more than $8.7 billion in 1980, after which it dropped substantially due to the oil glut (*ibid.*).

As these amounts indicate, there has been a spectacular increase in the volume of foreign aid over the past two decades, but they mask some important facts. Although the United States remains the largest donor, its contributions relative to those of other major donors have declined steadily. In the early 1960s, the United States share amounted to more than 60% of total bilateral ODA, but by the early 1970s, this proportion shrank to less than 30%. With reference to the United Nations target of 0.7% of donor GNP for ODA, the United States made its closest approximation in 1965, when its percentage was 0.58%, but this percentage has declined over the years to an estimated low of 0.23% in 1984, compared with, in this same year, estimates of 0.77% for France, 0.45% for West Germany, and 0.35% for Japan. Over the years, the highest percentages have been maintained by the Scandinavian countries and the Netherlands. Although the largest contributor, the United States ranked lowest among OECD donors in percentage of donor GNP in 1984 (ibid.).

The growth of the total amount of concessional aid from the OECD countries has slowed substantially, and indeed the total decreased by 6% in 1981 and has increased only modestly since then. Clausen (1985a:9) says that the "growth of official development assistance has fallen below even minimal expectations . . . [the] ability [of the low-income countries] to offer even modest hopes to their citizens, to reduce poverty, and to sustain growth depends vitally on a much more robust increase in aid for long-term development." The growth of ODA is declining just when the poorest countries, which are most dependent on ODA, may need it most, considering the abysmal projections for their economic growth rates. During 1981–1982, official development flows (including nonconcessional flows from multilateral agencies) represented 82% of the total net capital receipts of the low-income countries; in 1983, such flows still accounted for 40% of the total net capital received by all LDCs, even though some LDCs have "graduated" from aid (International Bank for Reconstruction and Development, 1985). As indicated in Chapter 2, advocates of basic-needs programs called for increases in financial assistance from the DCs that would be gradually raised to average an additional $20 billion annually over the next 20 years to match domestic efforts by the LDCs, if such programs are going to work. The prognosis for resource transfers on this scale is gloomy indeed.

As with most other issues of the development dialogue considered in this discussion, polemics characterizes much of the literature on foreign aid. At one extreme, aid has been assailed as actually harmful to the LDCs; at the other it has been hailed as indispensable to their development. Between, as in the case of the MNCs, there have been a variety of attempts to assess the positive and negative effects of aid; again as in the case of the MNCs, these attempts have been severely constrained by the paucity of adequate data and by the difficulties of tracing the ultimate effects of a particular type of assistance on a particular sector in a recipient country (Krueger, 1986). Ranis (1973) believed that aid, even though it has constituted only a fraction of total external investment in the LDCs, has had a major catalytic impact on the performance of the LDC economies through its influence on the efficiency of total resource use.

Griffin (1978), however, holds a different view. He maintains that much of foreign aid has been channeled disproportionately to the middle-income countries and that large and very poor countries, such as India and Bangladesh, have received far less aid than either their numbers or their need suggest as equitable. Moreover, there is no evidence that within the poor countries aid has gone, on balance, to the poorest people. According to Griffin, a significant proportion of aid has been used to supplement consumption rather than investment, and therefore the impact of aid on the rate of economic growth has usually been rather small. In effect, the LDCs have borrowed capital in part to increase their consumption.

Griffin is critical of foreign aid because there has not been enough of it to make any difference and because it has done little to contribute to the reduction of poverty. P. T. Bauer, on the other hand, sees no role for aid because he sees nothing wrong in economic inequality. Bauer (1981:23–24) claimed that "the pursuit of economic equality is more likely to harm than to benefit the living standards of the very poor by politicizing life, by restricting the accumulation and effective deployment of capital, by obstructing social and economic mobility at all levels, and by inhibiting enterprise in many different ways." And because all these effects are likely to be affected adversely by the flow of aid, "there can be no general presumption that in practice aid is more likely to promote development rather than retard it" (Bauer, 1976:110).

Altogether, of total bilateral aid of $17 billion in 1979, $11 billion went to middle-income countries. After reporting these amounts, World Bank staff (International Bank for Reconstruction and Development, 1981b:56) concluded: "The economic and humanitarian merits of a reallocation to the poorer countries are obvious, but political considerations have so far precluded such action." Multilateral ODA partly offsets the bias of bilateral aid against low-income countries, but as indicated earlier, multilateral aid constituted only 32% of all ODA at its peak in 1977–1978 and has decreased since then. The World Bank's International Development Association (IDA), which has disbursed about 84% of its aid to low–income countries, has had to cut its program substantially due to shortfalls in funding, which are considered below.

The International Bank for Reconstruction and Development

(IBRD), the International Finance Corporation (IFC), and the IDA comprise the "World Bank Group." They are legally and financially distinct from each other, but are all under the same management. The IBRD was established in 1945, and its first task was expected to be financing the rebuilding of Europe's war-damaged economies. With the initiation of the Marshall Plan, however, substantial funds for the European recovery were provided by the United States through the Economic Cooperation Act passed in 1948 (Goldthorpe, 1984). The IBRD then became an agent for the transfer of resources from the DCs to the LDCs to finance mainly infrastructure projects (such as roads and railways, telecommunications, and ports and power facilities). Since the mid-1960s, it has made consistent efforts to turn itself into a multilateral development institution devoted to both financing and influencing the direction of economic and social development in the LDCs. The IBRD states as its "one central purpose: to promote economic and social progress in developing nations by helping raise productivity so that their people may live a better and fuller life" (World Bank, 1985b:3).[16]

The World Bank finances its lending operations primarily from its own borrowings in the world capital markets. For the first decade of its existence, the bank relied overwhelmingly on the United States capital market, but in the 1960s, substantial sums were borrowed in West Germany, and by the 1970s, more than half the funds were raised in Japan, as well as in Germany and other European countries (Baer, 1974). Between 1946 and mid-1982, the bank lent a total of over $105 billion for about 3000 projects in more than 100 countries (World Bank, 1985b). In 1985, total lending commitments by the IBRD and the IDA were about $14 billion and total borrowings were about $11 billion (World Bank, 1985a).

A substantial contribution to the IBRD's resources comes from its retained earnings and the flow of repayments on its loans. IBRD loans generally have a grace period of 5 years and are repayable over 20 years or less. The interest rate on its loans is calculated in accordance with its cost of borrowing. These loans are directed "toward developing countries at more-advanced stages of economic and social growth. . . . Each loan is made to a government or must be guaranteed by the government concerned . . . and the IBRD's decisions to lend must be based on economic considerations" (World Bank, 1984:3).

The narrow definition of "credit-worthiness" imposed by the IBRD's charter eliminated most of the poorest LDCs from being candidates for its loans. Thus, through the years, IBRD loans have been made to the middle-income LDCs, a practice that still holds, as indicated in the IBRD's list of borrowers in 1984–1985 (World Bank, 1985a:194–195). The low-income countries could not afford to take on the interest rates and maturity periods of IBRD loans, let alone the conditions set by commercial loans, even if such loans had been offered to them. In 1960, the IDA was established to provide concessional assistance to low-income countries. In contrast to the IBRD, the IDA is a development fund in which eligibility for loans is based on need as measured by per capita income levels. Between 1961 and 1982, 81% of the IDA's lending commitments went to LDCs that as of 1980 had per capita incomes below $410, compared with only 8% of IBRD funds, and by 1983 this share of IDA commitments increased to 89% (International Bank for Reconstruction and Development, 1984, 1985). The funds used by the IDA come mostly in the form of subscriptions, general replenishments from the IDA's more industrialized members, special contributions by the IDA's richer members, and transfers from the net earnings of the IBRD. The terms of the IDA's loans, which are made to governments only, are highly concessional, since there are 10-year grace periods, 50-year maturities, and no interest, although there is a modest service fee. Without the IDA, the World Bank would be only a negligible source of assistance to the poorest countries and would have been forced to continue to limit that assistance to the middle-income countries with the best economic prospects. Nevertheless, the total of IDA loans is modest compared with that of IBRD loans. In 1985, for example, total lending commitments by the IBRD were about $11.4 billion, while the IDA total was only $3 billion, and this constituted a decrease of $547 million, or 15.3% from 1984 (World Bank, 1985a). Despite the critical need that the IDA was designed to meet, World Bank staff observe that over the years since its inception, "the predicament of low-income countries has not eased significantly; indeed, the recent recession in industrial countries has made it worse" (International Bank for Reconstruction and Development, 1984:49).

As indicated earlier, the poverty-focused development perspectives that emerged in the mid-1970s were quickly embraced by the bank's leadership and led to a flood of literature produced by the bank emphasizing the importance of attacking poverty by improving the productive capacity of the poor and meeting their basic needs. In an address on poverty in the Third World, Clausen (1985b:8) maintained that since the bank began to focus on poverty in the 1970s, it not only has urged continued efforts to accelerate economic growth in the LDCs but also has made special efforts to include low-income people within that process of growth: "The Bank's poverty-focused projects have shown that it is possible to reduce poverty, not only by income transfers, but also by drawing the poor directly into the growth process." Much of this assertion may be rhetoric, but the bank's practice, at least with respect to its IDA commitments, appears to match the rhetoric.[17]

Of the poor countries that have received IDA loans, 27 have now "graduated" to IBRD borrowing. Similarly, about 20 countries that borrowed from the IBRD no longer do so, and some of these countries are now sources of funds for both the IBRD and the IDA (World Bank, 1985b). Nevertheless, IDA funds have been subject to increasing constraints since 1982. Up to that year, IDA commitments increased by 8% a year, but in 1982, lending declined to a level 30% below that of 1980. This decline was due to a delay in receiving contributions to the IDA's sixth replenishment, a delay in which the United States figured prominently and which has been exacerbated by the reduced size of the seventh replenishment to $9 billion as compared with $12 billion in the sixth replenishment (International Bank for Reconstruction and Development, 1985). At $9 billion, the seventh replenishment "represents a major reduction in the concessional resources available to the world's poorest countries . . . 40 per cent lower in real terms than the IDA-6 agreement reached in 1979" (International Bank for Reconstruction and Development, 1984:49). These reductions have of course resulted in a substantial decline in IDA lending, and a further decline in real annual lending is likely over the next few years (International Bank for Reconstruction and Development, 1985). According to Clausen (1985b:11), "Donor governments are redirecting their foreign aid money away from development purposes toward their own national security purposes, and away from the poorest of the poor countries to those developing countries in which they have greater commercial or political interests— the middle-income countries."

Stryker (1979) points out that despite its claim that its decision–making process is based only on economic considerations, the World Bank is essentially a political institution. The bank may be owned by its 151 member governments, but 5 of its executive directors are appointed by the largest stockholders, namely, the United States, the United Kingdom, France, West Germany, and Japan, while 16 other executive directors are elected by the Board of Governors (which consists of one governor for each member country). The United States, as the largest contributor, provides 22.4% of the bank's subscribed capital and has 20.6% of the voting power, and the bank's presidents are chosen in the American White House (World Bank, 1985b).

The bank has its share of critics, of course, but some of them are ready to point out its virtues as well as its limitations. Whatever may be his unfavorable views of the bank, Stryker (1979:328) concedes that "the Bank has forged to the forefront of development thought today. The direction and distribution of lending operations are being subjected to moral and intellectual trends to an ever greater extent." Ranis (1981:352), although also a critic of the bank, says "that the Bank almost singlehandedly tried to stem the tide of growing fatigue with the problems of resource transfers to the third and fourth worlds and the tide of growing disinterest in the fate of the two-thirds of humanity on the part of industrialized countries, increasingly beleaguered and preoccupied with their own problems." And Wood (1984:702) concludes: "The World Bank is imperfect, and in some ways it is part of the problem, but it is the main institution Third World countries have to claim external resources on concessional terms, to exercise some voice over capital transfers, and to grapple with the complex issues of development strategy."

CONCLUDING OBSERVATIONS

"Growth with equity" may now hold center stage in development thinking, but as the discussion in this chapter has shown, the pursuit of this objective, both internationally and domestically, is beset by substantial problems and constraints. National and international priorities in agriculture have helped to offset some of the deleterious effects of urban bias. There is now a worldwide surplus of food, but hunger and malnutrition continue to afflict many millions in the LDCs. If growth with equity is to occur in reality as well as in rhetoric, then what the world needs is not only accelerated agricultural, as well as industrial, production, but also international reforms in the direction of a more balanced distribution of economic and political power between DCs and LDCs and domestic reforms to increase access of the poor to economic resources and to participation in decision-making about the development process. Such reforms could also have the effect of enabling the LDCs to become more self-reliant.

In view of the increasing interdependence of DCs and LDCs in the world economy, their needs will be best served if cooperation rather than confrontation is maximized in their relations. Particularly severe problems that need to be addressed, in the first instance by the DCs, concern trade barriers, capital flows to the LDCs, and restructuring of the LDCs' external debt. The model of a new international economic order that was so prominent in United Nations discussions in the 1970s may not have much currency today, but the problems with which its proponents were concerned are still with us and call for an agenda of policy reforms that will foster the growth with equity that now receives so much emphasis in the development dialogue.

The rhetoric of the bilateral and multilateral donors is already re-plete with the conviction that the focus of international assistance must shift to the poorest countries and to the poorest people in those coun-tries. Some attempts have been made to match this rhetoric in practice, most notably in the World Bank's IDA program, but there are many competing interests that impose substantial constraints on moving in this direction.

Increasing the volume of aid, as Streeten and others have advo-cated, is essential to effective implementation of development programs focused on growth with equity. Adequate external funding, however, may be a necessary condition, but is hardly a sufficient condition. In the poorest countries, external assistance can strengthen the forces working for broad-based development, but foreign donors can never take the initiating role. Unless LDC governments can demonstrate a clear politi-cal commitment to poverty-focused development and to carrying out the necessary structural reforms, no amount of foreign assistance will be of significant use in attacking the problems of poverty. The best the exter-nal donors can do is to ensure that their assistance is channeled to countries that are in fact making this commitment. If foreign aid is to be a genuine agent of development, the criterion of equity will have to be central in the process of international resource allocation, but this princi-ple alone is not likely to provide sufficient motivational force for the donor countries to provide aid.

Nearly two decades ago, the Pearson Commission (Pearson *et al.*, 1969) described "aid disillusionment" as pervasive among the DCs. If anything, such disillusionment is more severe today and is matched by "aid weariness" on the part of many DC donors. The nature and magni-tude of foreign assistance are only one issue in the international di-alogue. Questions of aid are linked to broader questions of trade and reform of international financial arrangements. Prospects for more con-structive negotiations on these issues depend on better understanding on the part of both DCs and LDCs of the realities of global interdepen-dence, on increased awareness that attention must be focused on re-forms in the areas in which there are possibilities for mutual benefit, and on reaching a consensus that international and internal reforms are es-sentially complementary and both need to be pursued if the interests of international and internal equity are to be served.

In addition to financial aid, some reference must be made to the other principal component of foreign aid, namely, technical assistance. Technical assistance has been characterized by a two-way flow of con-siderable magnitude—one of professional advisors and technicians sent from the DCs to work for varying periods of time in the LDCs and the other of persons from the LDCs who are sent for training in the DCs, although some have been trained in their own countries at the expense of donors. Technical assistance has made some notable contributions in expanding education, eradicating a number of major diseases, and increasing the production of basic foods. But technical assistance has often failed to adapt its objectives and methods to local cultures and conditions and to actual requirements in the LDCs. Advisors have gone out imbued with the conviction that the concepts and methods in which they have been trained are unquestionably effective and universally applicable and without an appreciation of the fact that the advanced technologies of the DCs cannot usually be transplanted without considerable modification and adaptation to the particular economic, technical, and sociocultural needs of the LDCs. This ethnocentric view of technology transfer dominated development thinking at least until the early 1970s and was reflected in an emphasis on showcase universities, high technology and large urban hospitals in the health sector, and large-scale agriculture. Such enterprises did nothing to address the needs of the poor majorities and in some countries may in fact have contributed to development policies inappropriate to a variety of national interests.[18]

Expatriate advisors are no longer as eagerly sought after by the LDCs as they were in the past, particularly in Latin America and some parts of Asia. One effective use of donor funds available for technical assistance would be to take advantage of technical expertise already available in some Third World countries to help others less endowed, as in the United Nations program referred to earlier, "Technical Co-operation among Developing Countries." Among other potential benefits, this cooperation constitutes an opportunity for foreign aid to foster collective self-reliance. In any case, technical assistance is still a thriving enterprise. The World Bank, for example, provides technical assistance through a variety of channels, although the primary one continues to be the technical-assistance component of loans, which often include placement of resident expatriate advisors (International Bank for Reconstruction and Development, 1982).

A few words should be said about the problem of coordination of aid programs. The Pearson Commission (Pearson *et al.*, 1969) observed that international aid, with its profusion of bilateral and multilateral agencies, lacked direction and coherence, and that a serious effort was needed to coordinate the efforts of aid-givers and aid-receivers. They recommended that the World Bank take the initiative in creating arrangements essential to the efficiency and coordination of foreign aid. The need for more effective coordination among bilateral and multilateral aid-givers still exists and is more acute than ever in view of the current severe constraints on development assistance, particularly for concessional aid. But improvements in donor coordination are not easily achieved, since perceived interests among bilateral and multilateral aid agencies, as well as among aid recipients, may vary considerably (Hough, 1982). The World Bank is certainly in a position to facilitate coordination, but it would be unrealistic to accord it exclusive responsibility for performing this role. The bank does make substantial efforts in this direction by designing its projects in close collaboration with recipient governments and agencies and often in cooperation with other multilateral aid agencies. World Bank staff report (World Bank, 1985b) that 40% of all its projects also receive financial support from other aid agencies, both bilateral and multilateral, and from commercial banks as well. They say (ibid.:7): "Many of these institutions would not have participated in the development process on the present scale were it not for the Bank's leadership and expertise." The bank is strongly committed to improved coordination of ODA and prides itself on its role as a "catalytic agent" (World Bank, 1985a:49). Nevertheless, the bank may not be well suited to serve as the chief coordinator of the overall arrangements for giving and receiving foreign aid. Cran and Finkle (1981) point out that the bank's heavy reliance on its own project procedures engenders a commitment by the bank to maintain a high level of independence and control in relationships with other donor agencies, which contributes to disputes with other donors about how to advise recipient governments in program strategy and in conflicts over which donor is to support which project components. As Hough (1982:89–90) concludes, "There is indeed need for fresh thinking and new approaches to the requirements and opportunities for donor coordination."

A recurrent theme in this chapter is that of the need for a better knowledge base for understanding of the factors relevant to the prospects for implementation of equity-oriented development policies. To cite but three instances of this need: (1) With regard to international economic relations, there are no definitive findings about the nature of the gap between rich and poor countries due to the paucity of longitudinal and comparative data (Seligson, 1984b). (2) In the area of popular participation and community-level action, it should be emphasized that if appropriate policies are to be formulated to alleviate poverty, much more knowledge is needed about who the poor are, where they live, and how different types of rural groups gain their livelihood. (3) Finally, although there is increased understanding of the process of foreign aid, "this still leaves a large agenda for research . . . [which] has lagged far behind" (Krueger, 1986:74). Much more empirical research is needed to assess the impact of aid and its effects on development. Wherever feasible, LDC scholars should be encouraged and given every opportunity to work on these problem areas so critical to the well-being of the LDCs.

NOTES

[1]See, for example, *World Development Report 1980* (International Bank for Reconstruction and Development, 1980a) for a description of small farm projects in India and Brazil in which "small is productive."

[2]For a recent publication of the principal message of Lipton's book, see Lipton (1984).

[3]More than a decade ago, Mahbub ul Haq (1976:76) contended that if the LDCs did not undertake seriously the restructuring of their societies, the consequence would be "confusion, anarchy, and political instability. . . . To translate the new development strategies into practical political and economic policy action . . . would require a wholehearted political commitment, mobilization of a mass political movement, fundamental institutional reforms, and some very tough decisions and choices."

[4]Such incremental approaches are meant to refer here only to the need to design selective and flexible strategies that have the best chance of coping with adverse political reactions likely to be elicited by the introduction of policies aimed at redistributing economic and political power to include the poor. This interpretation should not be construed, however, as minimizing the need for a "package" approach aimed at genuine change in the condition of the poor through a concerted effort on a variety of fronts simultaneously if the objectives of equity-oriented development perspectives are to be realized.

[5]Streeten and Burki (1978) discuss these and other operational issues.

[6]One funding agency, the Inter-American Foundation, which is funded by the United States Congress, directs virtually all its support to projects focused on "popular participation." This agency's grants are made to "grassroots organizations" or to larger organizations that work with local groups (Inter-American Foundation, 1985). The International Development Research Centre (IDRC) of Canada is one of several assistance agencies working in all the major regions of the Third World that promote popular participation through support of "action–research" projects. An IDRC staff member says of action–research (Stromquist, 1984:24) that "it is through the community's involvement in the identification of its main problems, in the collective understanding of the dynamics of these problems, and in their eventual solution that both knowledge and action emerge."

[7]For a vivid portrayal of this story, see Leonard (undated). Other relevant examples can be found in Korten (1980).

[8]Grant (1977:v), in his foreword to the International Labour Office report recommending adoption of the basic-needs strategy, stated, however, that "for the first time, an international forum with a majority of participants from developing countries has insisted on the necessity of *internal* as well as interstate reforms." In any case, according to Streeten *et al.* (1981), at least the initial reaction of a number of LDC officials soon after the 1976 International Labour Office Conference was that the basic-needs approach was diversionary and intrusive. It should be noted that the term "international development assistance community," as used in this discussion, comprises the representatives of donor governments and multilateral agencies, and the officials of recipient countries, including development planners and policy-makers, who serve as the managers of development assistance funds.

[9]The presidents of Argentina and Brazil have established a tariff union, modeled on the European Economic Community, that is intended to increase and reorient trade between them and have declared that the union will be open to other democratic states in the region (*New York Times*, 1986).

[10]This discussion follows the World Bank's grouping of LDCs into low–income and middle-income economies, as described in Chapter 1. Within the group of low-income countries, there is a subgroup called the "least-developed" countries. According to L. Berry and Kates (1980), "least development" cannot be adequately explained by randomness. Most of the least–developed countries are in sub-Saharan Africa, the majority are located in arid or semiarid environments, and many seem physically or economically isolated to an extraordinary degree. See also Enloe (1980) and Ford (1980).

[11]Although it may be primarily at the level of rhetoric, the DCs also continue to maintain the dialogue about the imbalances in international economic relations. A joint declaration issued after an "economic summit conference" held in 1985 in which seven DCs participated prominently featured a series of problems in relations with the LDCs that the DCs proposed to address, including lower interest rates and the debt problem, trade barriers and rising protectionism, resource flows including the need for increased development assistance, and so on (*New York Times*, 1985a).

[12]Home countries are those in which the headquarters of the MNCs are based. Host countries are those in which the foreign branches or affiliates of the MNCs are located.

[13]For an argument that takes the opposite position on many of these issues, see Schmidt (1983).

[14]The OECD was preceded by the Organisation for European Economic Co-operation, which was set up by the European countries that were the recipients of Marshall Plan aid after World War II. In 1961, when Canada and the United States joined the organization, it was reconstituted as the OECD, and Germany and Japan also became members. The member countries of OECD now number 24. Also in 1961, 17 of these countries, which are the major contributors to ODA, set up the DAC of the OECD to coordinate aid and discuss development issues (Goldthorpe, 1984; International Bank for Reconstruction and Development, 1985).

[15]It is because the allocation of bilateral aid is so heavily influenced by political considerations and historical ties that such aid has often not gone where it is most urgently needed. Thus, the totals of capital flows have not necessarily been related to capacity for development and have not always favored development (Uri, 1976). Similarly, the aid provided by the Eastern bloc countries and by OPEC has also been narrowly channeled (International Bank for Reconstruction and Development, 1982).

[16]This is also the stated purpose of the IFC, which was established in 1956 to work with private investors to promote growth in the private sector of the LDC economies and to help mobilize domestic and foreign capital for such growth. Since foreign aid in this discussion is concerned essentially with concessional flows, the IFC is not included in the discussion that follows. All references to the World Bank should therefore be understood to include only the IBRD and the IDA.

[17]The bank's priorities in lending are consistent with the professed commitment to alleviation of poverty. In 1985, IDA lending for agriculture and rural development constituted 44.9% of total lending, as compared with 21% of total IBRD lending in this sector. IDA lending for education in 1985 accounted for another 13.6%, as compared with 4.5% of IBRD loans. All other sectors received small percentages of IDA lending compared with these two. The 1985 share of IDA lending for agriculture and rural development represented an increase of 6% over the total allocated in 1983 (World Bank, 1985a).

[18]For an early assessment of a number of these issues, see Jenney and Simmons (1954).

Links between Development Perspectives and Population Growth

As indicated in Chapter 1, scholars in the fields of population and of development largely went their separate ways until relatively recently, with few attempts to bring together the two fields. This divergence was reflected in the scant attention paid to population variables in economic and social development planning and in the relatively superficial concern with development issues in population studies. Until the mid-1970s, "population and development" served primarily as a slogan invoked at international conferences. Over the past decade, however, concern with the complex interrelationships between population and development has generated a voluminous literature, replete with controversy and rhetoric as well as scientific reports on systematic research and analysis.

DEMOGRAPHIC TRANSITION

An assessment of the links between development perspectives and population dynamics must begin with a consideration of the "theory" of demographic transition, which was first formulated in the mid-1940s.[1] Although this theory has been discussed extensively in the literature since then, there is a need to consider it here once again because for more than two decades, with few changes in its original formulation, it dominated demographic thinking about the nature of the role of development in reducing fertility,[2] much in the way that the modernization model (with which it has much in common) dominated development thinking. The basic paradigm of demographic transition is not so much a theory as a model that describes the demographic changes that occurred in Europe during the 19th century. In most versions of transition theory, the general character of the process experienced by the industrialized countries is depicted as a series of three "stages" at which mortality and

91

fertility behaved in particular ways in accordance with fundamental economic and social changes of "development," usually viewed as synonymous with "modernization," with low mortality and fertility prevailing at the point at which "development" was "achieved" and the demographic transition thus completed.

In stage 1, so the theory goes, there is an equilibrium of population size maintained by high birth and death rates. Given high mortality in the absence of the health and sanitation services and other features that characterize modern society, societies in stage 1 employed a series of "pronatalist props," as Caldwell (1976:323) called them, to keep fertility high. Otherwise, the high mortality rate would have led to population decline and eventual extinction. Over time, however, mortality began to decline in country after country as methods of death control became available, creating a situation in which both high fertility and low mortality were valued.[3] The equilibrium of stage 1 became potentially unstable, and this instability led to stage 2, in which there was rapid population growth resulting from an imbalance between continuing high fertility and declining mortality rates. The onset of stage 3 occurred when individual members of the population consciously began to control their fertility and the birth rate gradually declined toward equilibrium with the low death rate.[4]

Central to the thinking of the proponents of this demographic-transition model was the view that fertility decline lags behind mortality decline because it cannot occur until the traditional social and economic arrangements and institutions that support high fertility are eroded by the advent of the transformations wrought by modernization, which favors a reduction in fertility to levels that correspond with lower levels of mortality. The same process of modernization, largely equated with industrialization and urbanization, that brought down the death rates was seen as destroying the pronatalist props.

Despite the elaborate detail with which transition theory depicted the process of moving from high to low fertility, it generated little specific explanatory power because it had nothing to say about causation. Perhaps its principal weakness was that it could not define a precise threshold of "modernization" that would reliably identify a population in which fertility is ready to fall (Coale, 1975). As Ilchman (1975:25) put it: "The issues of how, for whom, when, what, how much, and for how long, are not in any way answered. Sequences of choices, their costs, and priorities are all eclipsed in the sweep of the demographic transition." Transition theory yields a proposition that, at a very general level, cannot be denied, namely, that fertility and mortality are high in preindustrial societies and low in industrial societies, and between pre- and postindustrialization, there is demographic transition (Coale, 1975). The policy value of this proposition, needless to say, is very limited indeed.

Subsequent historical research on fertility and mortality in 19th-century Europe, particularly the work of the Princeton group (Coale, 1975, 1976; Coale and Watkins, 1986), has left little of the original model intact. A major finding of the Princeton studies is that overall fertility levels in Europe before the demographic transition varied considerably from country to country and subregion to subregion. Moreover, as Freedman (1979) points out, the patterns of development conditions actually associated with fertility decline have turned out to be quite varied. It would appear that in the European case, cultural and linguistic factors are more closely associated with variations in fertility decline than is the cluster of modernization factors posited as central to transition theory.

Coale (1975:352–353) has summarized the generalizable remains of transition theory in the form of three broad preconditions for sustained decline in marital fertility:

1. Fertility must be within the calculus of conscious choice. Potential parents must consider it an acceptable mode of thought and form of behaviour to balance advantages and disadvantages before deciding to have another child. . . .
2. Reduced fertility must be advantageous. Perceived social and economic circumstances must make reduced fertility seem an advantage to individual couples.
3. Effective techniques of fertility reduction must be available. Procedures that will in fact prevent births must be known, and there must be sufficient communication between spouses and sufficient sustained will, in both, to employ them successfully.

As Teitelbaum (1975) observed, the European data show that a high level of development was ultimately sufficient to establish these three preconditions for a decline in marital fertility across Europe. There is no evidence, however, of any "threshold" levels of development that were necessary for this to happen, and it is evident that the preconditions for fertility decline could exist in situations of little economic development, as in parts of rural France and in Hungary.

According to Knodel and van de Walle (1979), who have reviewed historical fertility studies, the most striking finding to emerge from the research on the fertility transition in Europe is that it occurred under remarkably diverse socioeconomic and demographic conditions, and this diversity is to be encountered in the less-developed countries (LDCs) as well. They go on to say: "The historical record provides little assurance that efforts to reduce fertility or hasten a decline through raising the level of socioeconomic development will meet with early success (*ibid.*:226). . . . Too often . . . interpretations of the historical record are based more on theoretical preconceptions derived from the present than on an empirically grounded familiarity with what actually went on in the past" (*ibid.*:240).

It may be pointed out that the demographic-transition model, with its assumption that modernization has been the principal agent in reducing fertility, masked, among other aspects of reality, the fact that "modernization," by decreasing such practices as breast feeding and postpartum sexual abstinence, may in fact contribute to increased fertility. Nag (1980:579), for example, states: "The available evidence shows that the decline in the practices of breast-feeding and postpartum abstinence is generally linked with urbanization and the spread of education and that, in the absence of widespread use of modern contraceptives, such a decline leads to shorter birth intervals and increased fertility." In a recent review of the relevant literature, Dyson and Murphy (1985) consider a number of studies that report a long-term decline in fertility as being preceded by a rise, this rise being largely due to changes in four variables, namely, marriage patterns, breast feeding, postpartum abstinence, and disease-related sterility. They argue that predecline rises in fertility have sometimes been substantial and that both European and Third World populations have experienced them. They conclude (*ibid.*:432): "So a fertility rise has to be viewed as an integral part of the opening phase of transition. Indeed, the first sign of an impending decline is a rise, which often starts many years before the predecline peak. Thus the initial impact of the nexus of changes that eventually cause fertility decline is to so alter the balance of factors determining fertility that birth rates rise."

MODERNIZATION AND DEMOGRAPHIC TRANSITION IN THE DEVELOPING WORLD

The limitations of transition theory in explaining the European experience are compounded when its potential for application to the LDCs is considered. The central idea that modernization—usually equated, as indicated, with industrialization, urbanization, and, by implication, with growth in gross national product (GNP) per capita—is sufficient to bring about a "natural" and rapid fertility decline is even less generally applicable to the LDCs than it was to Europe because of the model's essential weakness in specifying what degree of "modernization," if any, is necessary to produce a decline in fertility, and when, how, and for whom. Moreover, Teitelbaum (1975) identified a number of very substantial differences between the LDCs and 19th-century Europe in a number of the socioeconomic and demographic variables central to transition theory. Some of these differences are: (1) In European countries, mortality declines were gradual and generally related to the social and economic development that was occurring, whereas in many LDCs, mortality declines have been much more dramatic. The declines in the LDCs were usually the consequence of imported technology only marginally related to the pace and level of development. (2) Fertility levels in most LDCs have been much higher than in early 19th-century Europe. (3) In the 19th century, the European countries could mitigate some of the negative effects of rapid population growth by massive emigration to the Americas and other parts of the world, an outlet not available on any such scale to most of the LDCs today. (4) As a result of these differences, which are mutually reinforcing, the rate of population growth and the momentum created for further growth by virtue of this rate are much higher in the LDCs than they were in the European countries. Consequently, the demands and constraints imposed by such numbers of people impede social and economic development and, presumably, the fertility decline that transition theory maintains such development would bring.

It should be evident by now that the modernization model, which for a time held such allure for development researchers, as described earlier, has been, if anything, even more attractive to population researchers. The model has been enshrined in transition theory as the principal mechanism for reducing fertility and eventually controlling global population growth. Indeed, it has been accorded such respect that its components have usually not been analyzed, and adherence to its ethnocentric, linear, and deterministic views have led researchers away from, rather than toward, an examination of the empirical reality of what is going on in the LDCs, away from an understanding of population change that can be obtained only by systematic study of the actual changes occurring in the LDCs of which population change is an integral part.

Moreover, just as the orientation to the modernization model led development researchers to assume that tradition is an opposing force— the obstacle that modernization must overcome if it is to arrive at its destination—so transition theory has looked on high fertility as an obstacle to be demolished by modernization as it rolls on to its destination. Caldwell (undated:17) says: "Almost within living memory, fertility nearly everywhere was as high as it has ever been, and this is still the case over much of the Third World. We should be able to investigate high fertility in its own right and not as an anomaly that has resisted change."

Writing about fertility research in Africa, Ware (1978) says that it is based on an implicit model in which industrialization, modernization, and urbanization result in changes in economic and social structure and attitudes, which lead to changes in family reactions and attitudes, which finally, by means of changes in the intermediate or proximate variables, result in lower fertility. She goes on to say (ibid.:59): "The equation of modernization with development is often false, for only the elite benefit from the former. True development, which can be expected to affect overall fertility levels, must affect the whole population, must improve not distort the distribution of wealth, and must affect the rural areas as much or more than the favored urban zones."

To the extent that fertility research was oriented to demographic-transition theory, the task of research was viewed largely as one of specification and statistical estimation of the relationship between socioeconomic variables associated with modernization and economic development, on one hand, and fertility, on the other. Modernization is a concept loose enough to have subsumed many economic and social changes, and different researchers have exercised their own biases in emphasizing particular components of the so-called "modernization process" in explaining fertility change (Hauser, 1979).

Studies of modernization and fertility have dealt mainly with societal-level variables, such as levels of literacy or education, average per capita income, proportion living in urban areas or engaged in industrial occupations, number of radios or newspaper circulation per capita, and indices of power consumption (Fawcett and Bornstein, 1973). Thus, K. A. Miller and Inkeles (1974) employed scales of "modern experience" variables developed in the Harvard Modernization Project as predictors of acceptance of birth control in four LDCs. These scales measured education–literacy, exposure to mass media, urbanism of residence (on a scale from village to major city), modernity of occupational experience (from cultivator to very experienced factory worker), and living standard (consumer-goods owner).

In another study, Oechsli and Kirk (1975) employed ten "development" indicators as an index of modernization in relation to mortality and fertility declines in 25 LDCs in Latin America and the Caribbean. These indicators—literacy, life expectation at birth, primary school enrollment, male labor in nonagricultural pursuits, urbanization, number of hospital beds, newspaper circulation, telephones installed, secondary school enrollment, gross domestic product—they combined into a composite modernization index. Oechsli and Kirk found close correlations between levels of "development," as measured by their modernization index, growth in GNP per capita, and fertility and mortality declines, but they noted that they could not easily distinguish between cause and effect in the complex of changes they labeled "modernization." Although they found that modernization, at some level, was associated with a given mortality level and that the birth rate tended to stay high until some critical level of development is reached and then tended to decline as development proceeds, they could not say that development "causes" declining birth and death rates.

The need for research on the historical record, as called for by Knodel and van de Walle (1979), rather than on ahistorical cross-sectional analyses, which focus on the presumed relationships between modernization and population change to the neglect of the role of tradition, brings this discussion to a consideration of Caldwell's efforts to restate demographic-transition theory. In a series of publications, Caldwell (Caldwell, 1976, 1978, 1982; Caldwell and Caldwell, 1978) advances a series of propositions to describe the nature of demographic transition from high to low fertility. His fundamental thesis is that fertility behavior in both pretransitional and posttransitional societies is economically rational within the context of socially determined economic goals and within bounds largely set by biological and psychological factors. He argues that there are only two types of societies, one of high stable fertility, in which there is economic loss to individuals for restricting fertility, and another in which there is often or eventually economic gain from such restriction. He argues further that the key determinant in demographic transition is the direction and magnitude of intergenerational wealth flows or the changing balance of the two flows—one from parents to children and the other from children to parents—over the period from the time people become parents until they die. In pretransitional (high-fertility) societies, the wealth flow is from children to parents, and in posttransitional (low-fertility) societies, the flow is from parents to children, so that except for sentiment, the rational economic choice reverses, in the course of the transition, from that of having as many children as possible to that of having few or none at all.

According to Caldwell, the conditions of stable high fertility, and of subsequent destabilization, lie largely in the nature of economic relationships within the family. The family that determines economic advantage and makes demographic decisions is not limited to the family members who live in one household, but rather encompasses those groups of close relatives who share economic activities and obligations. Within this larger and demographically more significant kin group, the locus of economic and fertility decision-making is of prime importance.

The traditional peasant economy is a familial economy, fundamentally different from the nonfamilial capitalist economy. Caldwell maintains that a familial mode of production has long persisted within the capitalist mode of production, as an (at least temporarily) more efficient method of producing part of the family's needs, while giving material advantage to the male head of household as the dominant decision-maker. Posttransitional fertility decline arises from the continuing disintegration of this submode and its reproductive relationships, as capitalist production successfully competes with domestic production and as social change transforms the relationships of production.

In Caldwell's view, it is "Westernization" rather than economic modernization and urbanization that is bringing about fertility decline in the Third World. The distinction here is that modernization is that degree of social change that inevitably accompanies economic change because the capitalist mode of production demands it, so that the factory worker must follow the labor-market rules rather than those that prevail within the familial mode of production. Westernization, on the other hand, is the social change that results from importing aspects of the Western way of life through cultural diffusion. The most important aspects thus being imported are the concept of the predominance of the nuclear family and the concept of concentrating concern and expenditure on one's children, which is the reversal of the intergenerational wealth flow. All this occurs through Western domination of schools and the international network of mass media. In essence, Caldwell (1976:358) concludes "that fertility decline in the Third World is not dependent on the spread of industrialization or even on the rate of economic development . . . and that it is more likely to precede industrialization and to help bring it about than to follow it."

Caldwell's description of the economic rationality of the large family in traditional culture seems convincing and is supported by his data, but much more documentation is needed for his view of the social process of Westernization through which the traditional family, in the absence of economic change, becomes the nuclear family. It suffers from the same "threshold" problem as does modernization: How much education and other cultural importation are needed to Westernize the rural populations of the LDCs and what degree of Westernization precipitates fertility decline? His notion that the concept of the nuclear family is beginning to take hold all over the world and that conversion to the Western nuclear family is a necessary prior condition for fertility decline needs more systematic investigation. Freedman (1979), for example, agrees with Caldwell on the possible major role of the dissemination of Western ideas in motivating a desire for small families, but that this may happen through the dissemination of the Western nuclear family pattern he sees as only one possible pattern, rather than as a necessary prior condition.[5]

Caldwell's qualifications with regard to the modernization model and his efforts to restate demographic-transition theory have been helpful, but in one respect at least he still shares with some other social scientists the notion, so prominent in the modernization model, that social change is synonymous with a shift from traditional to modern forms, particularly with respect to the family. Cain (1986c) reports, on the basis of his research in several rural South Asian communities, that whatever other changes may be occurring in these communities, the "traditional" joint family system persists and shows no indication of a shift to the "modern" nuclear family form that appears to be inexorable in Caldwell's thinking. Similarly, although in the view of Freedman (1986), the demographic transition has been completed in Taiwan, many aspects of the traditional Chinese family persist even though some aspects may be fading away. As Cain (1986c:387) puts it, "One can . . . anticipate the dogged persistence of such [family] systems through time." Both Cain and Freedman emphasize the scarcity of valid empirical research on the changing and persistent elements in household and family organization. Freedman (1986:98) concludes: "Most Third World countries have some form of extended family. Changes in their family systems are inevitable with development, but, as in Taiwan, these traditional systems may serve to mitigate some of the problems created by substitution of nonfamilial for familial institutional systems in the West. The case for a universal convergence to the Western model is not convincing, and the desirability of such a universal trend is in doubt."

Caldwell (1976:358) himself notes that "sociological and anthropological work is needed to define the extent of the true extended families of obligation and to measure the internal wealth flows. . . . The study of the changing family and the measurement of movement toward the social, emotional, and economic nucleation of the conjugal family are important. A combined social science assault will probably be needed on the circumstances and conditions of the reversal of the wealth flow—and on the time taken for the flow from the older to the younger generation to grow to such an extent that it exerts a real impact on fertility control decisions." Clearly, much more systematic research will need to be done on the traditional familial economy and on the process of decision-making in the traditional family before the predictive value of Caldwell's restatement of transition theory can be ascertained. To cite Caldwell (1982:300) once again: ". . . a full [sic] satisfactory theory of demographic transition is unlikely to be distinguishable from a fully satisfactory theory of social and economic change from a system of familial productive [sic] to one of nonfamilial production. In neither case will the theory be adequate unless it can explain not merely the fact of fertility decline but the timing of its onset."

This review of demographic-transition theory indicates that its central assumption that economic development, and the industrialization and urbanization it is presumed to generate, in the LDCs would follow the Western pattern and "naturally" bring down fertility is not valid. Historical research has shown that the preconception that modernization, with which development has been equated, would bring about demographic transition was based on substantially oversimplified notions of what are not only necessary but also sufficient preconditions for fertility decline. Consequently, transition theory has provided little in the way of policy relevance. Even if modernization could be linked in precise ways with fertility decline, it could still affect only the small elites that have embraced it in the LDCs and not the rural majorities that still characterize so many LDC populations. Cain and Lieberman (1982) have pointed out that Bangladesh, for example, will remain predominantly rural, with agriculture at the center of its economy, for the foreseeable future, and the same forecast can be made for many other LDCs.

Demographic-transition theory not only essentially obscured empirical reality but also fueled the view, so popular at the World Population Conference in 1974, that "development is the best contraceptive," a view that still has its adherents today—and by "development" was meant "modernization." There are, however, a number of different pathways from high to low fertility. Fertility can decline under a variety of cultural, social, and economic conditions, and it is misleading to assume that convergence with the experience that characterized some of the Western countries must precede such a decline. Since transition theory is not very applicable to the LDCs, it has left little conceptual heritage with which to interpret the statistical relationships found in the large body of cross-sectional research oriented to the theory. Furthermore, as will be seen subsequently, there is no broad consensus on a conceptual framework that could replace transition theory as a guide to cumulative research on the determinants of population change that could strengthen the policy value of such research.

EQUITY, POVERTY, AND POPULATION GROWTH

As shown earlier, the concern with equity in the satisfaction of basic needs expresses a view of development that differs sharply from a development strategy focused exclusively on economic growth. The use of growth of GNP per capita as the principal indicator of success in development has waned as experience has shown that substantial growth of average incomes by itself may have little meliorative effect on income distribution and access to the gains of development. Nor has the central proposition of transition theory—that economic development, as measured by growth of GNP per capita, is the sufficient precondition for fertility decline—been borne out by events. Brazil and Venezuela, for example, are countries that enjoyed relatively high economic growth rates, an average of 3.7 and 2.7%, respectively, between 1950 and 1975, but at the same time maintained badly skewed income distribution and high fertility (Morawetz, 1977).

The basic-needs approach and other equity-oriented perspectives focus on certain critical areas as targets for need satisfaction, namely, nutrition, health, education, and housing, and stipulate that these needs can be met only if there are increases in employment and income, in provision of public services, and in involvement of local communities. These are also areas that include the factors considered to be among the most important determinants of fertility. The advocates of the basic-needs approach, with some notable exceptions, do not often mention the population implications, but the coincidence between the principal dimensions in the basic-needs approach and the factors held to be the important determinants of fertility argues for bringing the implications of population change more systematically into development thinking. Moreover, as will be seen, there are several reasons for believing that demographic factors have influenced trends in income distribution. Both increase in average incomes and redistribution of income, which are among the principal goals of equity-oriented development, are intricately related to population change. No automatic relationships between development and fertility have been identified, but it is clear that what matters with respect to reversing population growth trends is not just economic growth, but a strategy of development that benefits the poor (Cassen, 1978b). Thus, there is increasing interest in looking at the relationship between fertility and those factors associated not so much with average income growth as with the gains of development.

The basic-needs approach and other equity-oriented development strategies emphasize structural changes to increase access of the poor to resources that will substantially improve their well-being, and such gains are associated with lower fertility. As Sewell et al. (1980:98) put it, this approach " 'economizes' by reducing fertility rates . . . when infant mortality is reduced and more children survive, when women are better educated, and when the community takes care of the old and disabled, the need and desire for large families is reduced."

A note of caution is needed here. Ohlin (1978) observed that population growth compounds the task of meeting basic needs, but it is nevertheless not, in general, the dominant concern (except in some cases, notably that of urban housing). In health and education, for example, present needs are so inadequately met that problems of appropriate objectives and organization take precedence over those of quantitative increases dictated by population growth. Even in the absence of population growth, the prevailing concerns in these fields would be very similar. This is not to say that population growth is of no consequence. Indeed, Ohlin emphasizes that fertility decline in the LDCs will be promoted or retarded by the degree of success achieved in meeting basic needs.

In fact, marked fertility declines have already occurred in a number of countries in which development changes have been in the direction of equity-oriented objectives and the populations are mainly poor and rural (Gunatilleke, 1984). Sri Lanka, Kerala (India), and the People's Republic of China are among the examples most often cited. It has been noted (Freedman, 1979) that they share at least the following changes: (1) Better health and greater life expectancy, so that fewer births are needed for the survival of the number of children desired. (2) Higher education for both boys and girls, with the likelihood that fewer better-educated children may provide greater satisfaction than more poorly educated children. (3) Welfare programs offering at least minimum subsistence for the poor majority, which may decrease dependence on children. (4) Communication and transportation facilities generating the information, services, and goods that have produced the other changes. In connection with this list, Freedman observes that just how much change in which subset of conditions is sufficient to motivate fertility declines is not known, but probably more than one combination will turn out to be sufficient. It has been argued that the cases offered as examples may not be generalizable, but the same pattern of fertility decline associated more with distribution of the gains of development than with growth of average incomes seems to be occurring in northern Thailand and probably in Java and Bali (in Indonesia) as well.

Marked fertility declines have also occurred, of course, in some LDCs that have ranked among the fastest-growing in the Third World in GNP per capita. The two most cited examples are Taiwan and South Korea, which had average annual economic growth rates of 5.3 and 5.1%, respectively, between 1950 and 1975 (Morawetz, 1977). It should be noted that vigorous national family planning programs have probably contributed to the fertility declines in the countries mentioned above and that Taiwan and South Korea are also countries in which the majority of the population has shared in the economic and social benefits of national development.

A noteworthy analysis of cross-country data published by the World Bank in 1976 and 1977, pertaining to some 87 developed countries (DCs) and LDCs, focused on a series of relationships between basic-needs policies and population growth (Morawetz, 1978). The analysis takes as its departure point the argument that policies specifically designed to improve the health and nutrition levels of the poorest people are likely to cause infant and general mortality rates to decline. But, the argument goes, a reduction in mortality rates is likely to lead to an increase in the population growth rate, which, in turn, may partially, fully, or more than fully offset the welfare gains from implementing the initial policies. This argument ignores, however, a second important aspect of the effect of basic-needs policies on population growth—their effect on fertility. Morawetz advances several reasons that basic-needs policies may eventually cause fertility rates to decline, even if the same policies do not lead to significant increases in per capita income. First, since parents are likely to be concerned more about the number of surviving offspring than about the number of babies born, a decline in infant mortality may lead, after some lag in recognition, to a decline in fertility. Second, an increase in the quantity and quality of education that is available may cause fertility rates to decline, both because parents' aspirations for themselves and their children may be raised and because parents may now have more positive attitudes toward (and better access to means of) birth control. Third, basic-needs policies are likely to cause an increase in the degree of equality of distribution of the national income, which in turn may cause fertility to decline, a proposition that will be considered presently. A country in which the poorest 70% of the population, who account for a disproportionately large share of population growth, receive, say, 30% of the national income is likely to have a lower fertility rate than another country with the same average per capita income in which the poorest 70% receive only 15% as their share.

The findings of the analysis are as follows: (1) Basic-needs policies, to the extent that they lower infant mortality rates, increase education, cause the income distribution to be more equal, and raise per capita income, may indeed bring about an eventual reduction in fertility as well as in mortality rates. (2) There does seem to be some slight evidence that reduced infant mortality and increased education interact in reducing fertility, but the data do not permit any precise estimate of the importance of such interaction. (3) There do seem to be lags in the effects of decreased infant mortality and increased education on the fertility rate, but the data shed little light on the determinants of the length of these lags.

Thus, although equity-oriented policies seem to carry with them the promise of eventual fertility decline, the critical question is how soon that decline will occur. The predictive value of the effect of broad-based development on fertility decline, in the sense of when it will occur, is no more enhanced by this analysis than it is by transition theory or Caldwell's restatement of that theory. It is apparently not true that implementing basic-needs policies necessarily sustains rapid population growth, but it is also apparently not true that governments that follow a basic-needs policy are already doing all that is necessary to slow down population growth (*ibid.*). Governments still need to take all measures in their power to reduce fertility rates as rapidly as possible to avoid population sizes that could have serious negative consequences for the development prospects of their countries. It seems evident that combining policies that foster broad-based development with large-scale, effective family planning programs will reduce fertility rates faster than would reliance on either strategy alone, just as the attainment of the objectives of broad-based development will be made easier by fertility reduction.

There is a voluminous literature reporting efforts to assess the independent program effects of family planning on fertility change. A detailed review of the differing interpretations of these effects would require going far beyond the scope and main focus of this book. Nevertheless, a brief consideration of this literature is in order, since, as just indicated, family planning programs have a critical role to perform, in conjunction with broad-based development strategies, in reducing fertility rates.

The variation in results and interpretations that characterize this literature can be largely attributed to the imposing methodological problems involved in measuring the impact of family planning programs on fertility. As Mauldin (1983:269) observes: "Perhaps the most serious problem is that on a national scale, one cannot know what would have happened without the family planning program. . . . On a national scale, one can construct models taking into account changes in socioeconomic factors, but different models give different results." Birdsall (1985:vii), also addressing the problem of identifying the impact of a program by estimating how fertility would have changed in its absence, says: "That requires systematically eliminating other possible causes of a country's fertility decline—such as increases in income, education, and life expectancy in the same period. In addition, information on the change in the availability and quality of family planning information and services is needed."

Between 1965 and 1975, a substantial number of family planning programs were established in the LDCs, and this circumstance offered the opportunity for generating a relatively ample information base. Two principal sources that have provided a basis for more precise assessments of the program effects of family planning are (1) a country-level family planning index originally based on the performance of programs in LDCs in 1972 updated to 1982 for 93 countries (Mauldin and Lapham, 1985) and (2) household and community surveys conducted by the World Fertility Survey that covered 41 LDCs around the world and by the Contraceptive Prevalence Survey project that included 43 countries (Population Information Program, 1985b). World Bank staff (International Bank for Reconstruction and Development, 1984:118) observe that the analyses made possible by these data sources "leave little doubt that the programs work."

Whatever may be the advantages of this data base, it does not preclude differing interpretations. On the basis of a study of 1980 crude birthrates and changes in these rates between 1960 and 1980 in 83 LDCs, Cutright (1983: 101) reports "that indicators of education, health and family planning program effort have a significant independent effect on fertility. The finding is true for all 83 countries combined, and for Asian and Latin American countries analyzed separately." Hernandez (1984, 1985) chooses a different interpretation from Cutright, at least in emphasis. He maintains (1985:80–81) that family planning programs "account—independently of the socioeconomic and cultural setting—for no more than 3 to 10 per cent of the variation in fertility change during the late 1960s and early 1970s in 83 developing countries" and that studies employing the best available research designs "find little or no program effect independent of the socioeconomic and cultural setting." Cutright (1986), Dodd (1986), and Warwick (1986) provide assessments of Hernandez's approach to analysis of the impact of family planning programs on fertility in the LDCs.

In any case, a series of reports on cross-national and country studies affirm that family planning programs do have identifiable independent effects. Mauldin (1983:289), in a review of the literature on the impact of family planning programs on fertility, concluded that "the consensus of most analysts appears to be that . . . there is considerable empirical evidence that large-scale family planning programs, when well-managed, have a substantial effect on fertility independent of the influence of socioeconomic factors." The conclusion to another review of this literature (Population Information Program, 1985a:J-733) states: "Family planning programs have clearly lowered fertility in a number of developing countries. Fertility has declined most in countries where strong family planning programs operate with government support in favorable social and economic settings. Even in relatively poor countries, however, moderately strong family planning programs have made a difference to fertility."

With regard to national or in-country studies, Zachariah (1983) found in a study of the state of Kerala in India, for example, that the principal determinants of Kerala's fertility decline were widespread improvements in health and education and an effective family planning program, consistent with Cutright's finding reported above. The analysis by Merrick (1985) of recent declines in Brazil, Colombia, and Mexico yields a partially different set of common threads in the experience of these three countries. He concludes that *both* supply (in the form of increased use of contraception) *and* demand factors contributed to the recent acceleration of these declines. With regard to demand, lower income classes, particularly in urban areas, have been increasing their consumption aspirations but have great difficulty in realizing them because of inflation and persistent income inequality, and so their adjustment has been to reduce fertility to enable them to allocate both time and monetary resources to material consumption rather than to children.[6] Broad-based development, changes in aspirations of the kind brought about by the changes identified by Merrick (and in Freedman's list of changes in China, Kerala, and Sri Lanka), and availability of and receptivity to efficient methods of contraception can all constitute key factors, and indeed are mutually reinforcing, in precipitating a fertility decline. As Mauldin (1983:289) says, however, "Precise quantitative credit cannot be allocated among socioeconomic factors, institutional factors, and policies and programs."

It may be noted that family planning activities, with the exception of reversals or setbacks in a few countries, continue to expand in the LDCs. Mauldin and Lapham (1985) point to a modest increase, between 1972 and 1982, in program effort in over half the 93 countries included in their index and a more substantial increase in program effort in more than a third. The World Bank (International Bank for Reconstruction and Development, 1984) reports that about 85 LDCs encompassing about 95% of the Third World's population now provide some form of public support for family planning programs, and another source (Population Information Program, 1985a:J-734) states that "around the world, 127 countries, representing 94 per cent of the world population, provide government support for family planning. Of these, 95 are developing countries."

Poverty and rapid population growth are closely associated and mutually reinforcing, but neither is the necessary determinant or consequence of the other (Birdsall, 1980). Even though they may be related in important ways, it would be a gross oversimplification to conclude that high fertility is the cause of poverty or that reducing fertility has the direct effect of ameliorating poverty. Rodgers (1984) has reviewed the literature on the two-way relationship between population growth and poverty in the LDCs. He concludes (*ibid.*:169) that "high fertility and high rates of population growth tend to have adverse effects on the incidence and evolution of poverty, but that these effects tend to be relatively small." He qualifies this, however, by noting that there are cases in which there is evidence of little or no effect, while other cases show larger effects.[7]

As the discussion of Caldwell's work shows, for the rural poor in many LDCs, high fertility makes good economic and cultural sense. In general, however, the higher a country's per capita income, the lower its fertility and mortality. Among LDCs, those of sub-Saharan Africa and of the subcontinent, Bangladesh, India, and Pakistan, have the highest levels of fertility and mortality and the lowest incomes, while the DCs have the lowest levels of fertility and mortality and the highest incomes (Birdsall, 1980). But the negative association between fertility rates and income, at least at the country level, does not hold consistently. Mexico and Brazil, among middle-income LDCs, had relatively high fertility (until recently), as do still the high-income oil-exporting countries of Iran, Libya, and Venezuela, while a number of low-income countries, such as Indonesia, Sri Lanka, and China, have relatively low fertility.[8] Birdsall (*ibid.*:13) says: "The exceptions call attention to certain factors which mediate the simple negative association. . . . These are the distribution of income within a country; the availability and distribution of health and educational services . . .; and with regard to fertility, the access of the poor to family planning services."

Fertility decline by itself will not solve poverty problems; more direct attacks on poverty and slow economic growth are necessary. Nevertheless, it can be said that in many LDCs, particularly those with low levels of economic and natural resources, the degree and scale of future poverty could be reduced with lower rates of population growth (*ibid.*).

Fertility rates are declining in many LDCs, but given the built-in momentum generated by the large proportion of children and adolescents in LDC populations (who in turn are a consequence of the high fertility and declining mortality since 1950), population growth will continue well into the next century regardless of what is done now to reduce fertility. This momentum is one of the most severe problems the LDCs will have to cope with in the long run (Teitelbaum, 1974; Conde, 1978; International Bank for Reconstruction and Development, 1984).

Very substantial growth lies ahead for the LDCs on almost any assumptions. The growth potential of a population depends on the size of the generations that successively reach reproductive age. For young populations, such as those in most LDCs, the dynamic effect of the age structure ensures a growth rate that will continue for most of a century even with substantial declines in fertility.

If the gains of development are to be enhanced for the coming generations, everything possible must be done to head off subsequent increases of even greater magnitude than those already projected on the basis of built-in momentum. Consider the following calculations and projections.[9] It took more than 1500 years for world population to double from 300 million in 1 A.D., but in 35 years, between 1950 and the present, world population nearly doubled from 2.5 billion to about 4.8 billion (International Bank for Reconstruction and Development, 1984). As Demeny (1985a:5) puts it: "It took almost all of human history until the industrial revolution to reach the size of one billion; adding the second billion took some 120 years, the third 33 years, the fourth— between 1960 and 1974—just 14." World population will have grown to about 6 billion by the year 2000 and probably to about 9 billion by 2050 (International Bank for Reconstruction and Development, 1984). Most of the increase in world population since 1950 has been in the LDCs, from about 1.7 billion in 1950 to over 3.5 billion in 1984. Of the 6 billion projected for the year 2000, about 4.8 billion will be living in the LDCs (it is to be hoped that many of these countries will by then be "developed" rather than "developing").

For the LDCs as a group, annual population growth rates rose from 2.0% in 1950 to 2.4% in the mid-1960s, when they apparently "peaked." Since then, the average growth rate for the LDCs has slowed to about 2.0% a year (ibid.). This decrease in the average growth rate is due almost entirely to the decline in China's birth rate; population growth rates in the LDCs actually vary between 2.0 and 4.0% a year, compared with 1.0% or less in the DCs. According to World Bank staff (International Bank for Reconstruction and Development, 1984:74): "Population growth beyond the year 2000 depends critically on falling fertility in the next decade or two. . . . Under any assumption, the populations of most developing countries are likely to increase by 50 per cent or more by 2000." According to Demeny (1984:122–123), "In many areas the brunt of the 'population explosion' is yet to come." Elsewhere, Demeny (1985a:21) notes that fertility declines may be under way in countries or subnational regions in which about 1.7 billion of the LDC population lives, but "in populations numbering about 1 billion, fertility transitions have not yet begun." In any case, absolute annual increases in the size of the world's population were slightly less than 72 million in the late 1960s, 77.4 million 10 years later, and estimated at 80 million in 1985–1986 (ibid.). Most of the increase is occurring in the LDCs (International Bank for Reconstruction and Development, 1984).[10] Growth rates are declining, but they apply to increasing numbers due to built-in momentum. In one review of world population trends, Tabah (1980:386) concluded: "It is in fact during the next decades, when the population will have more than doubled, that the effect of demographic growth will weigh heavily on the other major problems of development: nutrition, employment, the threat to ecological equilibrium, and the exhaustion of certain nonrenewable resources, predicted in some instances to occur a number of years before the demographic transition will have been achieved."

Although poverty means not only low income but also a cluster of deficits associated with low income, such as lack of education, poor nutrition, and high morbidity and mortality, income is clearly a critical factor to be considered in the relationship between poverty and fertility. At the most general level, all the evidence seems to point toward the proposition that fertility will decline as economic and social development bring improved well-being to the poor majorities in the LDCs, which decades of economic growth have failed to do. But the idea that income itself can have a direct relationship to fertility has been very difficult to test (Simon, 1976). Even if there is a causal relationship, the question is whether it could operate with sufficient strength and speed to justify a policy of income distribution. Clearly, there are other justifications for implementing such a policy, which were extensively considered earlier in this discussion.

There has not been much empirical research on the relationships between population dynamics and income distribution. Earlier studies by Kocher (1973) and Rich (1973) mobilized evidence to show that other things being equal, fertility and mortality declines tend to occur earlier and rates tend to be lower in populations characterized by a greater degree of socioeconomic equality, and concluded that equalizing the distribution of income reduces fertility.

Repetto (1978, 1979) has done extensive work on this proposition. His analysis, based on cross-sectional data from a number of developing countries, attempted to document the contribution of economic inequality to rapid population growth through its effect on birthrates. He argued that a more unequal distribution of income within a community implies a higher aggregate birthrate and a faster rate of population growth, and that for a community at any level of development, as measured by average income per capita or some similar index, the overall birthrate of the community will be lower the more equally distributed that total income is.

Societies in which economic gains are limited to a small elite, while the vast majority lead marginal lives of insecurity and deprivation, display high fertility. Any fertility declines under these conditions are usually concentrated within the small fraction of the population that has received most of the economic benefits, so that the declines do little to reduce the rate of population growth in the society as a whole. At low levels of income, increases in living standards result in rapid fertility declines, while at higher levels, there may be little change in fertility and possibly some increase. So it is impossible to refer generally to the effect of economic improvements on birthrates. The point is that the economic status of those who experience the improvement is a key determinant of that effect. The impact of income growth on birthrates depends on who gets the income; i.e., it is the distribution of income that matters.

Boulier (1982), among others, reviewed Repetto's evidence in support of the hypothesis that income redistribution decreases fertility and found it unconvincing. Indeed, he flatly concluded that there is no evidence for the proposition that reductions in income inequality induce declines in fertility. Repetto (1982:177–178) defended his work against this criticism: "Would world fertility decline be unaffected if all income growth in the next decade accrued to the OECD countries, or the OPEC countries? . . . Would fertility in the villages of Bangladesh be unaffected if all the income growth went to the 10 percent who own 60 percent or so of the land? If not, distribution matters. The problem is to understand better how much and why it matters." Although Flegg (1979) also questioned the validity of Repetto's assessments due to conceptual and methodological limitations, he concluded (ibid.:472), on the basis of his own analysis of a sample including 47 LDCs, that the " 'demographic transition' of these countries will be expedited considerably, if accompanied by more equal distributions of income."

Repetto may not have made the case that income redistribution in itself is a sufficient condition for fertility reduction, but then neither has the case been made in this sense for any of the other determinants of fertility that are deemed important. Repetto may not have been able to answer the question of how and to what extent fertility responds to income-redistribution programs, but he has established the importance of the problem and laid the groundwork for further work on it.

The effects of income redistribution on fertility reduction remain unclear, but looking in the opposite direction, i.e., the influence of fertility differentials on income distribution, the effects may be somewhat more discernible. Birdsall (1977) affirms that high fertility increases the inequality of income distribution among families. She says that parents with less education and income are more likely than others to have large families, and where there are economic and social restrictions on upward mobility, the relatively more rapid increase in numbers of the poor can adversely affect efforts at income redistribution. This consequence is even more likely to occur where there is concern with increasing the distribution of opportunities, such as educational opportunities, rather than with redistributing income directly, since a disproportionate share of poor children will come from the large families least able to take advantage of such opportunities. If the norm of large family size persists in future generations, the poverty associated with large families is likely to be perpetuated and to exacerbate the difficulties of implementing poverty-focused development policies. The other side of the coin is noted by Coale (1978–1979:411): "The usual initial restriction of family limitation to the more privileged segments of the population tends to perpetuate . . . the concentration of income in the next generation by giving the children of the well-to-do a favorable home environment, easier access to schooling, and, to the extent that there is inheritance of property, lesser division of their already disproportionate claims on wealth."

The large fertility differential between high- and low-income groups, then, would appear to lead to perpetuating, if not actually increasing, skewed income distributions. As Birdsall (1977:77) concludes: ". . . an unequal distribution of skills emanates in turn from growing up in and perpetuating a large, poor family. The issues involved go to the very heart of the problem of economic development." Breaking the cycle requires not only fertility reduction but also adequate access of the poor to employment and earnings opportunities and amelioration of the deficits in education, health, nutrition, and other services to which the poor are subjected.

Given the paucity of both theory and empirical research for analysis of the interactions between fertility and income inequality, convincing generalizations are still not within reach. The effects of demographic factors on income distribution, and vice versa, are mixed and inadequately understood. Although it does appear that higher fertility is associated with greater economic inequality, it is not clear whether the direction of causation is from fertility to inequality (Rodgers, 1978, 1983). If Repetto is on the right track, the reverse causation may be just as likely.

At least a few words need to be said here regarding employment in the Third World. With ever larger numbers entering the labor force, problems of unemployment and underemployment will become greatly exacerbated beyond those that already exist unless poverty-focused development policies can generate programs for creating employment and increasing income for the poor that will give them much greater access to the gains of development and convert population constraints into economic opportunities. For the low-income LDCs (excluding China and India, which are projected to remain at about present growth rates), the average annual growth of the labor force is projected to rise from 2.3% in the period 1970–1982 to 3.0% in the period 1980–2000 while the oil-importing middle-income countries are projected to experience just a slight rise in growth rates in 1980–2000 (International Bank for Reconstruction and Development, 1984). Given these projections of continuing growth in the labor force, and particularly the increase to 3.0% a year for the low-income LDCs, World Bank staff (*ibid.*:88–89) concluded that "it does seem clear that the size of the agricultural labor force in most of today's low-income countries will go on increasing well into the twenty-first century." According to Sewell *et al.* (1980), at least 40–45% of the labor force in the Third World is unemployed or underemployed, and there is virtually no likelihood that millions of jobs, perhaps as many as 500–800 million, can be created by the end of the century.

On the basis of a review of a series of case studies and of aggregate data on long-term employment trends, Portes and Benton (1984) argue, with regard to the industrial labor force in Latin America, that the rate of labor absorption by the urban sector is considerably greater than that indicated by official statistics. According to their analysis, there are a substantial number of workers employed under various covert arrangements in the "informal sector" who are not taken into account in the official tabulations. They see the informal sector as integral, rather than marginal, to formal-sector activities. Informal labor practices not only render aggregate employment statistics highly misleading but also are detrimental to the economic security of the workers subject to such practices. They conclude (*ibid.*:608): "The informal mode of employment continues to represent not only time-honored practice, but also the predominant instrument for dealing with variable labor demand in many industries and countries." If there is to be transition of the LDCs into industrialized societies, such transition "must await a drastic alteration in the balance of forces between the social classes and in the scope of state regulation."

In any case, it is evident that employment policies by themselves will not be sufficient to make the necessary degrees of difference in employment opportunities for the poor majorities in the LDCs; providing such opportunities will also require increasing the pace and scope of overall social and economic development. In the words of Sewell *et al.* (1980:82); "The challenge is thus not simply to develop effective *em-*

ployment policies, but also to work toward overall *development* strategies capable of providing adequately productive and remunerative jobs for as many of the Third World's poor as possible" [emphasis in original]. For this reason, equity-oriented development must focus not only on employment, but also on enlarging access to assets and to opportunities for human capital formation for the poor majorities in the LDCs.

CONCLUDING OBSERVATIONS

Development policies that seek to reduce poverty and population policies aimed at reducing fertility go hand in hand. It is extremely unlikely that social science research will eventually identify any fundamental solutions to the problem of reducing fertility that would not involve major social and economic structural change as well (Miro and Potter, 1980). Analyses of what has happened to absolute poverty in the LDCs over the last 25 years indicate that there are greater absolute numbers of poor people; whether the proportion is larger is less certain (Streeten, 1978). Development policies in part explain this increase in absolute number of the poor, but the social and political structure, cultural traditions, the extent of human capital formation, the distribution of assets, and international trade relations have all played a part in influencing the relationship between economic growth and poverty reduction, although the relative importance of each of these elements is difficult to ascertain. Many of these factors are also related to fertility reduction, particularly education, income, and land tenure, and if better health and the reduction of infant mortality, more productive employment, and improved status of women are added, the determinants of fertility and of poverty are fairly well subsumed.

Attainment of the objectives of broad based development may indeed facilitate reduction of fertility, but these objectives are not in themselves a sufficient condition for such a reduction in the short run (Coale, 1978–1979). The uncertainties that becloud the nature of the relationships between fertility and its determinants and the unresolved question of the length of lags between changes in these determinants and the occurrence of fertility decline do not evoke much confidence in the aforementioned slogan that development by itself is the best contraceptive. The objectives of equity-oriented development strategies must be assiduously pursued in any case, of course, since they are desirable in their own right.

Their attainment will be made easier by the reduction of fertility, however, so there is an imperative need to move ahead in evaluating and improving policy measures that can be undertaken for the specific purpose of reducing fertility in the short run. These measures include family planning programs and their interactions with aspects of social change; the incorporation of family planning programs into other development programs, such as health, rural development, and education, where this may enhance the effectiveness of family planning; the use of incentives; and other interventions that may have more immediate fertility-reducing effects.

NOTES

[1]Caldwell (1976:323) maintains that modern demographic-transition theory was "born almost in mature form in a paper written by Notestein in 1945."

[2]The meaning of "fertility" in this discussion follows customary demographic usage; namely, it refers to the rate, or frequency, at which women bear children. More specifically, the fertility rate (also called the general fertility rate) is the number of live births per 1000 women aged 15–44 years (in some countries, the age range used is 15–49) in a given year.

[3]Although the demographic paradigm attributed mortality declines in Europe largely to death control, it should be noted that development-related factors in addition to health and sanitation services contributed to these declines. Prominent among these factors were improved transportation and communication facilities, the shift from home- to factory-based employment, and the advent of scientific agriculture. Freedman (1979) has noted some of these factors, both in Europe and in such LDCs as China and Sri Lanka, as well as the state of Kerala in India, that motivated lower fertility in these places; they facilitated mortality declines as well.

[4]This description of the stages of demographic-transition theory largely follows that of Teitelbaum (1975).

[5]Knodel and van de Walle (1979:239) also attach considerable importance to the role of cultural diffusion. One of their conclusions is: "Although the European experience confirms a loose relationship between socioeconomic modernization and fertility decline, it also suggests that there was an important innovation–diffusion dimension to the reproductive revolution that swept the continent."

[6]With regard to Mexico, the fertility decline has been particularly dramatic. By 1970, Mexico's population was growing at a rate of more than 3.5% a year. In 1984, the population growth rate was estimated to be about 2.2%. Alba and Potter (1986) present an impressive argument that although many of the economic supports for high fertility began eroding toward the end of the 1960s, the national population policy and accompanying national family planning program initiated in the 1970s exerted a substantial downward influence on Mexico's fertility.

[7]Rodgers (1984:169) further qualifies this "conclusion" by calling it a "basic theme," since "conclusion would be too strong a word." This qualification is consistent with his characterization, at the beginning of his book, that its "topic is one in which ideology and preconception, rather than empirical considerations, tend to predominate" (ibid.:1). In reviewing Rodgers's book, Mueller (1985) emphasizes the diversity of research findings regarding population–poverty relationships, which she attributes to the diversity of statistical techniques employed and also to the need to identify the relevant structural

and contextual reasons for the diversity. In a paper that reviews relationships between poverty and a range of demographic variables including fertility, Lipton (1983:69) qualifies his conclusions as highly tentative and notes that his paper seeks "merely the demographic correlates of poverty, rather than, as yet, the direction of causes and effects."

[8]Coale (1978) observed that Mexico, according to transition theory, should have shown a major reduction in fertility by the early 1970s in view of its impressive rates of economic growth between 1940 and 1970, but by 1970, Mexico's population was growing at the rate of 3.5% a year. Alba and Potter (1986:58) state that "the kind of development pursued in Mexico between 1940 and 1970 yielded . . . impressive gains in conventional indicators of economic growth and modernization [but] failed to produce an environment that was conducive to low fertility and the small family." And they conclude (ibid.:69): "The Mexican experience from the 1940s to the 1960s suggests that rapid development does not automatically engender early fertility decline if the course of development is not such as to alter the economic and cultural basis for high fertility."

[9]On the usefulness and limitations of population projections, see Keyfitz (1981) and Demeny (1984).

[10]For projections of the percentage distribution of world population between LDCs and DCs for the year 2000 and beyond, see Demeny (1984).

Population and Development
A Selective Overview

In the preceding chapter, an effort was made to identify the links between various development perspectives and population growth. Doing so required a review of demographic-transition theory because this theory constituted the dominant demographic model employed to account for the role of development in reducing fertility. It was concluded that this model generated little specific explanatory power because it had nothing to say about causation and thus could not define a precise threshold of "modernization" that would readily identify a population in which fertility is ready to fall. Coale's revision of transition theory identified three broad preconditions for sustained decline in marital fertility, namely, that fertility must be within the calculus of conscious choice, reduced fertility must be perceived as advantageous, and effective techniques of fertility reduction must be available. These may be preconditions for fertility decline, at least as pertains to the European experience, but the question remains as to what combinations of variables at specific levels result in the establishment of these preconditions and what levels or patterns of development are required for these preconditions to be sufficient as well as necessary to bring about fertility decline. Similarly, Caldwell's restatement of transition theory makes a convincing case for the economic rationality of the large family in traditional culture as a powerful support for sustaining high fertility, but his thesis that "Westernization" ultimately destabilizes the conditions of high fertility is also vulnerable to the "threshold" problem, since it does not specify what degree of Westernization precipitates fertility decline. Moreover, conversion to the Western nuclear family is by no means a foregone conclusion, and in any case there is no evidence that such conversion would be sufficient to induce a substantial fertility decline.

In this chapter, the discussion focuses on other conceptual frameworks and approaches concerned with fertility and various sectors of development. Given the voluminous literature about these relationships

117

that has appeared over the past decade, and the complexity that characterizes this field, no attempt has been made at comprehensive coverage.[1] Rather, the chapter is a selective overview that highlights some of the contributions and limitations of this literature.

CAUSAL ANALYSIS

As in many other fields of the social sciences, consensus in the field of population and development is not easily come by, but most persons concerned with the field would probably agree to the following general propositions: Enhanced development, where it includes economic growth and the more equitable distribution of its gains, is likely to be accompanied by declining fertility; reduction of fertility is not an end in itself, but rather a means to facilitate these goals of development, since rapid population growth slows down development; and in a variety of circumstances, integration of population activities with those of other development programs may enhance the effectiveness of both. This is a short list, and as a guide to policy intervention it has no value at all because of its generality. But it does provide a starting point.

Studies of the determinants and consequences of fertility have employed either a "macro" approach in which geographic divisions are usually the units of analysis in aggregate models or a "micro" approach focused on households and individuals. From these studies, there has emerged a consensus on at least a few factors that tend to be associated with fertility reduction, namely, female education and employment, decreases in infant mortality, and greater equality in income distribution to the extent that it increases the well-being of the poor. But consensus stops here. In the interpretation of these findings, there is no agreement on which of these factors, if any, is both necessary and sufficient for a fertility decline, or on the relative importance of one or another factor. There are various explanations of why the results of fertility research are subject to this and other uncertainties, and they can be advanced at different levels.

To begin with, much of this research was oriented to demographic-transition theory, which, as has been shown, essentially obscured empirical reality. Second, attempts to attribute fertility decline to one or another factor are unlikely to be successful. The causal connection between a particular factor and fertility is complex and certainly indirect, since it must operate sooner or later through one or another of three variables, namely, sexual intercourse, conception, or gestation and parturition. These "intermediate variables," as they were called by Davis and Blake (1956), are the only direct means by which fertility change can occur. Higher incomes, better education, improvement in the status of women, reduction in infant mortality, and other benefits of economic and social development do not themselves directly affect fertility. Any effect they have can come only through their capacity to change one or more of the intermediate variables.

Over 30 years ago, Davis and Blake (*ibid.*) provided a classification of these means of fertility control. Their framework specified 11 intermediate variables in the three categories of intercourse, conception, and gestation. To indicate how limited are the means to fertility control, the components of their scheme are presented here:

Intercourse variables
  A. Those governing the formation and dissolution of unions in the reproductive period:
    1. Age of entry into sexual unions
    2. Proportion of women never entering sexual unions
    3. Amount of reproduction period spent before, between, or after unions
  B. Those governing the exposure to intercourse within unions:
    4. Voluntary abstinence
    5. Involuntary abstinence
    6. Coital frequency (excluding periods of abstinence)

Conception variables
    7. Fecundity[2] or infecundity as affected by involuntary causes
    8. Use or nonuse of contraception
    9. Fecundity or infecundity as affected by voluntary causes (e.g., sterilization, medical treatments)

Gestation variables
    10. Involuntary pregnancy interruption
    11. Voluntary pregnancy interruption

Bongaarts (Bongaarts, 1978, 1982, 1983, 1986; Bongaarts and Potter, 1983) systematically analyzed the variations in impact of these 11 variables and succeeded in identifying seven "proximate determinants" that can account for most of the fertility differentials among populations, namely, "marriage (and marital disruption); onset of permanent sterility; postpartum infecundability; natural fecundability or frequency of intercourse; use and effectiveness of contraception; spontaneous intrauterine mortality; [and] induced abortion" (Bongaarts and Potter, 1983:5). Bongaarts further refined this framework to identify the four primary proximate determinants of fertility differences among populations or subgroups within a population: proportion married, contraceptive use and effectiveness, prevalence of induced abortion, and duration of lactational immunity from conception. These proximate determinants are the only direct means through which economic, sociocultural, and institutional factors can affect fertility. According to Bongaarts (1978:105): "If an intermediate fertility variable, such as the prevalence of conception, changes, then fertility necessarily changes also (assuming the other intermediate fertility variables remain constant), while this is not necessarily the case for an indirect determinant such as income or education. Consequently, differences among populations and trends in fertility over time can always be traced to variations in one or more of the intermediate fertility variables."

Economic, sociocultural, and institutional factors are the determinants of the proximate variables, but as noted, there is no general agreement as to how these factors operate to influence the proximate variables and in turn fertility. The important contribution of the Bongaarts model has been to reduce, and thus simplify, the number of intermediate variables that must be taken into account without losing any of the comprehensive character of the Davis–Blake scheme and at the same time to make the link between these variables and fertility more amenable to quantification. The Bongaarts model cannot explain a change in fertility brought about by a change in a proximate determinant, but it does substantially facilitate identification of where to look for the explanation. Of the proximate determinants, Bongaarts (1986) asserts that a substantial increase in the use of contraception is responsible for the notable declines in fertility in the Third World. Mauldin and Segal (1986:12) note that the prevalence of contraceptive use in the less-developed countries (LDCs) is very closely associated with fertility levels, but they also note that this "prevalence is closely associated with the education of women, age at marriage, and with other factors that affect the levels of fertility."

In addition to the difficulties imposed on attributing fertility decline to one or another economic or sociocultural factor by the indirect nature of the relationship, these difficulties are compounded by the likelihood that several relevant factors may be changing at the same time. These factors are linked in intricate ways, and they often move together over time so that their independent effects are difficult to isolate. As Cassen (1978b:29–30) says: "The longer one studies fertility the less one would care to attribute alterations in it to any simple single cause. Rather there is a set of mutually interacting causes all of which are part of a broad process of societal change."

A third reason for the variability in the interpretation of the findings of fertility research is that the relationships between fertility and its determinants and consequences vary among regions, countries, and different socioeconomic, occupational, and cultural groups within countries. The conditions, correlates, causes, and consequences of fertility rates in different countries vary sufficiently so that attempts to reduce fertility will have to take into account the particular institutional, sociocultural, and material environments in which reproductive behavior takes place, as well as the type of development policy being pursued (McNicoll, 1978, 1980). Much of the research to date has taken these environments as givens and has focused on individual and household characteristics largely to the exclusion of these environments (Population Council, 1981).

An enormous range of factors have been identified as determinants and consequences of fertility, reflecting the complexity of the relationship of fertility to the economic, sociocultural, institutional, and psychological factors that are also part of the broad process of social change. A United Nations task force, for example, has engaged in constructing a framework for the conceptualization, measurement, analysis, and formal representation, through modeling, of interrelationships between population and development (United Nations, 1981a,b). The framework comprises a 61×61 matrix for the mapping of linkages among 15 main development objectives, 10 population variables, and 36 other variables reflecting the broader economic, social, cultural, and political aspects of the development process.

Since attempts to attribute population change to any simple single cause are likely to be futile, what needs to be done is to arrive at a more precise understanding of how a particular cluster of causal mechanisms operate in the determination of fertility. As Hawthorn (1970:70) has observed, "So long as the relative contribution of various determinants is unknown, so it is impossible to begin to suggest a mechanism that can account for the change." Simply knowing that there is a statistical association between education or socioeconomic status and mortality and fertility only provides the starting point for searching for the explanation of the relationship. Particularly apt is the statement by Hawthorn (ibid.:84) that "the relatively plentiful data on differential fertility by social class or socio-economic status can at best *specify* the questions that we need to ask; they can never *answer* explanatory questions" [emphasis in original].

One major approach to the sociology of fertility has been to attribute the causes of reproductive behavior to the norms, prescriptions, and values, i.e., expressed desirable end states, to which such behavior is oriented. Hawthorn does not believe that norms and values should be considered as causes of fertility levels. Although he acknowledges that fertility cannot be explained without taking norms and values into account, he maintains that a sociological theory of fertility must go beyond the norms and values to an explanation of how they were generated by the sociocultural and economic environments in which they developed.

Hawthorn formulated a three-factor explanatory model comprising variations in resources (income), costs, and tastes or preferences, in part derived from Easterlin's work (to be considered presently), to condense the vast array of supposedly independent variables that affect fertility through the proximate determinants. He singled out educational level, religious affiliation, and female employment (with some qualifications) as most prominent in affecting fertility intentions. Other factors, when found to be related to fertility intentions, are so related through mechanisms that can be better expressed in terms of the interaction among resources, costs, and tastes. He concludes (*ibid.*:110), however, that "to say simply that fertility can be explained by the interaction of resources, tastes and costs is not to state a testable theory; it is, rather, to specify what variables a theory must contain. It is only when specific values are attached to each variable (including fertility itself) that a testable and potentially explanatory theory can emerge."

The views that the attainment of broad-based development objectives will everywhere be made easier by the reduction of fertility (a proposition to be considered further below), and that high rates of population growth are a global problem, are by now widely accepted, but there are divergent views that will be taken into account in the subsequent discussion. Hawthorn (1978:14) pointed out, however, that "it does not follow that this problem can have any general solution. The balance between fertility and infant mortality is very different in different poor societies. The other conditions of high fertility are equally different. . . . Practically, it makes little sense to devise a general solution." At the regional level, Kirk (1971) observed that quite different levels and kinds of development are associated with fertility reduction in, say, East Asia, Southeast Asia, and Latin America. Furthermore, as indicated above, relationships between fertility and its determinants and consequences also vary among countries and among different groups within countries. It follows that when the same problem is analyzed in more than one country, it cannot be assumed that sociocultural, economic, and political factors will have exactly the same effect in all countries or even throughout each country (Urzua, 1978). It seems clear, then, that if population research is to have policy relevance, it will have to be at the least country-specific to arrive at findings informative enough to yield recommendations for policy-makers. There have been increasing calls for village-level studies (Jones, 1978; Miro and Potter, 1980; Population Council, 1981; Urzua, 1978) as a way to document more concretely the economic, sociocultural, and institutional contexts of fertility behavior. Jones (1978:40), for example, says: "The problem now is to bridge the interpretive gap between statistical relationship and causative reality. Focused, in-depth, village-level studies have more potential for producing insights and identifying causal relationships that only come to light with extended residence in the study area. Some of these could then be tested in a broader geographic setting."

This is not to say that comparative or cross-cultural work is of no value. On the contrary, comparative treatment may very well strengthen particular explanations by placing them in a larger framework of what works and what does not, but only if the research documents the empirical reality of the setting in which reproduction occurs. Such work should be sufficiently specific to serve as the basis for policy decisions in that particular setting and at the same time permit more general conclusions.

ECONOMIC AND SOCIOLOGICAL APPROACHES: EFFORTS AT CONVERGENCE

Beginning with Becker (1960), economists have been elaborating models of consumer choice as their contribution to an understanding of the determinants of fertility. Simply stated, this approach is oriented to the proposition that families will move toward having fewer children as the costs of having children increase. Children are viewed as "consumer goods" by their parents, and thus fertility becomes amenable to analysis in the income and price framework of economic demand theory. As described by McGreevey and Birdsall (1974), the essential distinction is between the income effect, which increases the demand for children, and the price or substitution effect, which reduces the demand for children by increasing the price of children relative to other goods, thus inducing higher-income families to substitute other goods for children.

The microeconomic approach has probably yielded some important insights, but it has also been subject to criticism on a number of counts (Goldberg, 1975; Turchi, 1975; Population Council, 1981; Cain and Lieberman, 1982), such as the narrow commitment to the direct effects of income, the assumption that parents' decision-making is always rational, the frequent dependence on sparse data, the doubtful relevance

to problems in the LDCs, and the exclusive focus on the internal workings of the household while abstracting from the psychosocial, sociocultural, and institutional contexts in which the households are located. Perhaps this abstraction constitutes the most severe limitation, as
indicated in the following comment (Population Council, 1981:313): "If
one accepts the assumptions of the theory, the internal workings of the
household are revealed; but the theory is silent on what is going on
outside the household. To some extent, economists are constrained by
poor and incomplete data, and it is quite likely that better tests of the
theory and sharper insights would follow from better data. The problems of limited scope and abstraction from the larger setting remain,
however, regardless of the quality of the data."

Easterlin (1968, 1975, 1978) has attempted to broaden the microeconomic approach and to bridge the gap between this approach and
sociological approaches by introducing measures of "taste" as a significant variable in the relationship between economic factors and fertility.
In the original Becker formulation, and for his followers, tastes (or preferences) were treated as given and immutable, but Easterlin replaced
this notion with the idea that tastes, which determine utility and cost
under a given pattern of income and prices, change throughout the life
cycle. Easterlin viewed tastes as a sociological as well as an economic
variable. As he put it (1975:55): "It is through tastes or subjective preferences that attitudinal considerations stressed by sociologists operate,
such as norms regarding family size and 'quality' of children. . . . The
overriding emphasis of economists, however, . . . has traditionally been
on price and income variables rather than on preferences, and in this
way they have subordinated consideration of tastes. . . . The formation
of tastes should have high priority in fertility research and . . . such
work would help bridge the economics and sociology of fertility."

In a later paper, Easterlin (1978) presented an analytical framework
that attempts to integrate the approaches to fertility analysis of both
economists and sociologists. In his framework, the fundamental variables are demand for children as the outcome of tastes, income, and
prices; potential supply of children as the outcome of natural fertility
(i.e., fertility that prevails in the absence of deliberate attempts to limit
family size) and the prospects for child survival; and the costs of fertility
regulation, both psychic costs (the displeasure associated with the idea
or practice of fertility control) and market costs (the time and money
necessary to learn about and use specific techniques). In Easterlin's
framework, these three sets of variables are the codeterminants of actual
fertility. In his version of demographic transition (*ibid.*:132), "the transition to modern fertility levels occurs because modernization shifts the

representative household from a situation approximating an excess demand for children to one of excess supply, thereby generating a motivation to limit fertility and avoid unwanted children."

In this same paper, Easterlin accords attention to the LDCs as well as the developed countries (DCs). He sees the forces of modernization leading both to greater motivation to limit fertility and to making fertility regulation easier by lowering its subjective and market costs.[3] Although he writes of an evolution from premodern (read "LDCs") to modern conditions in which the balance between motivation for fertility regulation and its costs tips in favor of fertility control, he is cautious about its inevitability. Referring to the LDCs, he observes that for many reasons, the pattern of fertility decline would be likely to be different from one place to another, that there are differences in the initial premodern conditions from which societies start and in the trends in the various aspects of modernization, and that in the LDCs there are influences that were absent from the earlier experience of the DCs.[4]

The elements of the Easterlin framework are relatively more precise and specific than those comprised in demographic-transition theory, but here again the same "threshold" problem appears. Easterlin says that when the balance between motivation for fertility regulation and its costs tips in favor of fertility control, "a 'threshold' of fertility regulation is crossed and family size moves downward" (ibid.). But what are the particular combinations of Easterlin's fundamental variables at specific levels that constitute the necessary and sufficient conditions to precipitate a fertility decline? He can make the case that this threshold has been crossed in the DCs, but he himself raises doubts as to whether, when, and how this will occur in the LDCs.

The Easterlin framework has made a genuine contribution in taking tastes or preferences into systematic account as one of the fundamental variables in the calculus of parental decision-making, thus bringing microeconomic theory closer to the real world. But tastes, in his view, are shaped by religion, education, place of residence, norms, values, occupational status, income, and family-building experiences—in short, by the whole array of social, cultural, psychological, and economic factors that influence the individual as he or she moves through the life cycle. If all these factors can be bundled into tastes, then it appears to be a residual category in economic analysis to be left to the noneconomic disciplines that take these variables as their normal beat. Commenting on another version of the Easterlin framework (Easterlin, Pollak, and Wachter, 1980) that is essentially the same as the one described here, Hawthorn (1981:702) said that the difficulty with the Easterlin model "is that it is consistent with such a variety of possible explanations of changes in fertility (or the absence of such changes) that it effectively fails to forbid any." In any case, the Easterlin model has increased awareness of the need to bring together economic and sociological approaches and has become very influential in the study of the determinants of fertility, as attested by the central role it has been accorded in the conceptual framework that guided the work of a major review of the determinants of fertility (Bulatao and Lee, 1983a), to be considered below.

The Davis (1963) "theory of change and response," like Easterlin's focus on tastes, constituted an attempt to reconcile the microanalyses of the economists with the macroanalyses of the sociologists. Davis's argument is a rather sophisticated version of demographic-transition theory. Reviewing the demographic transition in Japan and northwest Europe, Davis maintained that families adopted a "multiphasic response" to persistent high rates of natural increase resulting from past success in controlling mortality to maximize their new economic opportunities and to avoid relative loss of status. The multiphasic response for coping with natural increase includes delayed marriage; the use, within marriage, of means of fertility control such as abortion, sterilization, and more frequent resort to contraception; and international emigration. The multiphasic effort to reduce population growth occurred simultaneously with a spectacular economic growth, and according to Davis (*ibid.*:362), families acted to reduce their fertility not as a response to "absolute need or to some cultural idiosyncracy such as a particular 'value system' or 'custom,'" but to maximize their economic welfare and protect their social status relative to other families in their reference group. In other words, they were motivated to reduce fertility by personal pressures, not by societal or cultural pressures. They perceived how an adaptive response in their own demographic behavior could serve their interests and acted accordingly to serve those interests even if in doing so they contravened their traditional norms and values. Thus, their responses were individual responses to opportunities for enhancing economic and social status.

In assessing Davis's theory, Matras (1973) pointed to the by now familiar limitations of demographic-transition theory. He affirmed that it is important to know that individuals can improve their economic and social status and at the same time contribute to an aggregate effect in slowing population growth, but he went on to say (*ibid.*:463–464) that "the theory of multiphasic response raises as many questions as it answers . . ." since "it is more important to know which response will be adopted . . . in different populations, just as it is important to know what the timing of the responses will be in relation to the stimuli for population growth, and what the differential patterns of response are in different sectors of a population. But perhaps most important, we need to know what factors—social structural, historical, economic, and environmental—are connected with different patterns of demographic responses to population growth." And Burch (1975:130–131) observed that Davis's "theory is atemporal in that the events described proceed on no well-specified schedule. Nor is it clear whether certain key events may or must precede others."

If Davis's theory has any application to the situation in the LDCs, it is only with reference to the elites. The opportunities offered by spectacular economic growth that characterized the situation in Europe and Japan, which families felt they had to grasp by altering their demographic behavior or else face loss of social status and consumption, have not of course reached the poor majorities of the population in the LDCs.

In concluding this section, consideration should be given to a concerted effort to achieve better understanding of fertility change in the LDCs conducted by a panel of scholars from a variety of disciplines. Their labors were published as a collection of 40 chapters in two volumes (Bulatao and Lee, 1983a). The conceptual framework for the study is essentially the one presented by Easterlin (1978) and described above, although it departs from Easterlin in "avoiding where possible the strong assumptions that framework makes" (Bulatao, 1983:1) and in incorporating "concepts and insights from different disciplines . . . [and] is based on work in economics and public health, in psychology and anthropology, in sociology and statistics" (ibid.:2).

The two volumes reporting the work of the project were prepared by the Panel on Fertility Determinants of the Committee on Population and Demography, which was established by the National Research Council of the National Academy of Sciences. The conceptual framework adopted by the panel, as presented by Bulatao (ibid.), groups influences on fertility according to Easterlin's three categories of the supply of children, the demand for children, and fertility regulation and its costs. The framework expands on these categories by including among the basic components reproductive history (which covers both nuptiality and childbearing experience), socioeconomic characteristics (education and income among others), and the influence of social institutions (although 11 are listed, only some of them are considered in the chapters under this heading). In the penultimate chapter, Bulatao and Lee (1983b) employ this framework, in an overview, to organize knowledge about the interacting influences on fertility in the LDCs and to summarize the research evidence, as mobilized by the papers prepared by and for the panel. In effect, their analysis points to demand for children as the major cause of variations in fertility levels.

According to Bulatao and Lee (*ibid.*:758), "The framework can accommodate all hypothetical influences on fertility," and they note that "past fertility research appears to fall rather naturally into these three categories" (i.e., demand, supply, and regulation costs). Despite the marked dependence on the Easterlin model, they state (*ibid.*) that "although this framework may seem at first to assume an economic model in which couples make optimizing decisions, in fact no such assumption is necessary; indeed, 'demand' and 'supply' as used in the framework are only loosely related to the corresponding economic concepts." They also note that the framework is intended to serve, not as a theory, but as a rough classification scheme. Social institutions receive consideration in this study, primarily in a chapter by Potter (1983), and some socioeconomic characteristics, such as education and female employment and income, are the subjects of particular chapters, but the fertility impact of some key sociocultural factors, such as ethnicity and religion, receives little attention in these volumes. Regarding these factors, Bulatao and Lee (*ibid.*:783) maintain that they "have such different meanings across societies that it is difficult to discuss them without considering the effects of variations in social settings." This may be true, but sociocultural factors merit greater attention in attempts to understand influences on fertility.[5] Finally, it may be noted that the framework explicitly excludes from consideration the consequences of fertility levels and trends.

Bulatao and Lee follow Easterlin closely in the prominence they accord "modernization" in their description of the process of fertility change and its role in arriving at the threshold at which fertility decline is precipitated, but are careful to qualify their picture of the way fertility responds to the process of modernization by stating that it is speculative. They conclude (*ibid.*:785), however, that "this speculative picture is consistent with the arguments and evidence reviewed here, though it is far from being an established view." Hollerbach (1982), a member of the panel, analyzed a number of the views of the linkage between changes in the process of fertility decision-making and the nature of the demographic transition and concluded that none of these views has much empirical support thus far.

The concluding chapter of the panel's publications presents an agenda for research on the determinants of fertility in the Third World that constitutes a valuable source for further work in this field, particularly with respect to setting priorities. There are a number of comprehensive reviews in these volumes of the interrelationships between fertility and development sectors that are substantial contributions to the literature.

EFFECTS OF POPULATION GROWTH ON DEVELOPMENT

The economic consequences of rapid population growth for development are still far from understood. But then the lack of precise knowledge about how population growth affects economic development should be expected when it is taken into account that the process of economic growth and development is itself not very well understood. As Miro and Potter (1980:102) observe, ". . . no conclusive findings as to the quantitative relation between fertility and income per capita over time are available today. This should not come as a surprise, considering that agreement on, and understanding of, the factors responsible for economic growth in general are notably lacking."

It would seem, however, that the question of the impact of population growth on the growth of average income should no longer hold center stage, since the shift in priorities to equity-oriented development strategies makes it considerably less imperative to have improved knowledge about the precise nature of the relationship. As King *et al.* (1974:23) suggested, ". . . the effect of population growth on the quality of development—as measured by such social indicators as the number of people who are adequately fed, become literate, share equitably in income growth, and are productively employed—is more important than its effect on the growth of average income." Nevertheless, the question of this latter effect constitutes the focus of a continuing debate.

The relationships between rapid population growth and poverty on one hand and income distribution on the other are reviewed in Chapter 4 and so will not be considered again here. Relationships between population growth and a number of other development sectors are discussed in Chapters 6 and 7.

As has been indicated, the view is widely held (some dissenters will be mentioned presently and are discussed further in Chapter 8) that attainment of the objectives of broad-based development will be made easier by slower population growth.[6] Rapid increases in numbers and a high dependency ratio impose heavy burdens on an economy and mean that a much greater share of a society's resources must be diverted to responding just to the accelerated expansion of the population's needs—to simply maintaining, if possible, existing levels of living— rather than improving the well-being of the population.

A fuller exposition of the consequences of rapid population growth for particular development sectors is undertaken in Chapters 6 and 7 and for economic and social development in general in Chapter 8, but some observations are in order here. After a detailed review of the consequences of rapid population growth, World Bank staff (International Bank for Reconstruction and Development, 1984:105) concluded: ". . . the evidence discussed . . . points overwhelmingly to the conclusion that population growth at the rapid rates common in most of the developing world slows development." Prominent among the negative effects are those on the formation of human capital at both the family and the societal level and the limitations imposed on the quantitative and qualitative improvement of formal schooling.

With respect to rapid population growth as an obstacle to educational progress, Jones and Potter (1978:12) point out that in LDCs that are making strong efforts to expand the proportion of the school-age population covered by the education system, the contribution of population growth to the increase in educational costs over the 1980s is likely to be on the order of 30–50%. They also say (ibid.:11): "The increasing importance of knowledge and skills as societies and economies evolve and develop makes educational development a key component of all development plans. Education is not only expected to lead to socio-economic progress by equipping the population to participate fully in a modernizing economy, it is also expected to influence the growth and structure of the population."

Earlier, it was noted that some LDCs have made substantial economic progress even though their fertility rates have remained high. That they have reflects the fact that the negative effects of rapid population growth do not necessarily impede all economic development. Obviously, other influences are also at work. Coale (1978) examines one such case, that of Mexico, and addresses the question of whether there is evidence that despite impressive economic progress, the continuation of high fertility has been a detriment to the quality of Mexican life. In other words, is there evidence that important progress would have occurred if fertility had fallen rather than remaining constant or even rising slightly? Between 1955 and 1975, the population of Mexico doubled, and fertility was slightly higher at the end of this period than it had been at the beginning (although, as noted earlier, after 1975 fertility began to decline rapidly). Nevertheless, in 1975, the Mexican population was more than 72% literate and more than 60% urban, income per capita had nearly doubled since 1955, and life expectancy had risen to about 65 years and was still increasing. Coale maintains, however, that if fertility had fallen beginning in 1955 according to one of the projections he made at that time, there would have been about 25% fewer persons under 15 years of age in 1975. The smaller numbers would have yielded many advantages for the whole population, including less crowded living conditions, better food, better parental care, and the possibility of some 15% higher income per equivalent adult consumer.

The very rapid increase in the child population also had some dramatic consequences for the extension of education, as Coale shows. Enrollment in primary school rose from 2.25 million in 1950 to over 8 million in 1970, but the number of children not enrolled in school increased from 3.75 million to 4.42 million in 1970 despite continuing allocation of substantial resources to education.

In their study of the interrelationships between population growth and development in Mexico over the past four decades, Alba and Potter (1986) show that despite the steady expansion of the Mexican economy, the gains this expansion promised for development were dissipated by the effects of rapid population growth as the mechanisms for accommodating this growth, particularly in agrarian reform and land distribution, in generation of employment, and in provision of housing and public services for the urban poor, became increasingly eroded. They conclude (*ibid.*:70) that their "analysis of the Mexican experience demonstrates the ways in which rapid population growth can exhaust an expansionary style of development. In the long run this type of economic–demographic accommodation is unworkable."

The mainstream view that economic development will be facilitated by slower population growth has not gone unchallenged. Boserup (1965, 1981) and Clark (1967) have been two of the more prominent proponents of the view that population growth is beneficial for economic development. Boserup developed the theme that population pressure on resources has stimulated agricultural innovation and technological change. Clark similarly contended that population density encourages economic and technological progress and that the world has immense physical resources for agricultural and mineral production still unused that could support growing populations.

At present, the leading advocate of the beneficial effects of population growth is Julian Simon, who has pursued this argument in some detail in two books (Simon, 1977, 1981). The later book constitutes a popularized version of the earlier one, and it has gained him more exposure in the media than anyone else writing about population, with the possible exception of the doomsayers trumpeting the dire effects of the "population explosion."[7] To obtain some idea of Simon's views in the earlier book, consider the following (1977:491–492) quotation: "My over-all conclusion is: Economic Demography is a Cheerful Science. For more than a century economics was thought of as the 'dismal science' because of Malthus' vision that . . . population growth would always tend to bring society to the brink of starvation. But the analysis in this book argues that the opposite will happen—that increased population growth eventually helps raise the level of living even higher. . . . The fact that our economic system can support an ever-increasing number of people seems wonderful to me."

Like the earlier book, the message of the popularized sequel, entitled *The Ultimate Resource* (1981), is that the effects of population growth, at least in the long run, are mainly beneficial for DCs and LDCs alike. His conclusion (*ibid*.:348) is similar to that just quoted: "The ultimate resource is people—skilled, spirited, and hopeful people who will exert their wills and imaginations for their own benefit, and so, inevitably, for the benefit of us all." In arguing the case for the beneficial effects of population growth, he rejects the extensive literature on population and development research that counters this position because it does not take into explicit account the value of human ingenuity and endeavor. Ness and Ando (1984:179) refer to two extreme responses to the question of whether there is a population problem. At the affirmative extreme are the doomsayers, for whom "future generations are already consigned to death by massive famines." The doomsayers have "consistently been countered by those who see people as the most precious resource," a position they identify with Simon and say, "From this perspective, there is no population problem."

Some of Simon's arguments have been advanced before, such as the notion that technological progress is well served by population growth both because more heads are better than fewer for generating new ideas and because of economies of scale. Much of his argument rests on the thesis that a moderate rate of population growth is beneficial in the long run, although it may be harmful in the short run. But as Sirageldin and Kantner (1982:172) note: "His short run lasts for 60 years! A span longer than the life expectancy of most people born on earth in the year of [the book's] publication. Not many developing countries could afford or be able to wait that long for improvement." They also observe (*ibid*.:171) that "aside from the puzzling assumptions and presumptions in his formal attempt to model economic–demographic interrelations, Simon's book is filled with incomplete analysis, selective documentation, and false analogies." Preston (1982:177) observes that "by successfully attacking the purveyors of doomsday rhetoric and by failing to offer successful arguments at the other extreme, Simon winds up in effect strengthening the moderate orthodoxy." These quotations are from two of three detailed reviews of *The Ultimate Resource* published in a symposium, all of which are mainly unfavorable (see also Timmer, 1982).

Simon has defenders, however, among them Perlman (1982:494), who in his review of *The Ultimate Resource* says, "On the whole, I can think of no very recent book in demographic economics . . . that is so well documented and has so logical a core, and yet will begin to stir such passionate disagreement."

Simon's views on the positive contribution that rapid population growth can make to development have helped to generate a voluminous literature concerned with what has been called "the new population debate," which is considered in Chapter 8. Suffice it to say here that this discourse involves a revisionist approach that, although often ostensibly aimed at the rhetoric of the doomsayers, also rejects the orthodox stance that rapid population growth is a development problem, a view that Demeny (1986:486) says "has been the implicit assumption in the long-standing intellectual tradition of our [the demographic] profession."

SOCIOCULTURAL FACTORS AND POPULATION GROWTH

There are frequent references in the literature on population and development to the importance of sociocultural factors in explaining fertility decline in relation to changes brought about by economic and social development, but the role of these factors remains largely unstudied. One such reference by Hauser (1979:18) is illustrative of many: "This interaction [between fertility decline and developmental changes] does not take place in a vacuum; there are other factors that may play an important role in determining the outcome of particular changes. Among such other factors, cultural characteristics, especially value systems, probably deserve emphasis." Sociocultural factors may deserve emphasis, but they do not often get it. As Burch (1975:135) has written: "Culture can be quantified to some extent . . . but little effort has been made in this direction, and the leading theories of fertility decline . . . all try to transcend culture as a possible explanatory factor. . . . The prevailing view in demographic theory is that they [attitudes, values, and cultural definitions] are neither causally important nor manipulable save in a superficial sense. Emphasis is on structure, means, and economic rationality."

Coale's work on revision of transition theory is an exception to this neglect. As indicated previously, a major finding of Coale and his associates in the European Fertility Project is that overall fertility levels in Europe before the demographic transition varied considerably from country to country and subregion to subregion, and the patterns of development associated with fertility decline have turned out to be quite varied. In the view of Coale (1975:353), these differences must be attributable to cultural factors: "Unmeasured traditions and habits of mind may be the basis for differential resistance to the establishment of the first pre-condition [that fertility must be within the calculus of conscious choice] and may be one reason for the strong relation . . . between religion and fertility."[8] Anderson (1986:293), one of Coale's associates, maintains that a consistent finding of their research on fertility in Europe is that "nonsocioeconomic variables, such as religion, language, ethnicity, and region, explain much of the variability in marital fertility decline, even after socioeconomic variables have been taken into account." And Watkins (1986:448), another of the participants in this project, concludes: "The decline in marital fertility can precede significant modernization, simply defined, as it did in France and among some forerunners elsewhere: the European experience suggests that modernization is sufficient but not necessary. Nor is the response of fertility to the changes that define or accompany modernization always immediate: the lag may be quite variable and seems to be associated with longstanding cultural differences."

Freedman and Knodel and van de Walle are also among the few demographers who have accorded more than passing attention to sociocultural factors. Freedman (1979:79) says, for example, "Cultural factors—that is, factors not easily translated into the customary development variables—appear to affect both the demand for children and the readiness to accept birth control." Knodel and van de Walle (1979), looking at the findings of the research on fertility decline in Europe, conclude that cultural setting and tradition are likely to exert an independent influence on the response of populations to organized family planning efforts as well as to general development. They say (*ibid.*:237): "Matters would be far simpler if those particular cultural characteristics that are favorable or unfavorable were readily identifiable. . . . Unfortunately, there is very little firm knowledge concerning the cultural factors that have facilitated the acceptance of family limitation."

No one has to convince the anthropologists of the importance of sociocultural factors, of course. They have done useful work on population processes, but their views are not reflected perceptibly in the mainstream thinking that has been the subject of this discussion.[9] Polgar (1972), for example, questions the assumptions of transition theory that there was only one demographic transition, which is associated with the Industrial Revolution, and that "pretransition" times in human population history, i.e., prior to 1650, were characterized by unvarying high fertility. He says (*ibid.*:210) that "population history . . . shows humankind to have long engaged in practices that kept its numbers below the biological maximum of reproduction," but he also cites archeological findings that show sharp upturns in population growth—one, for example, that occurred 10,000 years ago associated with the agricultural revolution. Similarly, Cowgill (1975:521) argues that "population growth is not an inherent (or inelastic) tendency of humans. Rather, it is a human possibility which is encouraged in some situations and discouraged in others. In spite of ambiguities, data on ancient population trends clearly show many significant changes in growth rates and some significant periods of declining population."

Citing the work of Polgar and of Cowgill, among others, Scrimshaw (1977) suggests that this work suffices to establish the historical existence of values and behavior affecting family size. She says (ibid.:10–11): "What clearly emerges from all the literature on this subject is that the regulation of fertility is not a new idea. Only a handful of societies reproduce at the biological maximum. However, not all societies are conscious of their behaviors which affect fertility." She goes on to say that cultural values related to family size are expressed at the familial level in a variety of ways. Whether these values are recognized overtly or not, they maintain a range of family size and spacing that usually is adaptive for a particular culture, at least under the conditions that existed when the behavior developed.

Sipes (1980) took a sample of ethnographic studies of 20 preindustrial societies to test a wide array of hypotheses found in the literature concerning the effects of sociocultural factors in decreasing population growth rates. The variables involved in these hypotheses are grouped by Sipes in nine general subject areas: kin and social systems and relationships, position of women in the society, marriage and divorce, pregnancy and parenthood, sexuality, the supernatural, world view and horizons, education and literacy, and the value of children. Of the 64 hypotheses tested, only a small number were supported by the data. He concludes (ibid.:99) that his research shows how little is known about human fertility behavior and "that much of what we think we know is not so. There seems to be a great, complex and hidden mass of interactions between fertility/population growth rate and the rest of human behavior which we do not understand."

As Hawthorn (1970:97–98) has observed, "The difficulty with many of the socio-economic, social, and social–psychological factors that can be seen as affecting tastes is that they are also strongly related to the supply of income." A couple who are well educated are also likely to be more prosperous, and women are likely to have improved status at higher levels of income and education. Even in the case of religion, as Mandelbaum (1974) concludes for India, the relationship between religion and fertility seems to have as much to do with levels of income and education among the followers of a religion as it does with any specific precepts of that religion. Similarly, Balasubramanian (1977) says, also with reference to India, that the low level of fertility for Christians as compared with Hindus and Muslims is explained by the high level of education and income of the Christians. Cassen (1978b:50) observes: "It seems to be true that there is a general association of higher fertility with religions which do not favour contraception, such as Catholicism, or which favour high natality, such as the Muslim religion. . . . But it is also . . . true that *among* Catholics or Muslims the better-off, the urbanised, the better educated, those whose mortality is lower, have fewer children" [emphasis in original].

Although religious differentials in fertility have been identified in a number of studies, it is still uncertain whether religious affiliation can exert an independent influence on fertility, apart from income, as is the case with ascertaining the relative independence of other variables associated with fertility, such as education and female employment. Hawthorn (1970:101) reached the conclusion that until more is known about the interrelationships between religious belief and economic behavior, it is best to treat them as independent of each other, since "whatever the exact explanation, the fact remains that to some extent religious affiliation is a 'taste' factor not contaminated seriously by resource (income) variables."

The issue is not whether economic factors influence fertility. Of course they do. There has been advanced at length in this discussion the argument that attaining the objectives of broad-based development in reducing poverty will also be conducive to reducing fertility, just as slowing population growth is likely to facilitate realization of those development objectives. The economists have made a valuable contribution in their work on the economic values and costs of children by showing that, under certain conditions, high fertility is sustained because parents perceive the added economic value of additional children as greater than the cost of having them, whereas under other conditions, fertility declines because the economic value of children is perceived as decreasing or disappearing and preferences for other benefits of the good life compete effectively with the preferences for children. The real issue is that this focus on the economic calculus abstracts from the complex set of interactions that characterize the processes of population and development, and thereby leaves out of systematic consideration a range of what may be important sociocultural and institutional factors that mediate and are mediated by economic pressures and thus influence the ways in which economic pressures affect parental and societal decision-making. To acknowledge that "tastes" have an important bearing on the economic calculus is not much help if in fact tastes continue to be treated as a residual category.

The research findings on fertility decline in Europe show no consistency in the direct effects of income on fertility; the level of "socioeconomic development" was an uncertain predictor of the trend of fertility. Similarly, it was earlier indicated that marked fertility declines have already occurred in a number of LDCs in which economic development is still at relatively low levels. The variability in tastes for children is substantial indeed and cannot be explained by economic pressures alone. Noneconomic factors must be at work as well and must be taken into systematic account if the variability is to be explained. A group of scholars have recently made an impressive attempt to assess the findings of the World Fertility Survey with regard to reproductive change in the LDCs (Cleland and Hobcraft, 1985). In summarizing this assessment, Cleland (1985:243) says: ". . . what has been learnt about the possible causes of fertility decline from the study of differential fertility? In terms of thorough testing of specific hypotheses, the haul is a modest one. . . . Yet, taken *en masse*, the results are more consistent with an ideational theory of change, based on the spread of new aspirations or new attitudes towards family formation or birth control, than with a structural theory, which emphasizes changes in economic roles of family units, of women or of children."

Demographic as well as economic research on the factors that influence fertility have focused on what are customarily called "socioeconomic" characteristics, mainly income, education, the status and employment of women, and rural–urban residence, and have been mainly concerned with establishing the aggregate associations between these characteristics and fertility. Although termed "socioeconomic," the latter three factors tend to be treated more as economic than as social because they are intertwined with income, and they are usually viewed as important components of economic development. Along with infant mortality, they are thought to be the most closely related to reproductive behavior, and they are more readily identifiable than other social and cultural characteristics, particularly in being more amenable than the latter to survey research. In the view of Miro and Potter (1980), changes in social pressures generated by kin and community that may influence fertility behavior are less tangible than the aforementioned factors and thus often overlooked, while cultural attitudes and values are even less tangible.

Immerwahr (1977:187) maintains that "there are some real social characteristics that bear on fertility, such as those based on tradition,

custom and religion, though usually these are called *cultural* characteristics . . . [and] these cultural characteristics have roughly as much
importance as determinants of fertility as do the economic, though in
some cases they may masquerade as economic characteristics"
[emphasis in original]. In this vein, Knodel and van de Walle (1979)
argue the case for the status of women. They regard this as more a
cultural than a socioeconomic characteristic because the extent to which
women participate in the broader socioeconomic system beyond the
immediate and extended family appears to be determined more by religious and other cultural values than by socioeconomic development as
such. As one example, they point to cultural beliefs regarding the appropriate role of women and the implications of designing development
policies aimed at altering the subordinate status of women, which may
be particularly conducive to reduction of fertility.

Just as a high degree of male dominance and female subordination
in decision-making about reproductive behavior may provide strong
support for high fertility, other examples may be cited of sociocultural
factors that may play this role and may either be relatively independent
of economic factors or mesh with them in providing support for high
fertility. For example, a strong preference for sons obtains in many
LDCs. As Hawthorn has noted, this preference may be based on views
of economic necessity, but in a large survey in India, only 56% of parents
who felt they must have sons gave economic reasons. The rest gave as a
reason "carrying on the family line" (Immerwahr, 1977:189). Son preference as a reason for perpetuating the family name is a powerful motive
affecting fertility in Korea and Taiwan, and in the Chinese tradition,
sons are essential for the rituals of ancestor worship (Jones, 1977). Son
preference, it may be noted, is not a prominent factor in Thailand or
Indonesia. Immerwahr (1977) claims that even where sons are preferred
in order to provide economic support in old age, this preference may be
primarily the result of a cultural constraint. In Western society,
daughters may be valued for potential support in old age as much as
sons, perhaps even more so, but "in many strata of Indian society, by
contrast, a married woman's parents are often not supposed to accept
even a meal in their daughter's home" (*ibid.*:189).

To cite a few other examples, choosing a particular family planning
method may be a matter of sociocultural preference. In India, vasectomies were very popular with Hindu men, but relatively few Indian
Muslim men accepted them no matter how high the incentive payment;
similarly, in Sri Lanka, many Tamil men have accepted vasectomies,
whereas Sinhalese men rarely do so (*ibid.*). Catholicism in the Philippines fosters positive orientations toward children and large families in

all socioeconomic strata of the population, rather more so than in Buddhist Thailand, which may explain the higher family-size ideal in the Philippines than in Thailand, despite more serious problems of land shortage and rural tenancy in the Philippines (Jones, 1977). Another sociocultural factor linked to fertility is that of time orientation. Differential effects on decision-making about fertility may be expected on the part of those people who are oriented to the present and those whose orientation is toward the future. Finally, Jones (*ibid.*) mentions that Yoruba society (in Africa) positively values the noise and bustle associated with a large family and notes a parallel with Indonesia in this respect. This characteristic is also to be observed in the Philippines.

Although the sociocultural factors mentioned here tend to support high fertility, the anthropological work shows that regulation of fertility has been practiced by various groups and societies throughout human history when such behavior was perceived as adaptive, so that sociocultural supports for high fertility are not immutable.[10] As indicated earlier, there is need for further research to identify the sociocultural factors that facilitate as well as those that impede acceptance of limitation of family size.

As the evidence from the European studies and the other examples given show, there is no automatic relationship between economic change and reduction of fertility. The need for social and cultural change must be taken into account as well. If greater understanding of how sociocultural factors specifically affect reproductive behavior can be attained, perhaps the lags that have been observed between the timing of economic change and fertility change can be shortened. Jones (1977:31) says: ". . . fertility theories and models, if they are to help very much in understanding and, in particular, measuring the strength of factors influencing fertility, must be designed with the particular cultural, social and familial setting in mind. Cultural differences and value systems are not explicable merely by the particular stage different economies have reached, but rather have . . . an independent effect on marriage patterns and 'natural fertility' as well as on the perceived value of children and hence on fertility levels and trends." Referring to Easterlin's framework, Jones observes that it is broad enough to encompass all the diverse factors that impinge on fertility, but that in achieving this breadth, it loses specificity with regard to the particular factors that may be important in given settings.

Reference was made earlier to the increasing calls for village-level studies as a way to document more concretely the institutional, sociocultural, and economic contexts of fertility behavior, and Jones's recommendation for such studies was quoted. In the paper just cited, he indicates some of the kinds of data needed (*ibid.*:39), including more knowledge about changes in patterns of marriage and the causes of such changes, the power structures that characterize different kinship networks, the ways in which land is inherited, the division of labor in the family and how the household economy functions, and "perhaps most important of all, how the social and technological changes . . . reaching even the most isolated villages are altering people's world view and their evaluation of children."

If more can be learned about how fertility change occurs or does not occur in specific sociocultural contexts, perhaps ways can be found to induce fertility decline without waiting for comprehensive economic development to bring it about. Greater light on how people can be induced to change their reproductive behavior, the all-important policy question, will require systematic research on the role of specific sociocultural factors. It is not at all clear which of these factors are relatively more or less malleable or manipulable, but there is no better way of finding out than by subjecting them to research of the kind proposed here. Questions of manipulability are not easy to answer in this any more than in other problem areas of the social sciences, but they are clearly important for making policy choices.

In the aftermath of the World Population Conference in 1974, there has been a search for specific development policies, "selective interventions," that might have the effect of helping to reduce population growth rates. The policies most frequently mentioned are redistributing income in the direction of greater equity; broadening educational opportunities and improving the quality of education; improving the status of women and facilitating their access to employment; implementing basic-needs policies of the kinds considered in this discussion, and related efforts to reallocate resources, such as land reform; instituting social and legal measures to raise the age at marriage; and providing sources of security and risk insurance that will supplant children as such sources (Cain and Lieberman, 1982; Ridker, 1976; O. G. Simmons and Saunders, 1975; Taeuber, 1975). All these policies are likely to have at best long-term effects, and most are what LDC governments should be implementing anyway if they are committed to broad-based development. If fertility effects are to be achieved in the shorter term, they will have to be complemented by direct fertility policies, including family planning programs and incentive and disincentive schemes, that can mesh with the sociocultural and economic contexts of particular countries, subregions, and communities. Sociocultural factors are intimately involved in all these development efforts, but their specific role has yet to be subjected to systematic research and experimentation to ascertain the causal relationships involved and to help assess the relative importance of each of these direct and indirect policy measures with respect to fertility effects so as to identify the appropriate mix for a given place and time (Jones, 1978).

INSTITUTIONAL FACTORS AND POPULATION GROWTH

Thus far, in considering sociocultural contexts, the focus has been on perceptions, meanings, orientations, and values that appear to be fertility-related. This discussion now turns to another major component of sociocultural contexts, the role played by institutional (also termed organizational or structural) factors as they may affect fertility behavior. They are dealt with here separately from sociocultural factors because they are largely so treated in the literature. In one view (McNicoll, 1977), three levels or stages of analysis are distinguished in a strategy of research: institutional analysis, which focuses on the fertility-relevant components of social organization that mediate between individuals and families as decision-makers and national governments; evaluation of the local objective realities that actually face individual decision-makers or potential clients of development programs; and exploration of the meanings that are attached to these realities in a given sociocultural context, which is the level just considered. The second of these levels is seen as filling the gray area between institutional and sociocultural analysis.

Among mediating institutions that influence fertility, the family is clearly of major importance. But an understanding of the ways in which the family is important in determining fertility levels suffers from the same constraint as understanding the effects of sociocultural factors, namely, the lack of an adequate knowledge base. As Cain (1982:159) says, ". . . it is difficult to find statements in the literature that specify what it is about the family *per se* in these [LDC] settings, or changes in the family, that is of causal significance for fertility. More often, the family is depicted as an intermediate institution that is acted upon in the course of development; whose transformation accompanies rather than initiates change in reproductive behaviour."[11]

Cain sees the work of Caldwell as a major exception to this view. As indicated in the discussion of Caldwell's work, he regards demographic transition as centrally linked to transformation of the family through social change rather than through economic change as depicted by transition theory. Some of the limitations of Caldwell's interpretation and the questions it raises were identified earlier and will not be repeated here. Suffice it to say that Caldwell's emphasis on the hierarchical nature of relationships and on the importance of extended family ties in the pretransition family may have only limited generality. The variability of these and other aspects of the family makes it difficult to distinguish the social from the economic functions of the family as they relate to fertility.[12] To cite Cain (*ibid.*:175) again: "Caldwell is not at all alone in his assumption that networks of extended kin do perform such [economic] functions; indeed, this is a very common assumption. But in fact there has been little research conducted in this area, even by anthropologists."

Although a number of publications advocating an institutional approach to the study of population change have recently appeared (Population Council, 1981; Miro and Potter, 1980; Potter, 1983), the most eloquent and detailed description of this approach is to be found in a series of papers by McNicoll (1975, 1977, 1978, 1979, 1980). He provides (1977) what he calls a "rough listing" of mediating structures or institutions: (1) indigenous social groups, mainly kin groups; (2) local administrative organization; (3) socioeconomic stratification (by landholding, income, or occupation); and (4) other interest groups, usually unorganized, such as women, or particular age groups, such as children or the elderly.

McNicoll (1975) has argued that one way to integrate population and development strategies would be to focus on community-level determinants of economic and demographic behavior. He suggests that a major reduction in fertility could be achieved through a unified community-development program by designing policies to establish or reinforce autonomy and solidarity and to provide incentives at the community level that reward economic performance and demographic restraint. He cites historical instances, Japan in the Tokugawa era and China in the 1950s and 1960s, as societies that evinced the capacity for acting to advance their economic and demographic interests, as densely populated traditional agrarian societies, prior to their encounter with the strong inducements of urban industrialization. And in their analysis of population and development in Bangladesh, Arthur and McNicoll (1978) found that creating the conditions for implementation of this community-level strategy would require structural change, including transfers of political power, and the design of a coherent development strategy.

In a subsequent paper, McNicoll (1980) carried further his exploration of the ways in which institutional settings can influence decision-making by individuals about fertility and considered how the forms and dynamics of the institutional setting itself may be investigated, having recourse to the transaction-costs theory of institutional structure. He suggests that thoroughgoing structural transformation may not be the only way of bringing about needed institutional change and notes (*ibid.*:456) that "as understanding of the relationships between institutional forms and the nature of the transactions they encompass is deepened, opportunities for marginal intervention are likely to become apparent. In the case of fertility, the prospect of such opportunities remains a major hope for humane policy."

Analyses of institutional settings to distinguish those that generate or sustain high fertility from those that are conducive to low fertility are still few. As McNicoll (*ibid.*:459) observed, "Still lacking . . . are well-designed empirical measures of the forms and dynamics of fertility-relevant institutions." Potter (1983) has reviewed the sparse literature on the institutional determinants of fertility. He presents three broad categories of the routes, or mediating variables, through which changes in institutional context may influence fertility behavior: (1) by way of changing the economic costs and benefits attached to family formation and childbearing, focusing on the labor value of children and the institutional arrangements that affect the costs of children; (2) through changes in internalized values concerning marriage and fertility, brought about through exposure to institutions such as the education system, the church, and those that foster rising consumer aspirations (which send "messages" about "appropriate" reproductive behavior); and (3) by way of shifts in the administrative and social pressures that are brought to bear on individuals and families with regard to their reproductive behavior. In this last category, Potter addresses two questions: What sort of institutional arrangements are likely to foster local efforts to either restrict or increase natural population growth? What are the institutional prerequisites for the successful implementation of national efforts to orient fertility, as opposed to local population policies?

Recent empirical research on the economic value of children in rural areas of Bangladesh places emphasis on detailed knowledge of the institutional underpinnings of the costs and benefits of children. Cain (1981, 1982, 1983, 1986c) and Cain and Lieberman (1982) focus specifically on the value of children as insurance against risk. They depict the harshness and diversity of the risk environment in Bangladesh and the absence of effective forms of insurance. The traditional means of institutional support to minimize risk—namely, subsistence guarantees once embodied in landlord–tenant arrangements, patron–client relationships, access to underutilized land resources, and kin and neighbor networks—are no longer available, and new institutionally based forms of protection have yet to emerge. In this situation, they say, there is a positive reproductive incentive associated with children as insurance against risk. Cain and Lieberman (1982) suggest that no sustained fertility decline in Bangladesh can be achieved without eliminating, or substantially reducing, this incentive. Consequently, they argue that a direct attack on the risk-insurance–fertility nexus is not only a necessary but also a sufficient condition for a substantial fertility decline in rural Bangladesh. Taking into account the assumption that the national family planning program and other social welfare programs will continue to operate and improve in the future, they make the principal recommendation (*ibid.*:4) that the anticipated demographic benefits will follow "if government anti-poverty and employment-generating initiatives, currently encompassing a wide range of activities and policies, are reorganized and reconstituted as a guaranteed employment scheme offering secure income-earning opportunities to all in need."[13]

Cain and Lieberman's work illustrates the point made previously that understanding of how fertility change occurs or does not occur in specific sociocultural contexts may help to identify ways of inducing fertility decline without waiting for comprehensive economic development to bring it about. They observe (*ibid.*:14): ". . . solutions to the predicament of high fertility and rapid population growth must be sought in currently existing social and economic circumstances, without the presumption that overall 'development' is now proceeding, or will necessarily proceed, along the classical Western path. . . . The operative question should be: how does one achieve a significant fertility transition in the absence of Western-style economic development?"

CONCLUDING OBSERVATIONS

This overview shows that the current knowledge base yields only a very broad understanding of fertility change despite the substantial amount of work that has been done in this field, and there is no generally accepted conceptual framework by which cumulative research on the determinants and consequences of population change in the LDCs can be guided. As indicated, it makes little sense to strive for a general solution, even if it were possible, given the complexity of the interactions among population and development variables, the different levels and kinds of development associated with fertility declines, and the fact that the relationships between fertility and its determinants and consequences vary considerably not only among countries but also among different groups within countries.

When the same problem is studied in more than one country, it cannot be assumed that economic, sociocultural, and political factors will have identical effects in all countries or even throughout each country. Consequently, population research and analysis will have to be at least country-specific if it is to yield implications with policy relevance for policy-makers and development planners. The study of sociocultural and institutional factors is not very amenable to cross-sectional survey research, but to the extent that such surveys of the correlates of fertility behavior are country-specific, they can help to provide a knowledge base for the design of village studies in which the role of such factors can be documented at community and household levels.

Conceptual approaches to the study of change in fertility behavior have largely taken their departure point from demographic-transition theory and constitute revisions or restatements of that model, among the most prominent of which have been those of Caldwell, Coale, and Davis. Perhaps most influential, however, has been the Easterlin framework. judging by its persistence and pervasiveness in the literature. An early version of the Easterlin model (Easterlin, 1969) influenced the attempts of Hawthorn (1970), a sociologist, to formulate an explanatory model of the determinants of fertility, and a recent summation of the Easterlin model (Easterlin, 1983) provided basic components of the classification scheme adopted by the National Academy of Sciences Panel on Fertility Determinants (Bulatao and Lee, 1983a) in its massive study of the determinants of fertility in the LDCs. In attempting to elaborate the meaning of "tastes," even though it remains for him a residual category, Easterlin has moved the microeconomic approach closer to an opening toward the work of psychologists, sociologists, anthropologists, and, it may be added, the work of economists like McNicoll and Potter, who have focused on institutional factors. As Robinson and Harbison (1980:228–229) put it: "In the end, economic, social and psychological forces all interact in determining the actual fertility decisions of couples. Psychological variables shape the individual's reaction to external forces and stimuli; sociological variables shape the group's reaction to and control over individual behavior, while the whole process proceeds in a roughly economic cost–benefit 'expectations' framework."

None of the approaches that have been considered in this discussion has specified a particular combination of economic and sociocultural variables that could constitute, in a given instance, threshold levels of economic and social development that would precipitate a fertility decline. It is possible, of course, that no such levels exist. Cutright and Hargens (1984:470) point out, with respect to Coale's three broad preconditions for fertility decline in Europe (fertility must be within the calculus of conscious choice, reduced fertility must be seen as advantageous, and effective contraceptive techniques must be available), that it is unlikely that the social and cultural factors that changed perceptions of these matters in Europe "themselves are perfectly correlated with development, and it is therefore not surprising that fertility declines in Europe did not uniformly take place after a certain level of economic or social development was reached." Cutright and Hargens nevertheless take the view that the threshold hypothesis is a useful analytical tool in understanding fertility trends. In a statistical analysis of data on a number of LDCs in Latin America, they present evidence to support the hypothesis that fertility will decline from traditional high levels if threshold levels of life expectancy and literacy are surpassed, and they state that these effects are independent of measures of social, economic, and family planning program development. They draw the following policy implications from their research (*ibid.*:470–471): "To initiate fertility decline less developed countries still maintaining traditional levels of fertility need to increase levels of literacy and life expectancy before the motivation to reduce fertility will affect enough couples to result in an initial fertility decline."

As has been indicated, the mainstream view that rapid population growth has negative consequences for the implementation of the goals of economic and social development has been subjected to a revisionist approach in a recent spate of literature that encompasses what has been termed "the new population debate." Some highlights of this discourse are examined in Chapter 8.

Finally, conceptualization in the field of population and development needs to take into systematic account the sociocultural and institutional factors that are operative in the fertility decision-making context, factors that have been largely deemphasized in a number of mainstream approaches (Burch, 1975). Including these dimensions of the context may in fact help to bring order into the vast buzzing, blooming domain of what Hawthorn (1981:703) views as "the complexity, variation, and variability of the interrelations between demographic, economic, social, and political factors at the individual, household, sectoral, class, regional, and national levels."

NOTES

[1]For pioneering reviews of this literature, see Cassen (1976) and Birdsall (1977). Jones (1978) has done a review for East and Southeast Asia, and Urzua (1978) has done the same for Latin America. See also Miro and Potter (1980).

[2]Fecundity refers to the physiological capacity of a woman, man, or couple to produce a live child, whereas fertility refers to actual reproductive performance.

[3]In the view of Easterlin (1978:109), the elements of modernization that are relevant "in bringing about the shift to modern conditions of childbearing" are innovations in public

health and medical care; innovations in formal schooling and mass media; urbanization; the introduction of new goods; and per capita income growth. He also notes that "more recently in a few countries another aspect of modernization—family planning programs—has perhaps also played a noticeable role in influencing reproductive behavior." For further elaboration of his views on modernization, see Easterlin (1983) and Easterlin and Crimmins (1985).

[4]Neverthless, in Easterlin's most recent work (Easterlin and Crimmins, 1985), he continues to believe that modernization, which he depicts as the mirror image of Western society, is taking over the world. The following quotations are illustrative: "The fertility revolution is part of a much broader transformation, commonly termed 'modernization,' observed in a growing number of nations since the mid-eighteenth century" (ibid.:3). "In terms of human personality, modernization is characterized by an increased openness to new experience, increased independence from parental authority, belief in the efficacy of science, and ambition for oneself and one's children" (ibid.:4). "In the twentieth century, increasingly since World War II, the initial signs of modernization have become more widespread in parts of Asia and northern Africa and, more recently, in sub-Saharan Africa" (ibid.:4). For Easterlin, fertility reduction is equated with modernization, but as indicated in the previous chapter, there are a number of different pathways from high to low fertility, and it is misleading to assume that convergence with the experience that characterized some of the Western countries must precede such a fertility decline. As indicated in the text, Easterlin did entertain some doubts, earlier on, as to whether the LDCs would necessarily follow the same track as the DCs, but these doubts are not apparent in his later work. As for Africa in particular, Easterlin does indeed seem unduly optimistic. As O. Frank (1985:40) concludes, ". . . there is little indication that the types of change . . . hypothesized to have ultimately had anti-natalist effects in demographic transitions elsewhere are occurring or will occur in the immediate future, in Africa."

[5]In his chapter on cultural influences in the second of these volumes, T. H. Hull (1983:381) says: "Although this framework can be used to analyze fertility at either the individual or social level, it is not as useful for dynamic analysis of the complex interactions between the individual life cycle and the process of social change. In particular, it does not lend itself well to analysis of fertility decision making by people confronted with a variety of constraints and opportunities, a subject on which there is relatively little in the literature generally."

[6]There is a very large literature on this theme. For some clear expositions, see Cassen (1976) and McNicoll (1984). Also, see the chapter on consequences of rapid population growth in International Bank for Reconstruction and Development (1984).

[7]See, for example, Documents (1982) for the transcript of a television interview of Simon by William F. Buckley, Jr.

[8]Coale and his associates also invoke cultural factors in explaining their findings with regard to a number of Central Asia republics of the Soviet Union, where there was continued high marital fertility as late as 1970 despite the presence of a number of indicators of "advanced" levels of development. They attribute this continuation primarily to the persistence of traditional values sustaining the rejection of voluntary birth control. See Coale, Anderson, and Härm (1979).

[9]For a summary of anthropological views on culture and population change, see American Association for the Advancement of Science (1974). See also Marshall, Morris. and Polgar (1972), Spooner (1972), LeVine and Scrimshaw (1983), and Nag (1983, 1984a).

[10]Davis (1973:21) says: "Our mores were formed when societies could survive only with a birth rate thrice that required by a modern death rate. Built into the social order, therefore, are values, norms, and incentives that motivate people to bear and rear children.

These cultural and institutional inheritances form the premises of our thinking." Davis is writing here about United States society, but obviously this comment is, if anything, even more relevant for the LDCs. Davis's affirmation of cultural values as a support for high fertility should be compared with the earlier discussion of Davis's theory of change and response, in which he argues that people in Japan and Europe were motivated to reduce fertility by personal pressures despite opposing societal or cultural pressures. Whatever may be the limitations of Davis's interpretation, it does lend support to the idea that reproductive behavior can be adaptive and that cultural values are not immutable.

[11]Oppenheimer (1982) has developed and tested an analytical model of decision-making in the family with respect to fertility behavior that incorporates, in addition to economic dimensions, social factors such as norms, institutions, and reference group comparisons. Employing United States Census samples, Oppenheimer focuses on the family as the major unit of analysis and specifies how social factors are essential for understanding decision-making with respect to marriage and the timing of births, family size, and participation of wives in the labor force.

[12]It may be noted that while Caldwell's research leads him to argue that strong kin networks perpetuate high fertility, the research of Cain (1977, 1981, 1982) on Bangladesh and India leads him to the opposite conclusion, namely, that strong kin networks, by constituting a source of insurance as an alternative to children, may be conducive to fertility decline by preventing children from becoming the focus of parental concerns for security. In this connection, Burch (1979:183), in his review of the literature on household and family demography, says: "Empirical studies to date, while interesting in their own right as investigations of the interrelations of fertility and residential household formation, have largely failed to deal with the broader questions of how social and economic interdependencies among dispersed kin groups affect marriage and fertility decisions."

[13]Robinson (1986) has published a critique of Cain's thesis that children in Bangladesh constitute insurance for their parents against risk and that this "insurance function constitutes one of the main explanations of the high fertility" (*ibid*.:289). Robinson maintains that "however plausible, the risk-insurance hypothesis simply does not hold up, either logically or empirically" (*ibid*.:298). Consideration of Robinson's argument, or of the reply by Cain (1986a), is beyond the scope of this discussion. Suffice it to say that in his reply, Cain states that Robinson has misread his work and reaffirms his argument that children are an important source of security to parents. He goes on to say (*ibid*.:303–304), however, that he is uncertain "of the precise implication of this for reproductive behaviour" and calls for "comparative research on risk and insurance conducted at appropriate levels of analysis and intensive studies that focus on security issues in particular localities, on the role of children in mediating risk, on the criteria of fertility decisions, and on the material consequences of reproductive failure."

Sectoral Reviews I

6

Among the key development sectors that affect and are affected by population growth are natural resources, health and nutrition, the status and employment of women, education, and income distribution. The latter has already been considered in this discussion, and the others will now be reviewed one by one. Although considering these sectors individually violates the reality that they do not operate independently (and indeed interact with other sectors that will not be reviewed here) and can be understood and interpreted only in a larger context, to proceed otherwise would be to enter into the morass of attempting to relate everything to everything else. Nevertheless, it is necessary to keep in mind the qualifications specified by Cassen (1976:788) in his review of the interrelationships between population and development: "The explanation of fertility trends covers an enormous range of variables, reflecting the complexity of this area of human behaviour and its relation to biological, social, psychological and economic factors. . . . Fertility alters in relation to processes in society of which these factors form a part." In her review of the relationships between population growth and development, Birdsall (1977:91) concluded: "No one intervention can be expected to affect fertility in a simple downward direction: the relation between each variable and fertility is complex, as are the relations among these variables and their joint effect on fertility."

These reviews, of natural resources and of health and nutrition in this chapter, and of the status and employment of women and of education in the next chapter, cannot claim to be comprehensive, since the literature on each of these sectors is so voluminous. In each review, however, an effort has been made to identify the principal problems and issues that characterize the present state of knowledge and to address important research questions. The specification of priorities for research on the interrelationships of population and development and of appropriate methodological approaches has been left for Chapter 8.

NATURAL RESOURCES

The debate about the world's future has been dominated by two extreme views (Ridker and Cecelski, 1979; Russell, 1979). One is the "limited" view, which asserts that there are limits to economic growth and expansion set by the finite nature of the earth's resources, that these limits will soon be reached, and that the consumption of the world's resources by an affluent minority should be limited in the interest of the poor majority and of future generations. The other, often called the "cornucopian" view, maintains that continued economic growth is needed so as to spread its benefits to the poor majority, that the advances of science and technology can create resources to replace those that are depleted, and that in any case, even if scientific progress were to stop, the possibilities of substituting more abundant for scarcer resources are great enough to push the limits to growth into the distant future. Perhaps the best-known proponents of this expansionist view are Julian Simon and Herman Kahn (1984),[1] while the "limited" view has been stated dramatically by the *Limits to Growth* study (Meadows, Meadows, Randers, and Behrens, 1972) and the *Global 2000 Report* (Council on Environmental Quality, 1980).

The available knowledge base is too scant and ambiguous to provide support for either of these extreme views (MacKellar and Vining, 1985). Clearly, there are all sorts of limits to the unbridled continuation of a consumption-oriented, expansionist approach to the use of the world's resources, just as there are indications that continuing economic growth is feasible and desirable, particularly if the benefits of such growth are to be shared by the poor majority. But opinions and views differ widely among members of the scientific community, depending on what of the available evidence they find convincing. In fact, Tinbergen (1975) maintains that neither position can claim to be a scientific view and that both natural and social scientists working in this problem area must admit that they are still in a prescientific stage of understanding the problem and its solution—a stage before the stage of established and tested theory with which a sizeable majority of scholars could agree.

One dimension of this debate of particular interest to this discussion is the question of how population growth affects the nature and timing of resource and environmental constraints. The debate about the balance between population pressures and natural resources has been going on at least since the time of Malthus, but the conviction that population growth is the principal cause of resource depletion and deterioration was substantially reinforced by the apocalyptic predictions of the *Limits to Growth* study and the gloomy projections of the *Global 2000*

Report. These studies served a useful purpose in highlighting the need to adopt a longer time perspective in assessment of the issues, but their contribution to a firm knowledge base was severely limited and yielded more questions than answers. According to Clawson (1981:21), for example, *"Global 2000* is seriously flawed. Its processes are suspect, its data lacking, its inconsistencies too prevalent, and many of its conclusions unwarranted. Yet . . . it does identify some real problems which do need to be imprinted on the public consciousness." As Ridker and Watson (1979) have noted, substantial research is needed to fill in the abysmal gaps in our knowledge about the environmental consequences of human actions, past as well as future. In particular, research is needed in basic sciences, such as climatology, in monitoring environmental and ecological change to provide an early warning system, and on technological and institutional factors that improve society's ability to control difficult environmental problems.

With regard to the debate, Ridker and Cecelski (1979:4) observe that "the relevant question is not whether to grow or not to grow, but how to redirect present and future economic output in ways that will better serve humanity. Clearly there are physical constraints to population and economic growth, but most of them are distant enough to be managed by adequate planning, good will, and international cooperation." Typically, the issues have been regarded at a global or national level, which has obscured important dimensions of the problems involved, such as acute problems caused by population pressure on regions and localities as it affects patterns of agriculture, land availability, water resources, and forest management. To cite Ridker and Cecelski (*ibid.*:31) again: ". . . the sheer availability of land and water is not the central problem in feeding the world's growing numbers. Rather, it is the disparities in the distribution of people on the one side and production capacity on the other, plus the barriers that stand in the way of eliminating these disparities."

The debate has also tended to focus on the one-way relationship of the impact of population growth on resource depletion. Research and analysis for policy purposes is needed in subnational contexts, and at the micro level, on the dynamic interaction of the population–resource relationship, with respect not only to the ways in which population growth and distribution affect the use of resources but also to the ways in which access to and distribution of resources condition demographic processes.

When one looks at the dimensions of population growth in store for the world, it is not difficult to understand why the impact of population on resources has received by far the greater attention. Even medium growth projections indicate that by the year 2000, at least 6 billion persons will need to be fed, compared with about 5 billion at present. Population growth alone, without regard for other causes of increased demand, will cause demand for water, for example, at least to double by the year 2000 relative to 1971 in nearly half the countries in the world, and still greater increases would be needed to improve standards of living (Council on Environmental Quality, 1980). Viewed from the global level, population growth and poverty appear to be leading to serious long-term declines in the productivity of renewable natural resource systems, but this trend is not inexorable, since it appears that people can adapt, through changes in population distribution and/or in social and economic organization, to a changing resource base. A relevant example is that of China: How did the Chinese add 100 million people in the last two decades and still manage to feed them all?

Approaches to the population–resource relationship that take the position that the problems can be solved either just by slowing population growth or by increasing resources are too simplistic. Clearly, there is need to do both and to understand that a variety of factors affect the relationship. But it must also be emphasized that population increase is neither the sole nor always a principal determinant of resource depletion and degradation. Murdoch (1980) maintains that environmental degradation of marginal land through overuse and misuse is caused by poverty rather than population pressure, although population density may be a contributory factor. He says (*ibid.*:305): "Ecological deterioration in marginal food-producing areas in the LDCs [less-developed countries] is . . . in essence a problem of poverty. Even if environmental degradation were the result 'merely' of population pressure, it must be stressed that this, in turn, has its origins in the structural poverty of the rural population."

In general, the prevailing view is that population growth does in fact have a negative impact on the environment and that a deceleration of population growth is important because it would reduce the number and intensity of problems that have to be solved in implementing development strategies. There is little agreement about the degree of the impact or what role population growth plays in comparison with other factors, but World Bank (1985a:71–72) staff accord a prominent role to rapid population growth: "Degradation and destruction of environmental systems and natural resources are now assuming massive proportions in some developing countries, threatening continued, sustainable development. The collective actions of a world population approaching 5 billion now appear fully capable of causing continental and even global changes in the resource base upon which all national economies rest."[2]

They point out that it is in Africa that "the breakdown between people and their environmental support systems" is particularly acute. In this connection, Talbot (1986) reports on the role of population growth in the depletion of resources and environmental degradation in the rangelands of East Africa, particularly the Maasailand of Kenya, and observes (*ibid*.:441–442) that "increased numbers of people lead to increased numbers of livestock, which, in turn, lead to overgrazing, degradation of the range resource, and ultimate reduction of the ability of these lands to support both livestock and people . . . with consequent famine, loss of livestock, and, often, loss of human life."

In the case of deforestation, for example, growing populations increase the demand for food and farmland and extend agriculture into forested areas. Between 1900 and 1965, half the forested area in the LDCs was cleared for agriculture (Barnes and Allen, 1981). If present trends continue, both forest cover and growing stocks of commercial-size wood in the LDCs will decline another 40% by the year 2000 (Council on Environmental Quality, 1980). But deforestation has various causes in addition to population pressure on limited agricultural land, such as climate, poverty, rising fuel prices, and range and livestock management.

In a review of the relationships between population and ecology, Henriot (1976) concluded, with respect to nonrenewable resources, principally energy, that there is some empirical evidence to show that every increase in population does have its effect on the overall supply of such resources, but that increase in consumption due to rising levels of industrialization and affluence is much more significant. With regard to renewable resources, he states that there seems to be strong evidence, more so than in the case of nonrenewable resources, that pressure from increasing population causes ecological damage. Repetto and Holmes (1983) call attention to other conditions that operate in conjunction with population growth to bring about more rapid environmental deterioration than would population increase alone. These conditions include breakdowns in traditional systems of resource management, the commercial exploitation of natural resources, export demands arising in the international economy as a source of pressure on LDC resources, and inequality of access to natural resources in many LDCs.

The view that population growth is the principal cause of environmental degradation and that such growth should be reduced to retard this degradation is much more prevalent in the developed countries (DCs) than in the LDCs. Moreover, the limits-to-growth perspective, which calls for the reduction of both population and economic growth and has gained some ascendancy in the DCs, is not in the forefront for the LDCs. Rather, their concern is with enhancing economic growth and achieving greater equity. In pursuit of that economic growth, some Third World leaders see the DC emphasis on environmental protection, to be enhanced by population control, as future issues that distract from current needs to reduce poverty. As Henriot (1976:13) puts it: "Very simply, many in the developing world—and especially those in policy-making positions—are ready and willing to endure more pollution and a less esthetically-pleasing environment in order to meet the immediate needs of their people."

Reducing inequality in access to a developing country's natural resources, especially land, is essentially a matter of adopting national policies that pursue the objectives of broad-based development. International inequality can be reduced to some extent through positive responses by the DCs to the LDC quest for a new international economic order. The LDCs view the DC calls for environmental protection and resource conservation as ringing hollow when in fact the DC share in world consumption of resources so heavily outweighs that of the LDCs. With regard to consumption of commercial energy, to take one example, the DCs account for more than half of world energy consumption. On the average, the DCs use about 8 times as much commercial energy per person as the middle-income LDCs and more than 40 times as much as the low-income LDCs (International Bank for Reconstruction and Development, 1980a).

In view of these considerations, there is no justification for the DCs to increase further their consumption of the world's scarce resources. As Ridker (1975:39) says, however, "A reduction in the consumption of resources by developed countries would not automatically help developing countries. This reduction would be of help only if the sale of these raw materials by developing countries were not an important fraction of their export earnings . . . and if some means could be found to transfer to them in usable form the resources that the developed countries release by consuming less." Although transfers of material resources on any sizeable scale are probably not realistic, transfers of appropriate scientific and technical knowledge could make a strategic contribution to amelioration of international inequalities. Keyfitz (1976:35) has pointed out that escape from world poverty is not likely to be accomplished through schemes for division of the existing product, but by contributing knowledge that will expand the product: "Incentives can be devised to direct technology in environment-saving rather than environment-damaging directions. . . . No one can forecast how much time it will take to solve . . . the complex of [technical] problems, but that time . . . will be shortened by a larger and more immediate mobilization of scientific and engineering talent." As for population growth, this discussion has repeatedly advanced the argument that the LDCs have nothing to gain and much to lose from continued rapid population growth in their efforts to realize the goals of broad-based development, which include the most equitable and effective use of their natural resources.

In summing up their book on resource and environmental problems, Ridker and Watson (1979) observe that both population growth and economic growth intensify these problems. At a general level, both kinds of growth have a similar impact. There is an important difference, however, since in the case of population growth, there are no offsetting advantages—each additional person adds to resource and environmental pressures. "In contrast, economic growth can be used for different ends than it is put to now. Although it adds to problems that need solution, it also adds to the capacity to solve problems" (ibid.:410).

Consideration of the relationships between population growth and natural resources has been focused thus far on the ways in which population growth affects resource use and adequacy. The other principal question to be addressed is that of the ways in which access to and distribution of resources affect demographic behavior. The connections between resources and fertility, as in the case of other development sectors, are largely indirect and therefore difficult to measure empirically. As with other population–development relationships, the interactions between resources and population cannot be understood without taking into systematic account the sociocultural, institutional, and economic contexts within which they occur. The task is to understand how resource–population relationships are structured by these contexts and how access to resources is distributed within local and national systems, in which different groups of the population are asserting claims on the same resources.

Empirical knowledge about the effects of resource policies and practices on demographic behavior is scant in such areas as agricultural technology and irrigation and water management. With regard to technical change, it has been noted that attempts to increase agricultural productivity by means of labor-intensive methods would provide motivation for maintaining high fertility. Those concerned with equity-oriented development have favored labor-intensive methods and opposed agricultural mechanization on the grounds that the latter only exacerbates the disparities between the rich and the poor.

It has been argued, however, that if a broad demand for new technology focused on mechanization could be induced by financial reform aimed at assuring farmers of more equal access to capital markets, the new technology could promote broad-based economic growth. The factors associated with such growth, namely, increased wages and employment, rising demand for investment funds, and increased demand for "higher quality" children (because of the need for more skilled workers), would have fertility-reducing effects.[3] Pfanner (1978), for example, has pointed to the need to know more about the effects on fertility behavior of the Green Revolution and of the promotion of agricultural crop diversification through multiple-cropping. Acquiring this knowledge calls for detailed studies of the supply, demand, and use of labor, including the economic roles of women and children, as agricultural technology changes. As he says (*ibid.*:5): "What we lack are microlevel studies, case histories and surveys of individual farm households providing agricultural and demographic information for the same families. Such studies would help to better understand the options available to farmers and the reasons for choices regarding adoption of the new technology and family size and the link between the two."

One area, that of the relationship between land and fertility, has been the subject of a growing amount of empirical research. Access to land is central to the well-being of rural populations, so that rural policies designed to effect changes in the basic institutional arrangements that govern access to land could have a particularly substantial impact on fertility. To begin with, a number of economic and demographic historians have undertaken to explain the substantial decline in rural fertility in 19th-century America as due to declining availability of easily accessible farmland in an area as it became more settled and developed. This literature has been reviewed by Vinovskis (1984).

The land-availability model that has dominated the literature on 19th-century fertility decline in the United States postulates that parents expected to establish their children on nearby farms, but reduced their fertility when it became apparent that it would be difficult to achieve this goal. Easterlin (1971) was a major supporter of this approach, but subsequently questioned it in introducing the "bequest" model (Easterlin, 1976:65–66). He noted that "the provision for one's children does not necessarily take the form of land, whether at home, nearby, or far away." Instead, "what is sought is equal treatment of offspring in terms of money value. . . . It is, then, the prospective 'increase of capital,' an ever present concern of farmers, that chiefly governs the changing size of families. The less the prospective growth of capital, the more will a farmer feel pressure to start limiting family size."

Vinovskis (1984) asserts that the evidence for the assumptions on which both the land-availability and the bequest models are based is thin because little attention has been paid to the relationship between inheritance and the age at marriage. He says (*ibid.*:85): ". . . it has not yet been demonstrated that most parents consciously reduced their family size because of the expectation that they would have to make a significant bequest to each of their offspring when they reached adulthood or that children frequently benefited from such a practice when they were about to set up an independent household."

In a study of land availability and fertility in the center–south of Brazil, Merrick (1978) found some support for the hypothesis that land availability is positively related to higher fertility in new settlement areas and contributed to its decline in older areas, but this influence is not independent of the role of other aspects of socioeconomic structure, such as land-tenure patterns, the economic value of children, female literacy, and the shift of rural workers from subsistence farming to employee status. Merrick concludes (*ibid.*:335) that "the prospects for further decline in rural fertility in Brazil may well depend more on the course of public policy affecting access of the rural population to land than on its actual scarcity or abundance."

The land-availability approach has yielded useful information for analysis of rural fertility, but better measures of land availability are needed to take into account a wide range of factors that include not only access to and control of land but also the amount and quality of land available. Moreover, an adequate understanding of the relationships between rural development and fertility requires a broader research orientation than the relatively narrow focus on the effects of land availability on reproductive behavior (O. G. Simmons, 1984a). As Vinovskis (1984:92) observes: "One avenue of analysis that most economic and demographic historians have not taken very seriously is whether or not there may have been large changes in the attitudes and values of nineteenth-century Americans which might have led them to reduce their family size."

In a review of the work on land availability and fertility in the LDCs, Schutjer and Stokes (1982) conclude that the findings are consistent with the historical research on the United States. They say (*ibid.*:238): "In summary, the available evidence supports the notion that access to land at the national, regional, or individual farm level is likely to result in greater economic returns for child labor, and hence contribute to the maintenance of a higher level of desired family size than would prevail should land be less available." The evidence on which this conclusion is based is still fragmentary, so that the idea that the size of holding to which a household has access for farming influences fertility through altering the economic contributions of children must remain a hypothesis for the present.

Access to land does not, however, always have the effect of providing support for high fertility. In a series of papers, Schutjer and his associates (Schutjer, Stokes, and Cornwell, 1980; Schutjer and Stokes, 1982; Schutjer, Stokes, and Poindexter, 1983; Stokes and Schutjer, 1984) both review the literature on the connections between land and fertility and report on their own research on this relationship in the Philippines, Thailand, and Egypt. They identify two dimensions that seem to have significance for fertility behavior. One dimension, already indicated, is the size of landholdings, which has positive effects. The second dimension is land ownership, which has negative effects by substituting land for children as a source of old-age security. Moreover, the higher incomes associated with ownership may be expected to lead to greater investments in child quality, particularly additional schooling. The short-run effect is likely to be fertility-enhancing, but the long-run effect fertility-reducing.

In the view of Stokes and Schutjer (1984:197), the two dimensions are distinct because an individual, family, or household may have use rights but not ownership rights. Moreover: "The two dimensions lead to different streams of income. . . . Owners of agricultural land receive returns to equity based on their investment. . . . Tenants of various types may receive a management and labor return, but regardless of how secure their use-rights, they do not receive returns to equity. The two dimensions of land and the alternative income streams have disparate implications for fertility." According to their argument, the income stream associated with ownership has a distinct and separate impact on fertility because the return to equity that only owners receive provides an alternative source of old-age security and thus reduces, in the long run, one incentive for continued high fertility. Moreover, land ownership may also provide in the short run a form of social insurance against risk and adversity. As indicated in the discussion of institutional factors, it has been argued by Cain that there is a positive reproductive incentive associated with children as insurance against risk.

The evidence on the relationship of land ownership and fertility is even less firm and more problematic than that on size of landholdings and fertility. But such limited evidence as exists is generally consistent with the perspective proposed by Schutjer and his associates and indicates that increasing land ownership may make a significant contribution to fertility reduction. As indicated earlier, the interactions between resources and fertility are largely indirect, and access to land is no exception. The effects of landholdings and land tenure on fertility can in any case only be indirect, through their capacity to change one or more of the proximate determinants. As Stokes and Schutjer (*ibid.*:196) observe:

"The influence of land systems on fertility . . . may be seen through their impact on the economic contributions of children, alterations in the decision-making processes of parents (including changes in the perceived costs and benefits of children), and directly on the proximate determinants of fertility." Much more empirical research is needed to specify what the effects of size of holding and of land ownership might be in different institutional and sociocultural settings, so as to ascertain under what conditions the effects are complementary or work at cross-purposes.

Cain (1985) has taken exception to the research on landholding and fertility for a variety of reasons, focusing primarily on the work of Schutjer and Stokes. Some of his reasons are methodological, but his principal objection appears to be that this work is restricted to the household level of analysis and (*ibid.*:15) "it is most unlikely that major advances in understanding the determinants of fertility will result from further empirical replication of relationships at the household level." Instead, Cain calls for extending the scope of inquiry to take into systematic account the institutional context of individual reproductive behavior. Stokes, Schutjer, and Bulatao (1986) have responded to Cain's assessment, and Cain (1986b) has published a rejoinder to this response. As in the case of the dispute between Robinson and Cain on children as insurance against risk, noted in Chapter 5 (note 13), consideration of the details of this exchange on the issue of the relationship between landholding and fertility goes beyond the scope of this discussion. It may be noted, however, as would be expected, that Stokes *et al.* (1986:311) reaffirm the need for further research on this relationship with respect to "the direction, size and range of effects [that] need to be specified in a variety of institutional contexts." They point out (*ibid.*:305) that "in the majority of developing nations land tenure, land settlement and land reform represent important policy issues linked closely to national agricultural development strategies. To abandon work regarding the fertility implications of such policies would ignore an important aspect of the future social and economic well-being of current and future populations in the world's poorest nations." Cain (1986b:317), in his rejoinder, says: ". . . it makes little sense to focus analytic attention on small socio-economic fertility differentials . . . while, over a relatively short period, fertility declines dramatically and by comparable amounts across all socio-economic groups. While there is much room for debate on the causes of such declines, it is most unlikely that causal insight can be found in the factors that account for the empirical relationship between landholding and fertility."

It is possible, of course, that both land ownership and children may constitute insurance against risk and thus have implications for fertility. Cain (1985:10) comes close to this position when he observes "that it is more useful to think of land and children as complements rather than substitutes in providing security. . . . Children can serve as an important means of insuring against loss of land." And Stokes *et al.* (1986:308), although they emphasize that land ownership substitutes for children as a source of old-age security, point out that the land-security hypothesis "does not imply that landowners will desire no children," merely that "land ownership should *reduce* the importance of children as sources of old-age security and contribute to lower fertility" [emphasis in original]. In any case, the knowledge base regarding the relationships between landholding and fertility, as well as the role of children as insurance against risk, is still so thin that further investigation of these relationships can only be encouraged. Both Cain and Schutjer and his associates do at least agree on the need for longitudinal data for clarification of these relationships.

The perspective provided by the work just reviewed suggests that the expectation that a policy of land redistribution will invariably bring lower fertility in its wake is simplistic, but constitutes a departure point for identifying the particular conditions under which land distribution is likely to have either pronatalist or anitnatalist effects. Seligson (1979), for example, noted a potential conflict between land reform and population policies in Costa Rica in that he perceived land reform to have a potential pronatalist impact. He found that peasants with access to land had higher fertility and attributed this to the influence of land ownership, which he saw as stimulating the desire for more children to obtain free family labor. He did not distinguish, however, between the fertility of landowners and those with other types of access to land, such as renters and sharecroppers, nor did his analysis take into account the possibly different effects of land ownership and size of holdings on fertility. Consequently, to eliminate the conflict between land reform and family planning programs, he recommended that reform to give land to the landless should give them, not ownership, but a fixed wage in a "self-run communal enterprise" (*ibid.*:55). Given their perspective, Stokes and Schutjer (1983) responded to the Seligson proposal by urging caution in the design of fertility-sensitive land reform policies due to the multidimensional impacts of land. They agree with Seligson's emphasis on the need for understanding the connections between agricultural and population policies if they are to be effectively coordinated, but call for more precise information on the consequences for fertility of variations in land reform programs on the grounds that such information could facilitate coordination of land reform policies and population policies.[4] Such information could help to shed light on the causal direction of the land–

fertility relationship, i.e., whether those with larger holdings have higher fertility or those with high fertility are able to acquire access to more land. As Stokes and Schutjer (1984) point out, the cross-sectional nature of most of the research done to date precludes a choice among these alternatives.

In view of the political and other constraints that stand in the way of the structural change needed if rural poverty is to be reduced, land reform is not likely to be an available opportunity for a large proportion of landless workers who are the poorest of rural residents. Yet they are the ones most desperately in need. Cool (1979) estimated that in South and Southeast Asia alone, there were upwards of 200 million landless or near-landless rural workers. He claimed that on the available evidence, this number is likely to grow both absolutely and as a percentage of total rural households at an unprecedented rate well into the future. Their plight underlines the need for broad-based approaches to development that will bring them increased access to resources needed for enhancing their economic and social well-being, such as expanded opportunities for nonagricultural employment if rural incomes are to move upward, provision of public services for better health and nutrition and greater life expectancy, and investment in human capital, especially education for women and children. Moreover, to the extent that a large proportion of the population can share in the benefits of development, they will also experience fertility declines that will eventually produce a greater aggregate-level fertility decline.[5]

HEALTH, NUTRITION, AND FOOD

In the lead paper in a collection reviewing health and population in the LDCs, John Knowles (1980) began by asking the question of why health interests received such low priority in development planning over the years. Health expenditures still consume only a fraction of total government expenditures in LDCs (International Bank for Reconstruction and Development, 1985),[6] and the greatest part of this modest expenditure has been consumed in urban locations because, in most LDCs, the physician–hospital–high technology approach to health care has limited such care largely to urban elites (O. G. Simmons, 1982, 1983). Given the strong commitment of the medical profession to this approach, health services do not reach or are inaccessible to a large proportion of the population in need, perhaps as much as 80–85%. Services are sparse in rural areas and urban slums largely as a result of a gross maldistribution of facilities and personnel, and a poor balance exists between curative and preventive care, since curative, hospital-based, high-technology medicine in urban areas is usually dominant. According to Knowles (1980), the health problems of the predominantly rural populations are largely those attendant on malnutrition; the ease of transmission of infectious disease because of inadequate supplies of potable water, inadequate sewage disposal, and lack of hygienic practices; ubiquitous parasitic diseases; and family size and inability to plan for a desired number of children, appropriately spaced in time.

Just as physicians have helped to maintain health near the bottom in development planning priorities, so Western economists' views of health as a "consumption" expenditure rather than as a "productive" investment have had a similar influence (R. A. Smith and Powell, 1978). Concern with and awareness of the substantial benefits that improved health might generate are beginning to counterbalance the pervasive view that improved health is merely a consumption benefit that the poor countries in particular cannot afford. Instead, as Beenstock (1980:2) put it, "One can argue that there is an investment dimension to health which in principle at least is no different to other capital inputs." Contentions that improved health has beneficial effects on productivity seem very plausible. As R. A. Smith and Powell (1978:8) state: "It does not have to be proved repetitively by cost/benefit studies which are difficult to perform that a patient horizontal with the fever and weakness of malaria, pneumonia, or tuberculosis is less productive than his healthy vertical counterpart whose mental and physical attitude bespeak potential contribution to a country's development."

Nevertheless, empirical evidence for generalizations about the direct positive impact of health on production is sparse indeed. Grosse and Harkavy (1980), for example, observe that the literature is filled with contradictory findings. As in the case of other development sectors, it is the complexity of the relationships involved that makes so difficult the documentation of unambiguous findings. Barlow (1979) set out to address two questions: To what extent does health promote development, and to what extent does development promote health? He arrived at two general impressions, namely, that the relevant empirical studies are on the whole not very convincing and that it is difficult to draw broad generalizations from the empirical conclusions. He arrived (ibid.:47) at the discouraging conclusion that "the relationships between health and economic development are so complex that the definitive study in this area will never be made."

The model Barlow presents for the study of the links between health and economic development illustrates the complexity of the relationships. If these links are to be investigated, explicit account must be taken of at least five interacting variables: income, health, nutritional status, educational attainment, and fertility. Each one affects and is affected by the other four to yield 20 direct relationships, from each of which a number of possible hypotheses can be derived. Despite the amount of empirical work that has been done on these linkages, there do not seem to be any empirical studies that attempt to account for these five interacting variables in a single geographic area, which lack, of course, further limits the generalization potential of the work that has been done (Grosse and Harkavy, 1980).

Preston (1978a) has addressed the issue of the relative importance of specific health interventions and of levels of general development as determinants of levels of mortality. Clearly, both are important, but again, given the complexity of the multivariate nature of the process involved, precision in the matter of relative importance in a particular situation is hard to come by, and as Preston (*ibid.*:3) says, "For policy purposes, the critical issue is how cheaply a certain reduction in mortality can be made when produced by one source as opposed to the other."

In any case, the idea that development *per se* is the best remedy is no more valid for mortality reduction than it is for fertility reduction. As Caldwell (1986:210) concludes, on the basis of an analysis of how Costa Rica, Sri Lanka, and the Indian state of Kerala achieved substantial success in mortality reduction despite their low per capita income levels, "Low mortality for all will not come as an unplanned spinoff from economic growth." Although he identifies a number of reasons, he attributes this success primarily to the fact that in each of these three cases, top priority was accorded to education, particularly female education, and to health, particularly in rendering local health services efficient and available to the entire population.

In a study of mortality differentials in the two Indian states of Kerala and West Bengal, Nag (1981) found that the mortality level was consistently lower in Kerala for many decades and that the difference became even sharper in the 1970s. The empirical evidence from various surveys shows that the differences between the two states in nutritional standard, per capita income, distribution of income and assets, and industrialization and urbanization cannot explain the lower mortality level in Kerala. Nag interpreted the difference as due to a distinction that can be made between economic and social development. Economic development is usually measured by per capita income and income distribution, while social development may be construed as the development of such social services as education, health, and transportation through public policy measures. From the evidence, Nag concluded that

West Bengal is characterized by a higher level of economic development and Kerala by a relatively higher level of social development. The lower mortality in Kerala, according to Nag, can be attributed mostly to its higher social development and partly to its favorable environmental and hygienic conditions.

Similarly, Preston (1978a) concluded that although economic factors remain very important in differentiating among nations' mortality levels, "unstructured" economic change now appears to be an inefficient method of reducing mortality. Nations that have "structured" development in such a way as to increase levels of literacy and to spread public health and nutritional programs widely among the population have achieved remarkable advances in prolonging life. Preston cites Cuba, Kerala, and Sri Lanka as prime examples. As he put it (*ibid.*:15), "All three areas have in common governmental programmes that aim explicitly at upgrading the social and health conditions among the poorest sectors; each has achieved exceptionally high levels of literacy; and each has public health programmes that achieve a relatively egalitarian distribution of health services."

On the basis of a series of papers prepared by World Bank staff on the relationship between education and health, Cochrane, O'Hara, and Leslie (1980) found a stronger correlation between life expectancy and literacy than between life expectancy and any other single variable. They concluded (*ibid.*:3) that "the existing evidence at the micro and macro level in bivariate and multivariate studies in a wide variety of countries is quite consistent—more educated parents, even those with only small amounts of education, have healthier, longer-living children."

In pursuing the argument that "unstructured" economic development is usually quite inefficient for reducing mortality levels relative to "structured" development that would channel increments in income toward educational expenditures or preventive-health measures, Preston (1978a:13–14) stated that "it is reasonable to expect that the same conclusion would pertain to programmes seeking a direct impact on nutritional levels. Untutored development is almost certainly not the best pill if the goal is mortality reduction." In a similar vein, Reutlinger and Selowsky (1976:7) maintained that only policies deliberately designed to reallocate food or income can eliminate undernutrition, malnutrition being "unlikely to disappear in the normal course of development." Growth rates in national products and food supplies at constant costs should not realistically be expected to be adequate to eliminate undernutrition in the lowest income groups within any reasonable time (*ibid.*).

Before this discussion turns to the effects of health and nutrition on fertility, a few comments are in order about nutrition and development and about the relationships between health and nutrition. Like health, malnutrition only gradually became viewed as a development problem. According to Berg (1973:2), this late interest may be attributed in part to the traditional view of malnutrition as a welfare rather than a development problem. As Berg says, "Welfare is not ignored by development planners; but, except in emergencies, it falls outside their primary focus of attention." Another reason for its late arrival on the development agenda is that malnutrition is not dramatically visible. It has been identified as the world's number one health problem and is associated with more deaths and disease than the occasional famines, but unlike famine, which attracts worldwide attention, it is unobtrusive and lacks drama. Berg states that the most telling reason it is neglected is that its ravages are limited to the poor, and those who are better off are isolated from its effects. He goes on to say, "Malnutrition does not raise the pervasive concern of the politically and socially vocal classes that an ailment like malaria, which knows no class bounds, arouses." There is an exact analogy here with the case of poliomyelitis and tuberculosis in the United States (O. G. Simmons, 1958). Fund-raising for support of research on poliomyelitis was always on a much greater scale than for tuberculosis. When treatments for the latter were developed, professional interest far exceeded public interest, but when Salk developed his poliomyelitis vaccine, public interest far exceeded professional, and he became a national hero. The fact is that poliomyelitis rates and numbers of associated deaths were always relatively low compared with those of other mass diseases, while tuberculosis rates were at least four times as high and the number of deaths due to the latter substantially outnumbered those attributable to poliomyelitis. Tuberculosis and poliomyelitis were both public threats, but the crucial difference is that tuberculosis was relatively confined to lower-income groups, while poliomyelitis was not.

The two-way causation between health and nutrition has not always been taken into account, so that research findings on the relationship are sometimes rather dubious. With regard to the effects of health on nutrition, Barlow (1979) pointed out that certain diseases cause a decline in nutritional status. Diseases involving diarrhea cause a rapid loss of nutrients. Also, for example, the loss of appetite that accompanies some diseases may lead to under- or malnutrition.

As for the effects of nutrition on health, nutritional status is a significant determinant of health, since children of below-average weight for their height have lower levels of resistance to illness. In general, as Barlow (ibid.:63) said, "It is to be expected that undernourished persons will be more likely to suffer from those diseases which are associated with deficiencies of certain specific nutrients, such as rickets, pellagra, scurvy, and goiter." Berg (1973) stated that the bulk of child deaths in the LDCs are attributable to otherwise minor childhood infections that are aggravated by the children's malnourished state. He said (ibid.:35), "All this suggests that improved nutrition among those cohorts in the population experiencing high child mortality may be an important condition for reducing child death rates."

While in general good nutrition has a positive effect on health, firm knowledge about the nature and magnitude of that effect is still scant. Berg noted that many of the links among diet, performance potential, and economic returns are poorly understood and may remain so, given the complexities of human development and behavior.[7] Little is known, for example, about the relative damage caused by "different degrees of malnutrition at different ages and of varying durations" (ibid.:26). Berg (ibid.:27) went on to say that "the known numbers [in the LDCs] of those whose lives will be marked by illnesses that seriously strike the malnourished are so great, and the effects of malnutrition on educational and productive capacity so apparent, that investment in nutrition programs can almost be undertaken as an act of faith." Cassen (1976) discussed the well-known problems of measuring the extent of malnutrition. Much more research is needed to judge which measures are best adapted to the conditions of particular countries.

Edmonston and Martorell (1984) have formulated a conceptual scheme to describe what they consider to be the key aspects of the relationship between undernutrition and infant and child mortality in the LDCs. Their model suggests four main demographic–nutritional linkages, namely, nutritional status of infants and children and their mortality risk; breast feeding, infant feeding, and mortality; demographic aspects of breast feeding; and correlates of childhood nutritional status.

A central tenet of demographic-transition theory has held that a decline in infant and child mortality is strongly and rapidly linked to a decline in fertility. The theory, it will be recalled, based on the European experience, described three stages: a pretransitional stage in which a population achieved an equilibrium in size by maintaining relatively high birth and death rates, a transitional stage of imbalance created by continuing high fertility but declining mortality that led people to realize that the probability of their children's survival was increasing, and a final stage in which an equilibrium was reestablished as people began to control their fertility in line with lower mortality. Dominated by these notions, research focused on the relationships between the declines in vital rates and modernization and on attempts to document the details of the interaction between mortality and fertility. In the latter area, much of the work was oriented to the "child survival hypothesis," which held that the increased certainty of survival following declines in mortality should produce declines in fertility. In its earlier formulations, it was simplistically argued that as long as parents do not expect most of their children to survive, it is unreasonable to expect them to be interested in fertility reduction. As described by C. E. Taylor, Newman, and Kelly (1976), experience with or fear of child mortality may lead parents to have additional children, either to "replace" those who have already died or as "insurance" against expected deaths, from which it follows that improved child survival will increase motivation to limit births and thus lead to fertility decline.

C. E. Taylor et al. (ibid.), who were among the foremost proponents of the child survival hypothesis, subsequently qualified their earlier view. They revised their position to indicate, among other things, that reduced child mortality is not necessarily a precondition for fertility reduction, that there was little basis for suggesting that the postulated fertility reduction attributable to increased child survival expectations might compensate fully for the population growth effects of reduction in child mortality, and that if there is a significant effect, it would probably be indirect and subconscious rather than volitional.

Typically, declines in fertility have in fact been preceded by declining mortality.[8] As Cassen (1976:788) stated: "Cases of major fertility decline in the absence of mortality improvements are so rare in LDCs today that many regard the reduction of infant and child mortality as virtually a precondition for large reductions in fertility." Miro and Potter (1980:92) noted that "in cross-sectional analyses of countries or of political divisions within countries, the level of mortality . . . is found to be a significant predictor of fertility." Cassen (1976) also observed, however, that in many LDCs, mortality has declined markedly but fertility has declined very little or, as in some African countries, has even risen.

After a critical examination of the available evidence, Preston (1978b) concluded that infant and child mortality levels cannot explain fertility rates or family size and that reduction of mortality is not likely to be conducive to adoption of fertility control. He flatly observed (ibid.:15): "The picture is not attractive for those who look to mortality reduction as a means of reducing fertility through familial effects, let alone for those who advocate such measures . . . to reduce growth rates. Nor does it lend much support to models of fertility decision making that view couples as proceeding deliberately and with minimal encumbrances toward some target number of surviving children." Preston's conclusion is paralleled by that of Francine van de Walle (1986) with regard to the relationship between infant mortality and fertility in the European demographic transition: "At the end of this quest," she concludes (*ibid.*:233) after a thorough analysis of the data, "we cannot report that the historical evidence confirms that the declines of infant mortality led to the decline of fertility. . . . Both declines occurred in the course of modernization." Kunstadter (1979:72), in reviewing the Preston book, commented that "the results of these studies suggest that we can now state that the amount of fertility reduction to be expected as a direct result of mortality control is small and probably inconsistent. High mortality does not cause populations to grow; lowering mortality, by itself, will not cause populations to grow more slowly. . . . One hopes that it [the Preston volume] will serve as a tombstone, as well as a milestone, in the study of demographic transitions."

These assessments by Preston and Kunstadter do not mean that there is no replacement effect at all, as both explicitly state. A number of scholars (Barlow, 1979; Birdsall, 1977; Butz and Habicht, 1976; Jones, 1978; Schultz, 1976) cite evidence for what may be called an "incomplete replacement effect." Preston (1975) himself indicates that populations at the lowest levels (Senegal and Bangladesh) and highest levels (France) of socioeconomic development appear to display the strongest replacement effect, while countries at intermediate levels (Mexico, Colombia, Taiwan) show relatively weaker effects or none at all. The reduction of infant mortality has its own justification, of course, but it is doubtful whether research on the role of infant mortality as a determinant of fertility is likely to have much of a policy payoff. Since such factors as family income, education, and economic growth probably distort the results of attempts to measure the direct relationship between fertility and infant mortality, research on how these factors affect both fertility and infant mortality is likely to have greater potential policy significance. Jones (1978) observed that in East and Southeast Asia, for example, perhaps the one ubiquitous element in all the regions in which fertility has declined rapidly is a preceding substantial decline in infant and child mortality. But then infant mortality also declined in most regions in which fertility has not declined. Jones suggested that a decline in infant mortality may be a necessary precondition for sustained fertility decline, but not a sufficient one.

In any case, as Bongaarts and Menken (1983) and Chen (1983) propose, there is need for identification of a set of generally accepted proximate determinants the effects of which on mortality at the individual level could be studied separately and in combination, as is now possible in the case of fertility. According to Bongaarts and Menken (1983), there is a surprising lack of consensus about the relative importance of the determinants (both proximate and socioeconomic or sociocultural) of early mortality. Clarification of this issue could throw light on the complex interrelationships between fertility and mortality, since the research to date has yielded both negative and positive findings. Whatever may be the direct relationships between fertility and mortality, it is likely that the same set of social, cultural, and economic factors and various intervention strategies are affecting both birth and death rates (O. G. Simmons, 1982).

There are effects of health and nutrition on fertility, apart from mortality, that merit investigation. Research is needed on the links among breast feeding, helath, nutrition, and social and economic change. The extent to which postpartum lactation provides contraceptive insurance has been the subject of some research (Bongaarts and Menken, 1983; Butz and Habicht, 1976; Menken, Watkins, and Trussell, 1980; Nag, 1983; Winikoff and Brown, 1980). As Butz and Habicht (1976:215) put it: "It is known that mothers in many low-income cultures are aware, in general terms, of the contraceptive function of lactation. To the extent that they breast-feed in order to delay their next pregnancies, it is reasonable to expect them to substitute cheaper or more effective goods or services for their own time when such substitutes become available. The extent to which they do so is not known."

Virtually all the reviews of the effects of health and nutrition on fertility converge on the conclusion that these effects are relatively small and insignificant. Given the earlier discussions of the importance of economic, sociocultural, and institutional factors in explaining the variation in the proximate determinants of fertility, this conclusion should come as no surprise (cf. Bongaarts and Menken, 1983:49). As Winikoff and Brown (1980:173) observed, ". . . it is now becoming clear that feeding people better does not increase the birth rate." They went on to say that nutrition-dependent differences in fertility are comparatively small and are of only marginal significance in determining numbers of births and birth intervals.

Bongaarts (1979) reviewed in detail the evidence for the hypothesis that malnutrition inhibits fecundity[9] and found that it provides only very weak support. He did find that malnutrition can impair the function of the process of human reproduction and that this effect is strongest and most evident in cases of famine and starvation, when both fecundity and fertility are reduced significantly. But he went on to say (*ibid.*:21–22) that "moderate chronic malnutrition has only a minor effect on fecundity and the resulting decrease in fertility is very small. . . . It may be concluded that a large improvement in the level of nutrition in the underdeveloped countries will at most result in a slight increase in fertility." Like Winikoff and Brown, he observed that a concern for the fertility impact of food aid to the poor nations is unwarranted.

Like Bongaarts, Gray (1983) found, in his review of the relevant literature, that severe malnutrition can have a marked effect on fertility, but the effects of moderate malnutrition on fertility are not significant. As regards health and fertility, Gray observed that malnourishment and ill health frequently occur together and interact so that it becomes extremely difficult to distinguish between nutrition and health effects on fertility. Gray's principal conclusions indicate that there is strong evidence that demographically significant levels of infertility (as in some parts of Africa) are associated with a high prevalence of pelvic inflammatory disease, but with this exception, "health and nutrition have not been shown to have a significant direct demographic effect on fertility among large populations in the developing world" (ibid.:156).

Looking in the other direction, there is a substantial literature on how high fertility may affect the health and nutrition of mothers and children. The evidence, as in all the sectors considered here, may be uneven, at times thin, and sometimes ambiguous. A substantial number of scholars (Austin and Levinson, 1974; Barlow, 1979; Menken et al., 1980; Scrimshaw, 1978; Watson, Rosenfield, Viravaidya, and Chanawongse, 1979; Winikoff and Brown, 1980; Wray, 1971) have affirmed the proposition that apparently the only fate for a child worse than being born into a large poor family is also being high in the birth order.[10] Berg (1973) provided a dramatic illustration when he reported for India that children with three or more older siblings constituted 34% of the child population, but 61% of all cases of protein–calorie malnutrition. He went on to say that during the Bihar famine relief program in 1966–1967, the most severe cases of malnutrition were invariably children from large families: "Nearly four times as much serious hunger and nearly five times as much protein–calorie malnutrition were found among the younger children of large families" (ibid.:37). As Watson et al. (1979) said, higher parity entails progressively higher reproductive risks for the mother, and again, they affirm that health risks and developmental problems appear to occur more frequently in larger families than in small ones and more to children of higher than lower birth order. In this connection, family planning programs clearly have an important role to play, since they address the problems of high maternal and child mortality, which are two of the most serious health problems in the LDCs (Population Information Program, 1984a).

Winikoff and Brown (1980:172–173) state that short birth intervals are even more detrimental than high parity in increasing health risk.

They say: "It is also clear that closely spaced and frequent births not only jeopardize infant health but are associated with poorer maternal health and nutritional status. . . . High parity women are, in addition, subject to increased risk of complications in pregnancy and childbirth."

Cassel (1971) wrote about the high susceptibility to health deficits of those segments of a population who have had the least previous experience with living in crowded conditions (e.g., in the case of migrants). To cite Winikoff and Brown (1980:173) again: "High fertility also results in family situations where there is increased crowding in limited housing facilities and poor hygienic circumstances. Crowded housing predisposes to transmission of infection and reduces availability of household goods for each member of the family." High population density in a favorable environment may not create major health problems, but in a setting of poverty, there is a high probability that any infection will spread (International Bank for Reconstruction and Development, 1980b).

Birdsall (1977:69) wrote that rapid population growth increases health costs, as is the case for education and other services: "More people require more health services. High fertility rates have an immediate effect on costs of health services since obstetric and pediatric needs constitute a substantial proportion of total demand for health services." Nevertheless, rapid population growth is not the only cause of inadequate health care. Much of this inadequacy can be attributed, in most LDCs, to the physician–hospital–high technology approach to health care. A shift to a primary health care approach could provide coverage for those large proportions of the population in need, instead of only a limited number, an issue that will be considered presently.

Jones (1978) asked the question, in the case of Southeast Asia, of why a substantial proportion of couples continue to want large families if the costs entail, as depicted here, a litany of reduced consumption per family member, impaired intellectual and physical development of children, increased ill health and malnutrition for parents and children, and increased maternal and infant mortality. There is some possibility that people are not generally aware of the links between family size and these problems, but Jones discounted this as a major reason. The principal reasons that the advantages of having many children are perceived to outweigh the disadvantages are the pronatalist supports to be found in the economic, sociocultural, and institutional contexts of fertility behavior, as considered at length earlier in this volume. Caldwell, Cain, and others have pointed to the need for old-age security, insurance against economic risk, and a reliable source of labor as prominent among these reasons. Another prominent reason is that where women's role options are limited and male dominance is high, a woman's status depends largely on the number of children she can bear. As has been repeatedly indicated, the particular combination of these and other factors that support high fertility is likely to vary widely among and within different countries in the developing world. To gain a better understanding of these variations for policy purposes, there is need for research at the community and family levels, to be complemented by country- and region-specific surveys.

As discussed in Chapter 4, the principal dimensions in the basic-needs approach and the factors considered to constitute the source of the important determinants of fertility largely coincide. Implementation of equity-oriented development policies, together with family planning programs, seems to offer as a concomitant the promise of eventual fertility decline, although how soon that decline would occur is uncertain. The International Labour Office manifesto on basic needs that appeared in 1976 was soon followed by a call at a conference sponsored by the World Health Organization and UNICEF in 1978 at Alma-Ata (in the Soviet Union) for all nations to implement programs of "primary health care" (PHC) to work toward health for all the world's people by the year 2000 (WHO/UNICEF, 1978). This call for PHC was clearly consistent with the spirit of the basic-needs approach. Indeed, Beenstock (1980:6) argued that the common denominator of basic human needs is in fact health and that "the challenge is to see how far it is possible to evolve principles of development policy where health is used as an organising framework for analysing basic needs."

Reforms in health care delivery might yield as much improved health as would an immediate reduction in demand due to lower rates of population growth. Instead of services for only a limited number, a shift to a PHC approach could provide coverage for those large proportions of the population in need in the LDCs (O. G. Simmons, 1982). Such an approach would include the following components (D. E. Bell, 1980): major participation by the community to be served, with some of the needed resources mobilized by the community; orientation to specific locations in the sense of designing the program to fit the actual circumstances of different communities; involvement of paramedical personnel of appropriate kinds; inclusion of other elements besides medical care, such as nutrition, water supply, health education, immunization, and specific therapies; emphasis on maternal and child health, including family planning; and linkages to a broader array of development efforts in education and agriculture and other income-producing activities.

There are formidable constraints and thorny issues that beset the implementation of large-scale PHC programs.[11] Since the Declaration of

Alma-Ata, progress has been slow, in large part due to these constraints. In an assessment of progress in PHC programs since Alma-Ata, Gish (1983:5) reported that in most countries, PHC has as yet relatively little to show "on the ground." But he went on to say that this may not be as relevant as to note that "the most important result of the Alma Ata initiative has been its contribution to the view that 'positive health' is much more than a mere outcome of economic growth and the application of technology. . . . It is in the longer run that the full contribution and efforts of the primary health care 'opening' will be judged." In any case, both reduction of fertility and adoption of a PHC approach (which in itself would help to reduce fertility) are indicated if the benefits of development are to be reaped by all.

This chapter began with a description of the debate about the world's future dominated by two extreme views, the "limited" view of the nature of the earth's resources and the "cornucopian" view, which espouses an expansionist outlook that pushes the limits to growth into the distant future. A prominent dimension of this debate has been the relationship between population pressures and natural resources, which was considered in the earlier discussion, and, within this question, the nature of the relationship between per capita food supply and population growth. A metaphor has been employed to depict the relationship between food and population, namely, that of a "race" between increases in food supplies and increasing population. In this view, progress is made when the percentage gain in national or world grain supplies grows faster than the percentage increase in population (Brown, 1977).

At this point, a huge literature has been generated, much of it speculative, as to whether the race can be "won," with both optimists and pessimists in generous supply. Birdsall (1977:70), citing an earlier appraisal by T. W. Schultz, noted that many questions remain unanswered because long-range projections of food supply and demand depend on unknown factors, such as changes in income and in agricultural technology, as well as "the heterogeneity of agricultural conditions throughout the world and the political plausibility of redistribution." The answers are still not available. As McNicoll (1984) noted, underestimating the scope of productivity gains as keeping pace with or exceeding the rate of population growth has been a common error in economic–demographic predictions since Malthus, and the opposite view, that technological rescue is always at hand, is no less subject to doubt.

From a global view, it is possible that food supplies can match the rate of population growth for a long time to come, even with current technology (Cassen, 1976). As Brady (1982:847) observed, "The world is neither in danger of running out of food, as some assert, nor on the verge of eliminating hunger, as others contend." Gilland (1983), however, warned that the consequences of relying on an excessively optimistic assessment of the future population–food supply balance would be so serious that a conservative judgment is justified, which he thinks is required by the momentum of population growth. Conceding that estimates for global carrying capacity and long-range demographic projections are subject to wide margins of error, Gilland projects that a world population of 7.5 billion will be reached fairly early in the next century, close to his estimate of the limits of global carrying capacity.

D. E. Bell (1986), while noting that most agricultural experts are optimistic about the world's capacity to feed the next 4 billion people, identifies a number of obstacles that will have to be overcome if this is to be achieved, among which are the following: To ensure adequate food supplies, there will be need for a continuing flow of new food-production technologies; policies will be needed to provide incentives for farmers to adopt new food-production technology, in the form of adequate markets, prices, land tenure, credit services, and lines of supply; increased food production will impose substantial pressure on land and water resources, so that appropriate policies will have to be formulated to ensure that the natural-resource base will not be seriously depleted; and there is need to deal effectively in the LDCs with hunger and malnutrition that result from poor distribution of the food that is available, not from overall food shortages.

There have been other somber messages. Borlaug, Anderson, and Sprague (1982:23), for example, contended that food and population constitute an "unequal equation" and that "those of us who work on the food production front have the moral obligation to warn the political, religious, and educational leaders of the world of the magnitude and seriousness of the arable land/food/population problem that looms ahead." Similarly, Hjort (1982:14) reported that the rate of growth in world agricultural production has been declining faster than the decline in the population growth rate and that "if this pattern continues, in another 20 years or so global food production could slip behind population growth."

In the view of Murdoch (1980), employing the metaphor of a "race" is seriously misleading. He contends that rapid population growth and inadequate food supply have a common origin and a joint explanation. In his view (*ibid.*:6–7), population and food problems are symptoms of common causes, and "the same political, economic, and social machinery both drives rapid population growth and constrains food production. That machinery has created and maintained the *structural poverty of rural populations* in the underdeveloped world . . . and is the cause of both rapid population growth and inadequate food supplies" [emphasis in original].

The most widely accepted estimate of the number of malnourished people, most of whom are to be found in the LDCs, is about 460 million; malnutrition appears to contribute to between one third and two thirds of all child deaths, and perhaps even more in the poorest countries (*ibid.*). To the extent that the race metaphor dominates views about the relationship between food supply and population growth, the extent of chronic undernutrition and its consequences is effectively masked. Brown (1977) maintained that per capita consumption of grain could increase sharply while the availability of grain for those who need it most could fail. Concentration on actual consumption figures diverts attention from the fact that large numbers of people are already malnourished. As Brown (*ibid.*:11–12) said, "Consumption on the part of those with adequate incomes can rise while the number of malnourished also grows. We can appear to be 'winning the race' while the magnitude of human misery increases." Over the next decade and beyond, prospects for the poor majority to attain a minimally adequate diet appear dim. Hulse (1982:1294) stated that "the lowest income food-deficient nations, which represent almost two-thirds of the total population of the developing countries, showed a food deficit equivalent to about 12 million tonnes of cereals in 1975. In these same low-income countries it is forecast that by 1990 the food grain deficit may be six to seven times that of 1975."

Much of the optimism associated with food resources keeping up with population growth has been generated by the capacity of the DCs, taken as a whole, to produce surpluses for export. A number of agricultural experts find this a weak reed and have urgently advocated building indigenous capacity for food production (Brady, 1982; D. G. Johnson, 1976; Mellor, 1975, 1978; Williams, 1981; Wortman, 1976). According to World Bank staff (International Bank for Reconstruction and Development, 1984:91), "Various studies suggest that the gap between domestic supply and demand [for food] is projected to widen in the developing countries, particularly because of continued rapid growth in population and income." Increasing population will result in more demand for food, and the LDCs will be forced to import larger amounts.[12] Estimates of the probable amounts of these imports vary, but range up to more than 100 million tons a year by 1990, at an annual cost of about $20 billion (Murdoch, 1980). Large imports of food cause a severe drain on the limited foreign exchange that many of the poorest LDCs can earn and constitute a serious constraint on their economic growth. The balance between food and population is also more precarious than the global picture suggests, because food production around the world varies from year to year. Shortfalls in production in some years can cause greatly increased hardship, particularly when bad weather causes simultaneous reductions in various parts of the world. According to Barr (1981:1087), the low-income countries need a massive infusion of capital investment, research support, and education if they are to build infrastructures that have the capacity to produce, distribute, and market food supplies: "Other options serve only to prolong and aggravate current disparities."

It is clear that food consumption by large sections of the population in all but the richest LDCs is below what is needed for a minimally adequate diet. Hunger and malnutrition are due not so much to rapid population growth as to poverty. Those who need food cannot obtain it because they do not have the money to buy it or produce it, not because supplies are inadequate in some absolute sense. But increased income is not enough unless that income can reach beyond the established farmers to the poor to assure them, as indicated above, of access not only to new food production technology but also to markets, credit, and politically sanctioned benefits of broad-based development. What is needed, according to Mondot-Bernard (1978:78), is acceptance, as a major goal of any development plan, "of a guarantee of nutritional adequacy for the entire population."

As in the case of other key variables associated with fertility, Pinstrup-Andersen and Kumar (1984) note that food policy does not affect fertility directly but through intermediate factors, so the principal task is to identify the factors through which food policy is most likely to have fertility-reducing rather than fertility-enhancing effects. They attach the greatest importance to the level and stability of real incomes of low-income households and to the demand for and shadow cost of women's time.[13] Their principal recommendation (ibid.) is that the goal of fertility reduction will be most effectively realized through the design of policies that will maximize self-sustained economic benefits for low-income households and for the most disadvantaged in such households, namely, women and children, and this holds for the goals of improved nutrition as well.

NOTES

[1]The position of Simon and Kahn (1984:45) is as follows: "Environmental, resource, and population stresses are diminishing, and with the passage of time will have less influence than now upon the quality of human life on our planet. . . . Because of increases in knowledge, the earth's 'carrying capacity' has been increasing throughout the decades and centuries and millenia to such an extent that the term 'carrying capacity' has by now

no useful meaning. These trends strongly suggest a progressive improvement and enrichment of the earth's natural resource base, and of mankind's lot on earth."

[2]It may be noted that the World Bank itself, as well as the regional development banks, have been criticized by conservation organizations for neglecting what may be the negative environmental impact of some of their development assistance projects. See Shabecoff (1986) and Adams (1987).

[3]For reviews of these issues, see Boserup (1984) and Choi and Hicks (1984).

[4]On the problem of coordination of rural development policies and population policies, see O. G. Simmons (1984a) and Chapter 8.

[5]As noted earlier, about two thirds of the developing world's population resides in rural areas and includes the vast majority of the world's poorest people. Their reproduction rates are among the highest in the world, and the rural poor will account for most of the population growth in the LDCs throughout the remainder of the century.

[6]Indeed, the average percentage decreased from 6.1% in 1972 to 3.0% in 1982 in low-income economies and from 6.5% in 1972 to 4.7% in 1982 in middle-income economies. See Table 26 on central government expenditure in International Bank for Reconstruction and Development (1985:224–225).

[7]In a review of the consequences of malnutrition, one nutritionist, Calloway (1980:19), reached the sweeping conclusion that "virtually nothing that the scientific community has discovered about nutrition in this century has altered the prevalence of severity of the dominant form of malnutrition. We know a great deal about energy–protein malnutrition—almost everything, in fact, except what causes it and how to prevent it. And what it costs society not to do so."

[8]In considering the effects of mortality on fertility, one should not forget the obvious but important point that it was the dramatic decreases in mortality in the LDCs in the postwar period that largely led to rapid population growth. As Stollnitz (1975:221) observed: "Mortality trends in the past few decades have been the dominant cause of the greatest acceleration of world population in history. Although gains in longevity are encountered in all regions, rich and poor, their extraordinary pace in low-income areas has brought about enormous differences between actual population growth and its prospects in the economically developed countries, on the one hand, and the less developed countries, on the other."

[9]As noted in Chapter 5, fecundity refers to the physiological capacity to produce a live child, fertility to actual reproductive performance.

[10]In an interesting paper, Scrimshaw (1978), in questioning the traditional assumption that high mortality leads to high fertility, advanced the idea that it is parental "underinvestment" in unwanted, high-birth-order children that may result in higher levels of morbidity and mortality. She suggested (ibid.:397) that "high fertility may be accompanied by the acceptance or even the unconscious encouragement of high mortality."

[11]For discussions of these constraints, see Cassen (1978c), Joseph and Russell (1980), Population Information Program (1982), and O. G. Simmons (1982). See also Mosley (1983), who proposed an analytical model for assessing the effectiveness of PHC programs as well as for improving their operation.

[12]The average volume of cereal imports by the low-income economies increased substantially between 1974 and 1983, primarily in China, India, and sub-Saharan Africa, and in the case of middle-income economies virtually doubled between 1974 and 1983. See Table 6 on agriculture and food in International Bank for Reconstruction and Development (1985:184–185).

[13]The shadow cost of women's time is the demand for and economic productivity of women's time in food production, processing, marketing, and consumption-related activities as opposed to the time women allocate to child care.

Sectoral Reviews II $\mid$ 7

In this chapter, the discussion moves on to a consideration of the relationships between the status and employment of women and fertility and of that between education and fertility. In these sectors, as in those just discussed, assessment of the effects on fertility is enormously complicated by the fact that these effects are essentially indirect, as Cochrane (1979, 1983), for example, has demonstrated so effectively in the case of education, which has been widely regarded as perhaps the most strategic development-linked variable affecting fertility.

STATUS AND EMPLOYMENT OF WOMEN

It has been observed that in the development debate, the principal protagonists have effectively omitted any reference to the place of women in the development process (Ahooja-Patel, 1977, 1982). The human and economic costs of this neglect are high in many of the less-developed countries (LDCs), especially in rural areas. Dixon (1978) has referred to a Chinese adage that women "hold up half the sky," but until recently this acknowledgment has not prevented women from remaining virtually invisible in most development plans. Dixon went on to specify four factors that have contributed to the neglect of women by development planners: (1) Males dominate decision-making in international and national planning agencies, in which women are largely underrepresented or are not represented at all. (2) The productivity of rural women is "invisible" because their work is performed mainly in the informal sectors of the economy, in subsistence farming, and in the home. (3) Planners favor large-scale projects and show little interest in improving the primitive technology used by women in domestic and farm work. (4) Women have little capacity, because of their powerlessness due to economic and cultural constraints, to bring about policy changes that would help them share in the benefits of development. As Anker, Buvinic, and Youssef (1982:27) noted in their proposal for a program of research on the interrelationships between women's roles and demographic change: "By focusing on a 'missing link' in economic development—women and their economic behaviour—researchers should be in a better position to advise policy-makers interested in equity, poverty, development, employment, women and population issues."

In reporting on the proceedings of a seminar on women in development, Tinker and Bramsen (1976) stated that there was unanimity among the participants, who came from 55 developed countries (DCs) and LDCs, that in no country were women being equally integrated into the economies of their countries or into the decision-making apparatus, so that development efforts have tended to favor men at the expense of women in myriad ways. One of the earlier works to point out that women often do not share in the benefits of development programs and may in fact be affected negatively is that of Boserup (1970). Since then, this theme has become prominent in the rapidly growing literature on women in development (Charlton, 1984; Dixon, 1983). Tinker (1976:33), for example, claimed that the development process has tended to restrict the economic independence of women by eroding their traditional jobs through the introduction of new methods and technology. She attributed this negative effect to Western stereotypes of appropriate roles and occupations that are exported with foreign aid and bring "modernization [that] continually increases the gap between women's and men's ability to cope with the modern world." Similarly, Huston (1979:115–116), in her study of Third World women in six LDCs, stated that "Western modes of development—tending to emphasize urban growth and male employment—have increased disparities between men and women in all areas of life: physical and social mobility, economic and political status, and interpersonal relationships."

Writing about the impact of mechanization, Margaret Mead (1976) noted that where traditional agricultural conditions prevail, women are still the principal producers of food. Where technical change is occurring, however, women are being displaced by machines, which, the prevalent belief is, only men can operate. Consequently, with agricultural development, women are being converted from producers of food to consumers only. Drawing on evidence mainly from Africa, Palmer (1977) found that agricultural modernization tends to increase the workload of women where such modernization involves both additional labor-intensive work and high-productivity work, since women are usually relegated to the former and excluded from the latter. To the extent that they are allocated the labor-intensive, poorly paid, or totally unremunerated work, they experience greatly diminished access to the returns, in cash or produce, on their own labor and a consequent decline in their control over the family's purchasing power.[1] In an evaluation of a large-scale rural development project (fictitiously entitled the Nemow Project) concerned principally with the project's impact on women, Palmer (1979) provided a clear example of how development objectives can be severely hindered by neglect of women. She concluded (*ibid*.:78) that "the principal lesson of the Nemow Project is that many of the weaknesses in the performance of production, income distribution, education, health and nutrition can be traced back to women's lack of access to resources in their own right."[2]

The effects of urban and industrial development may be as adverse for women as are those of rural development. Industrial development may provide opportunities for more paid jobs for women, but result in their exploitation by offering them only low-level work in the lowest-paid sectors. Moreover, where discrimination subjects them to unemployment, they do not have even traditional work to fall back on as a recourse. In the long run, however, industrial development may yield beneficial effects for women. Whyte (1978) pointed out that industrialization leads to a decline in the importance of agriculture in a society's economy and to a similar decline in the family as a basis for economic production. To the extent that new occupational opportunities emerge for women, the traditional economic motivations for control of family members become less important, as does concern for marriage alliances and maintaining the family labor force, so that some of the disadvantages suffered by women in predominantly agrarian societies can diminish.

In fact, the knowledge base about the effects of development on women is too thin and ambiguous to yield generalizations about the conditions of development under which the status of women improves, remains the same, or worsens. Research on this question is plagued by the fact that women's participation in the economy is frequently underreported because of their involvement in the informal sector and because of their status as unpaid family workers (Boulding, 1983; Mueller, 1983; Vanek, Johnston, and Seltzer, 1985). As Powers (1984) pointed out, there is an acute need to develop indicators that accurately reflect the real productive roles of women in the economy, as well as the changing family situations and changing economic responsibilities that women are assuming. She went on to say (*ibid*.:5) that "these indicators should also differentiate among different socio-economic groups of women in the society so that it is possible to make comparisons within a society as well as cross-national comparisons. . . . They must also focus on a comparison of the situation of women relative to that of men and make it possible to measure changes over time in the situation of women, as well as in the relative situation of men and women." Sociocultural and structural variation compounds the difficulties in developing such indicators. For example, Smock (1977b:211), writing about the effects of development in Ghana, states that "Ghana's development has enlarged the range of options available to some women, but at the expense of eroding women's autonomy and increasing their subordination to men. Although many women now enjoy some of the fruits of Ghana's development, including the opportunity to receive a primary school education, the social position and status of women relative to men has declined." Ghanaian society appears to be moving away from the traditional situation of male and female spheres of work and social relations into a new and more integrated situation between the sexes in which women are less separate but at the same time less equal.

Greenhalgh (1985) argues, in the case of Taiwan, that the rapid and impressive economic development achieved there may have been at the cost of increasing inequality between the sexes in areas of personal autonomy and in possession of socioeconomic resources, namely, education, occupation, income, and property. In her view (ibid.:301), "This pattern appears to extend throughout the region that includes Hong Kong, Taiwan, Japan, (South) Korea, and even the People's Republic of China." Whether or not this pattern in fact does extend to the rest of East Asia, however, needs empirical documentation. With regard to China, the study of Wolf (1985), for example, provides some support for Greenhalgh's claim, although her findings point primarily to the preservation of traditional gender inequality, rather than an increase. In assessing the consequences of the Chinese revolution for women, she says (ibid.:26): "What concerns me is the frequency with which a revolutionary government has stepped aside from one of its most earnestly stated goals, gender equality. Though the revolution for women has never been repudiated, it has been postponed all too many times." And she concludes (ibid.:261): "In China, a woman's life is still determined by her relationship to a man, be he father or husband, not by her own efforts or failures." Wong (1974:252), however, presents a different view: ". . . the general rise in the social, economic, and political status of women is not only the 'natural' result of economic development—as in the developed industrial countries—but also the 'unnatural' result of ideological forces exerted by both the government and the women's organizations acting under party guidance. It is this ideological coloring which has given the Chinese women's movement its unique character."

Deficiencies in the knowledge base about the effects of development on women can hardly constitute a justification for not moving ahead now with formulations of development policy specifically designed to yield positive effects for women (see Buvinic, 1983). Charlton (1984:218), for example, identified a number of criteria for "defining what constitutes a good development policy for women," which should "contribute to improved standards of living for girls and women, . . . provide minimal skills, such as literacy and numeracy, . . . expand the choices available to women in productive, income-generating activities, . . . [and] maximize the ability of women to participate in making the decisions that influence their lives." With regard to policy formulation, Safilios-Rothschild (1985a:26), in a review of the relationship between socioeconomic development and women's status in 75 LDCs, observes that "women's share of paid employment cannot increase unless policies giving priority to men in the allocation of scarce paid employment are modified." One of her principal conclusions (*ibid.*:25) is that "women's access to paid employment seems to be the most sensitive indicator of the status of women in developing countries not only because it taps the key dimension of economic independence but also because high access to this resource presupposes social development and social structural changes that weaken the operation of the sex stratification system."

As a concept, the "status of women" is hardly unidimensional and is certainly elusive. Dixon (1978:6–7) defined it "as the degree of women's access to (and control over) material resources (including food, income, land, and other forms of wealth) and to social resources (including knowledge, power, and prestige) within the family, in the community, and in the society at large." She went on to say that there is no way to arrive at a culture-free definition of "status," particularly one that reflects its many dimensions. The use by Whyte (1978:10) of the concept is similar to Dixon's, as "a broad and inclusive term that may cover the differential power, prestige, rights, privileges, and importance of women relative to men." Whyte's study used data from 93 "preindustrial" societies to make cross-cultural comparisons of the status of women relative to men. His findings make untenable the assumption that there is such a matter as *the* status of women cross-culturally, as well as the assumption that if women occupy a favorable position in a given area of social life, such position will necessarily be related to favorable positions in other areas. His findings also point out that there is no single best indicator of the status of women nor any particular key variable that affects the status of women. He maintained (*ibid.*:170) that "each aspect of the status, roles, and relationship of women relative to men must be examined and explained separately, unless future research shows a cross-cultural reality that is very different from the patterns we have discovered."

Whyte's work underlines the importance of cultural and structural factors in explaining the variety and diversity in the status of women, which are hardly to be explained by any simple biological determinism. Consistent with the perspective developed by Whyte, Oppong (1980), among other writers, viewed women as holding a configuration of statuses that not only obtain at one point in time but also change through the progress of their lives. She formulated a conceptual framework for research on women that identifies seven major roles that women perform in social life, namely, mother, worker, producer, wife, kinswoman, community member, and individual women (who may pursue individually chosen goals for her self-satisfaction). She stated (*ibid.*:4) that documentation of these roles "is vital for an understanding of demographic issues, including fertility and labour force participation, and for the design and execution of policies meant to affect these."[3]

Whatever may be the variety and diversity that characterize the status of women in different societies, inequality in the status of men and women is pervasive and usually characterized by male dominance. Giele (1977) stated that virtually no society in the world provides women equal status with men, and Rosaldo and Lamphere (1974) also noted that male dominance is to be found in all contemporary societies even though there are substantial variations among societies in the degree and expression of female subordination. Whyte (1978:180) was convinced that his analysis of preindustrial societies is mirrored in the life of women in modern societies, so he concluded that "there are no magic keys such that one particular breakthrough for women in legal rights, job participation, or sexual liberation will bring about general equality in all of social life. The obstacles to equality in various spheres will continue to be different and will have to be attacked separately."

The situation of women in Japan may be a case in point. According to Pharr (1977), postwar reforms eliminated prewar legal provisions that restricted the freedom, rights, and range of opportunities open to women and have led to high enrollment rates at all levels of education, increased entry into the labor force, higher voter turnout than among males, and a growing desire to play the decisive role in choosing a marriage partner. Growing numbers of women are taking advantage of these new opportunities, but (*ibid.*:251) "of those who do so . . . most continue to plan their lives with the primary goal of becoming wives and mothers. Japanese society still judges the adult woman primarily on the basis of her performance in the wife–mother role."[4] It seems clear that if women are to achieve equal status with men, substantial sociocultural as well as structural transformations will have to be implemented to provide women adequate access to material and social resources.

In the developing world, gender inequality is probably most deeply ingrained in the Muslim countries, in which it is powerfully reinforced by the patriarchal kinship, political, legal, and religious systems (Mernissi, 1976; Allman, 1978; Sadik, 1985). Within the Muslim world, the women of Bangladesh must be among the most severely disadvantaged.[5] Smock (1977a) found that despite this circumstance, Bangladeshi women do not feel oppressed because their acceptance of the structural and cultural attributes of purdah (seclusion of women from public observation) continues to make tolerable the limitations on their freedom of choice and opportunity: "Women, no less than men, endorse the precepts that sanctify an inferior and dependent status for them. Both men and women consider women's subordinate position natural, inevitable, and proper" (*ibid.*:121). An analysis by Cain, Khanam, and Nahar (1979) indicates that although Bangladeshi women undoubtedly value the status they achieve by maintaining high standards of purdah, they are quite aware of their insecurity and the high risks they face as the pressure of increasing poverty weakens male bonds of obligation to support women. In this deteriorating situation, women do what they can to hedge against risk and to create independent sources of security. According to Cain *et al.* (*ibid.*:433), "The best insurance for women . . . is to produce sons, as many and as soon as possible. . . . The risks that patriarchy generates for women are . . . independent and powerful incentives for high fertility, and given the strength of underlying patriarchal institutions, they present a significant obstacle to government population policy initiatives" (see also Cain, 1984).

A prominent theme in the literature on the status of women is that broadening women's role options would be conducive to lower fertility. Without access to opportunities for roles other than or in addition to motherhood, a woman's status depends largely on the number of children she can bear (Germain, 1975). In this pervasive concern with the relationship of women's status and roles to fertility, a principal focus has been on the relationship between women's labor-force participation and fertility (Kupinsky, 1977a; Standing, 1978, 1983; Weller, 1984). There is little consistency in the research findings regarding this relationship, leading Safilios-Rothschild (1978) to suggest that these contradictory findings can be understood better within a larger analytical framework that identifies the ideological and structural characteristics of the relationship between spouses. As she bluntly put it (*ibid.*:2): "Women's gainful employment outside the home does not begin to make a dent on their fertility unless the ideological nature of the husband–wife relationship and the structural relations between men and women in the society are such that women's work is similarly evaluated and paid as men's work."

If gender equality is to prevail, not only must women's work become as socially acceptable and materially rewarding as men's, but also, as indicated earlier, women must be accorded adequate accesss to and control over other resources as well. S. Zeidenstein (1979:310) observed that "both a woman's point of view about preferred family size and her willingness to act on this performance are influenced by her access to valued resources, her control over them throughout her lifetime vis-à-vis males, and the economically based social pressures to fulfill an accepted role." With regard to rural women, Palmer (1979) maintained that if the basic-needs approach is to be genuinely effective for them, it will have to open up redistribution of land and other assets for women as well as men beyond the level of the domestic unit and provide equitable economic and occupational opportunities for women.[6]

Precisely because women are less likely than men to own land or to have legal rights to land use, Dixon (1985) argues that there is need for a policy of rural development that would pay special attention to increasing opportunities for women in nonagricultural employment, i.e., in small-scale rural industries, construction, marketing, and upgraded service jobs. Moreover, she maintains (*ibid.*:18) that such "expansion of the employment opportunities for rural women . . . is not only a valuable end in itself, but also a means to enable women to transcend the inherent pro-natalism of patriarchal kin-based institutions."

N. E. Johnson (1984) reported that in Bangladesh, the institutions of purdah, kinship, and Muslim law preserve the gender inequalities of family production by granting women access to land only through men, while in India women can cultivate their own holdings. She noted that the limited success of land reform in several Indian states has benefited women financially and may partially account for the lower fertility in these states than in Bangladesh. Improving women's occupational and educational opportunities, ownership of assets, and participation in rural development on equal terms with men has its own justification, but adding the fertility-reduction potential to such development projects increases the benefits of the projects relative to their given costs.

Research on the relationship between female labor-force participation and fertility, undertaken in urban, industrialized settings in the DCs, tended to support the proposition that increased labor-force participation is associated with reduced fertility (Kupinsky, 1977a). Thus, the findings encouraged the view that female employment should be promoted as a powerful means of reducing fertility (Standing, 1983). Both economists and sociologists offered hypotheses to explain this inverse relationship (McGreevey and Birdsall, 1974). The economists focused on the opportunity cost of children, i.e., the income forgone by women who are not in the labor force because they are bearing and rearing children, so that the effect for working wives would be a decreased demand for children because of increased opportunity cost. The sociological explanation focused on role conflict, namely, on the notion that where mother and worker roles are most incompatible, an inverse relationship between female employment and fertility is most likely to appear (Dixon, 1976; Mason and Palan, 1981). In this situation, women are forced to choose between labor-force participation and the number of children they bear, so that if they wish to continue to work, they will opt for fewer children.

Research on the employment–fertility relationship in the LDCs indicates that the applicability of these hypotheses to the Third World is questionable and has yielded only ambiguous evidence (Mueller, 1982). As Dixon (1976:297) said, "The evidence holds primarily for nonagricultural work in the modern sectors of towns and cities—exactly the type of work that is extremely rare in the [developing] countries. . . ." Presumably, the degree of incompatibility between worker and mother roles is determined largely by a number of factors related to the location of work, i.e., whether at home or away from home, and/or to the type of child care available. With regard to location, there does not appear to be any consistent inverse association between urban industrial employment and lower fertility, on one hand, or a positive association between household-based rural employment and higher fertility, on the other. As Standing (1983:521) observed: ". . . establishing a causal relationship between more urban, modern types of employment and fertility levels is problematical. More modern, urban jobs may actually facilitate and subsidize childbearing, providing high incomes that enable women to afford children, and providing maternity leave and pay."

As to the question of child care, the role-incompatibility hypothesis usually assumes that patterns of child care are much the same everywhere and that if mothers cannot provide the care, then "mother substitutes" must be employed. Mason and Palan (1981) pointed out that this assumption violates the reality in much of the rural sector in LDCs, where children themselves often provide the "child care." Oppong (1983:564) noted that ". . . one of the most pervasive findings from historical and cross-cultural evidence on socialization is the extent to which children have traditionally been cared for by siblings, grandparents, and other kin. . . ." If women are willing to have children care for themselves or their siblings, they may have little sense of role incompatibility in working outside the home and thus would not reflect inverse employment–fertility relationships (Mason and Palan, 1981).[7]

To examine the compatibility between women's work and fertility according to the type of child care, Standing (1983) identifies a number of conditions under which fertility levels are least likely to constrain women's work activities, among which are: when there is an extended family with close ties to facilitate sharing of child care among members of the family, when the cost of the domestic labor to undertake child care in lieu of the mother is low, and when the family perceives the amount of desired input of parental time to be small.

It may be noted that the role-incompatibility hypothesis was derived essentially from the earlier perspectives oriented to the modernization model and demographic transition. The fact that much of the research in the DCs showed an inverse relationship between female employment and fertility (although not consistently so) led to the assumption that modernization, as it presumably spreads through the Third World, would invariably bring with it the industrialization of employment and consequently the inverse employment–fertility relationship (Mason and Palan, 1981). In a series of studies of women's roles and status in 8 DCs and LDCs, however, there was no correlation between the level of economic development or the degree of industrialization and women's employment (Smock, 1977c). Similarly, in her study of 13 LDCs in the Middle East and Latin America, Youssef (1974:5) found that in none of the countries was the relationship between levels of economic development and female labor force participation "repeating the pattern of the now-industrialized West."

The principal reviews of the voluminous literature on female employment and fertility all come to the same conclusion: There is no consistency in the empirical findings regarding the relationship; thus the nature of the current available evidence remains ambiguous (Kupinsky, 1977b; Safilios-Rothschild, 1977; Standing, 1978, 1983; Weller, 1984). In a number of LDCs, no inverse relationship has been found, including such different countries as Bangladesh (Chaudhury, 1978), the Dominican Republic (Gurak and Kritz, 1982), Mauritius (Hein, 1982), and Taiwan (Stokes and Hsieh, 1983). V. J. Hull (1977) reported contradictory findings on the relationship in the major countries of Southeast Asia. Also, a review of studies on female labor-force participation and fertility in Latin America showed no consistent inverse relationship (Davidson, 1977). The inverse relationship was fairly predominant in large cities, but virtually absent in small towns. Cleland (1985:239), in his review of marital fertility decline in the LDCs, reported that the World Fertility Survey "has failed to establish in a decisive manner an individual-level effect of female employment on fertility."

It is evident that there is rarely any simple direct relationship between female labor-force participation and fertility. As has been indicated, this is the case with virtually all the other major variables associated with fertility. In any particular country or setting, the interaction between female employment and levels of fertility is likely to be influenced by factors that affect both employment and fertility and cannot be understood in isolation from such other factors as the nature of the status of women, the type of family and kinship unit, education, motivation and work commitment, the prevailing norms concerning the employment of women, the occupational structure of the society or community, and women's access to occupational opportunities. Moreover, as Standing (1978:183) observed, "The conflicting results can often be traced to the widely varying methodological approaches that have been adopted in empirical studies and, in particular, differences in the number and type of control variables employed." Thus, one may conclude with Kupinsky (1977b:369) that the answer to the question of whether the fertility of working women is lower than that of nonworking women remains "a definite maybe! There is no consistent pattern, either in the less developed countries or the more developed countries, among all subgroups of working women."

Even where the inverse relationship between employment and fertility has been found, the fact that the finding has usually been based on cross-sectional data inhibits determining the causal direction of the relationship, as indicated earlier with regard to other variables associated with fertility. Cross-sectional studies usually leave unclear whether women have fewer children because they work or work because they have fewer children. In reviewing the evidence for the United States, where the role-incompatibility hypothesis was largely developed, Kupinsky (1977a:222) concluded that "the direction of causality is problematic and no single dominant causal path exists for all women under all circumstances."[8] He qualified this conclusion somewhat in stating that there is considerable evidence that "for some women the dominant causal path is from employment to fertility." The reading by Dixon (1978:7) of the literature led her to a different view, however. She said, "Recent research has leaned heavily toward the interpretation that, in almost all settings, fertility influences female labor-force participation more than vice versa." Standing (1983) concludes his review of the state of knowledge about the work–fertility relationship by maintaining that the literature is constantly finding sufficient reason, but no efficient cause. He proposed (ibid.:533) that future research "set up clean theoretical frameworks, pose alternative interpretations of observed relationships, and find better ways to refute some hypotheses in favor of others."

Safilios-Rothschild (1985b) pointed out that the high degree of intercorrelation between the indicators of women's access to valued resources makes it difficult to assess the relative importance of each of the indicators. Nevertheless, she viewed them all as important intermediate determinants of fertility, since they are so strongly related to the proximate determinants. On the basis of an analysis of socioeconomic indicators (data collected for 75 LDCs for 1970 and 1980) of women's access to such resources as food, health care, education, paid employment, and specialized training, among others, she concludes that women's access to paid employment and literacy seem to be the most important indicators. She emphasized (*ibid.*:22), however, that "only in-depth community studies can definitely help determine the improvement in which one dimension of the women's status is the necessary and sufficient condition for fertility decline." After reviewing the problems involved in the measurement of women's status, Mason (1984:23) concluded: "In sum, then, although a wide range of variables have been suggested as indicators of female status in the Third World, the validity of many of these indicators is unclear. . . . Even the most theoretically sophisticated studies may have trouble empirically assessing the impact of women's status on fertility or mortality patterns."

In any case, it is fair to say that the available evidence about the female labor–fertility relationship may be too ambiguous to support policies aimed at reducing fertility by increasing female labor-force participation. Nevertheless, improving the status of women by increasing their opportunities for labor-force participation and for ownership of assets on equal terms with men has its own justification. Moreover, gender equality in production and in decision making regarding reproduction is certainly more likely to enhance the potential for fertility reduction in the long run if not in the short run.

EDUCATION

As described in Chapter 1, Western views in the 1950s and 1960s on how the LDCs were to solve their social and economic problems focused on promotion of development, such as had been experienced in the West, which was equated with economic growth as measured by increases in per capita income. Approaches to education in the Third World were strongly influenced by this optimistic and simplistic perspective. Consequently, Western models of formal schooling were exported wholesale to the LDCs without their suitability being questioned. During the 1950s and early 1960s, there was great confidence in education as the main means of facilitating development. As Torsten (1980:xiii–xiv) noted, "Because development was to be reflected in gross national product, the main concern was with size and quantitative expansion, and, to this end, ambitious enrollment targets were set." Although universal literacy was and remains a political objective in many LDCs, expenditures on primary education were frequently regarded during the 1950s as a diversion of resources from training that would contribute more to economic growth. DC economists and LDC planners believed that economic growth could be impeded because of the lack of trained manpower at high and middle levels, so they favored the kinds of secondary and higher education that would presumably meet the manpower requirements of the industrial sector.

Manpower planning was initiated to cope with the anticipated problem, but now, several decades later, the result is that the LDCs are confronted with unemployment of the educated as perhaps their major educational problem (Blaug, 1979; Carnoy, 1980). As Carnoy (ibid.:153) stated: "Many developing countries face an apparent excess of highly educated labor; the average level of education in the labor force has increased, but so too has the average level of education among the unemployed. Furthermore, unemployment shows no signs of diminishing, even though the unemployed are in theory more adequately prepared than formerly to participate in the growth of the economy."

The euphoric confidence in education in the 1950s and 1960s was followed by more than a decade of criticism and disenchantment with formal education.[9] As J. Simmons (1980a:61–62) concluded: ". . . the assumptions which were used in the past need to be seriously questioned. Few planners and educators can say that the outcomes of the educational investment of the past two decades have made the contribution to either growth or to development that they had expected." The financial investment by the LDCs in education over the past few decades has been very heavy indeed. Their total public expenditure rose in real terms (in 1976 dollars) from about $9 billion in 1960 [2.4% of their collective gross national product (GNP)] to $38 billion in 1976 (4% of GNP). Costs vary widely by region, and school attendance in some parts of the world remains low, especially among the poor, in rural areas, and by girls. Among those in the LDCs who do enroll, 40% on average drop out before the fourth year (International Bank for Reconstruction and Development, 1980a).[10] It may be noted that the average expenditures for education as a percentage of total central government expenditures decreased substantially between 1972 and 1982 in low-income countries, although not in sub-Saharan Africa, and decreased slightly in middle-income countries (International Bank for Reconstruction and Development, 1985). According to Schultz (1985:1), "School expenditures in some low and middle income countries have recently not increased as rapidly as enrollment."

J. Simmons (1980a) pointed to two different explanations of why the

educational record is not better despite the massive investment that has
been made. One argument maintains that formal education systems in
the LDCs are irrelevant to those countries' needs. The proponents of
this explanation call for reform of education systems to meet the needs
of both the poor and the rich in more efficient ways and believe this can
be done without shifts in political and economic power. Those who hold
to the other explanation argue that although present education systems
do not address the priority needs of the poor majority, they are satisfying the priority needs of the elites to maintain political and economic
power, and that this explains why so many plans for educational reforms to increase the benefits to the poor have never been implemented.
Citing Adam Curle, J. Simmons (*ibid.*:62) said that "education . . . does
not so much free men from ignorance, tradition, and servility, as fetter
them to the values and aspirations of a middle class which many of them
are unlikely to join." It should be noted, however, that when the drive
for development in the Third World began, there was resistance, not
only on the part of elites but also by the masses, to making existing
education systems more relevant to development needs. As Ward
(1974:xvi) observed, ". . . the masses, offered education for the first
time, would accept no substitutes for places in the same inherited system that had given so many social and economic advantages to the
national elites."

The notable shift in development objectives, in the early 1970s, from
an exclusive preoccupation with economic growth to objectives concerned with equity and the reduction of poverty as well, which has been
repeatedly considered in this discussion, has begun to be reflected in
changing priorities in education. The shift in this sector is a change in
priorities away from education as fueling the engine for economic
growth, with the emphasis on sheer numbers to be enrolled in higher
levels of formal schooling, to an emphasis on the distribution of educational services and equality of access to education consistent with the
shift in perspective to broad-based development. Although secondary
and higher education have important roles to play, the value of general
education at the primary level is now more widely appreciated. World
Bank staff (International Bank for Reconstruction and Development,
1980a:48–49) noted that primary education is of particular importance in
overcoming absolute poverty; the rates of economic returns on primary
education are high. There are also favorable effects on equity. As primary education becomes more pervasive, additional spending will be
increasingly concentrated on rural areas, girls, and the poorest urban
boys. "In general, primary education tends to be redistributive toward
the poor. In contrast, public expenditure on secondary and higher edu-

cation tends to redistribute income from poor to rich, since children of poor parents have comparatively little opportunity to benefit from it" (*ibid.*).

In this connection, it should be stated that education does not necessarily create the gap between the rich and the poor or between the elite and the masses, but does serve to perpetuate or exacerbate these inequalities. Children of the rich everywhere have greater access to education, and particularly to higher education. Coleman (1965a:31) called this "the law of unequal development advantage" and went on to say: "The process of uneven development tends to continue according to its own logic and dynamic unless countervailing influences, such as egalitarian political policies, provide for equal access to education, or deliberately allocate resources not only to ensure regional equality, but also to 'level up' the less developed areas."

In looking at education in the Third World, there has been an unfortunate tendency to regard it as largely a homogeneous enterprise in which the only differences are quantitative (Coleman, 1965b). Such homogeneity may obtain at the primary school level, but at the secondary and higher levels of education, there is a wide variation in types of education, not only as to content but also in the impact of these different types on the perspectives and behavior of the recipients of this education. As would be expected, this variation reflects the great variety and diversity of cultural, institutional, and economic contexts and configurations among Third World countries. And just as education has been regarded as a homogeneous enterprise, so development has been viewed as a homogeneous process. These perceptions and assumptions of homogeneity have fueled the debate over what curriculum content contributes most directly and instrumentally to development. Coleman (1965c:528), however, was saying more than two decades ago: "By now it is abundantly evident that developmental requisites are not necessarily the same or even congruent in the different institutional spheres— educational, economic, and political; indeed, they may be and frequently are at variance, and sometimes even conflict with one another. Rapid educational expansion does not necessarily give rise to either economic growth or political development; economic growth has occurred without extensive educational development, and, in many instances, it has been politically destabilizing."

Although there is increasing awareness of the need to focus on considerations of equity if education is to play an influential role in development, a concomitant change in priorities is still largely to be effected. As J. Simmons (1980b:235) concluded in his review of the papers in an edited collection: ". . . for most developing countries, adherence to the current policies of educational investment will result in increasing inequality between the rich and the poor and little improvement in the efficiency of school systems. . . . If the objective is greater equality and efficiency, then a central problem is how to redefine the relationship among the actors in the reform process—the haves and have nots—to assure that both groups participate in the identification of their needs and the management of the investment programs."

In addition to the inequality between the rich and the poor, there is also a pervasive urban–rural inequality. Edwards and Todaro (1974:25) pointed to the urban bias in economic development as contributing to a related bias in education systems, i.e., "a strong orientation toward the educational needs of the modern urban sector." Unlike the assessment by Simmons that priorities have yet to change, Edwards and Todaro shared the more optimistic view that priorities are already changing in saying that the shift in development perspectives from economic growth to poverty-focused development has led policy-makers in a growing number of LDCs to evaluate education not only by its contribution to economic growth but also by its effects on poverty, employment, and income distribution. They maintained (*ibid.*:26) that the education system may at any stage of development exacerbate existing inequities or facilitate wider participation in the benefits of economic growth, but "it is unrealistic to expect the educational system itself to play a major role in directly redressing inequities which stem from factors outside of its control, namely distorted incentive systems, malfunctioning labor markets, and the political abuse of power." J. Simmons (1980b:235) stated, consistent with this view, that educational reform requires implementation of "a package of reforms which extends beyond the educational system to the labor market and the political arena."

Before moving on to a consideration of the relationship between education and fertility, it seems advisable to emphasize once again the need for thoroughgoing educational reform, through innovation and experimentation as spelled out by J. Simmons (*ibid.*). Only through such reform can education come to constitute a key component of broad-based development by enabling the larger population, rather than a small privileged minority, to acquire the knowledge and skills needed to participate fully in the process of economic and social development. The observations of R. M. Miller (1974:89–90) are apropos: "Education must . . . become less formal in the sense of taking account of local conditions and assisting people in a process of development that includes working out new roles for themselves. . . . What we need to turn attention to are alternative forms of education that are developed in relation to local needs and that utilize local skills. . . . The nonformal educational models of the developed world are often wildly inappropriate to conditions in developing countries."

In the literature on the determinants of fertility, perhaps the most widely accepted generalization is that of the inverse relationship between education and fertility. As in the case of the other links between development factors and fertility, it is tempting to settle for clear, simple, and linear relationships. Nevertheless, as has been shown in the case of the relationships between fertility and other development sectors, it is not possible to characterize them in any simple way. Since education affects fertility through a wide array of factors, it is not surprising that its effect is not consistently inverse.

In her review of the literature on fertility and education, Cochrane (1979) presented evidence to indicate that education may cause fertility to increase or decrease. The decrease is greater in relation to the education of women than of men and in urban than in rural areas. But education is more likely to be associated with an increase in fertility in countries with the lowest level of female literacy. The principal question addressed by Cochrane (1979, 1983) is that of how education operates through other variables. As she pointed out (1979:5): ". . . education by itself cannot directly affect actual fertility behavior but must act through factors such as preferences for large families, knowledge of birth control, health of parents and children, and so forth." She said (*ibid.*:55): "The distinction between direct and indirect effects is unclear . . . perhaps because it is difficult to conceive of how education by itself can alter fertility without acting through either biological or behavioral variables."[11]

It is true that the existence of a generally inverse relationship between education and fertility is fairly well documented. In his discussion of the findings of the World Fertility Survey, Cleland (1985:239) reported that "WFS individual-level analyses have furnished massive confirmation that higher levels of parental education are associated with the greater use of birth control and lowered marital fertility. Though the relationship varies considerably across countries in magnitude and form . . . the link persists . . . and it holds in both urban and rural settings." In an analysis of the data on education and fertility in India, for example, Jain and Nag (1985:49–50) found that "female education in India monotonically increases the use of contraception and age at marriage, both of which, in turn, decrease fertility," and they concluded that "advancement in female education can be expected to influence fertility behavior even without simultaneous changes in other factors such as increased opportunities in the paid labor force."

The neat model of the inverse relationship does seem to hold true for South Korea and Taiwan (Jones, 1978), for example, but in Southeast

Asia and in a number of African countries, there appears to be conflicting evidence. In Thailand, Goldstein (1972) found an inverse relationship between years of schooling of women and mean number of
children born in both rural and urban areas and concluded (*ibid.*:436)
that "overall, education plays a key role as an instrument of fertility
reduction." In the review by Jones (1978) of the findings for Southeast
Asia, some studies show the inverse relationship, but others, in
Thailand, Indonesia, Malaysia, and the Philippines, show a more or less
weak inverted U-shaped relationship between education and fertility.
Fertility is slightly lower for uneducated women than for women with a
few years of schooling and declines again at levels of education beyond a
few years. Similarly, with regard to Africa, Ware (1978:55) observed that
there is general agreement that a minimal degree of education serves to
raise rather than to lower fertility: "Evidence from an increasing number
of high-quality data sources show that women with primary education
have higher fertility than women with no formal education at all, and
that at least some secondary education is needed before fertility begins
to fall."

Although the explanations for this humpbacked pattern are speculative, they seem plausible. As noted by Cochrane (1979), some education seems to improve the health of women sufficiently to increase their
chances of conceiving and carrying their births to term. In a similar vein,
Ware (1978) suggested that women with primary education are better
nourished, more aware of hygiene, and generally healthier, so that they
experience less fetal wastage and thus have more live births.[12]

Ware touched on an important issue when she noted that the vital
question still to be answered is why education should have such a
powerful influence on women's fertility behavior. As she said (*ibid.*:78):
"Since secondary education for the majority of women [in Africa] is a
distant prospect and primary education may even serve to raise fertility
levels in the short term, it would be very rewarding to have more information as to precisely where the antinatalist effect of education is located." Mason (1984:52–53), in her review of the literature on the status
of women and fertility, accorded high priority to two factors as determinants of fertility: "understanding the full range of impacts that women's
schooling may have on their status as well as their fertility" and "the
position of women within the family or household."

In a review of the literature on education and fertility, Graff (1979)
placed principal emphasis on how education is conceptualized as an
independent variable and contended that the common ways in which
education is viewed account largely for the role it is typically found to
perform. As indicated earlier in this discussion, and as elaborated in

detail by Graff, simplistic and linear models view education as a homogeneous enterprise, consistent with the linear view expressed in the modernization model that high fertility is a traditional phenomenon that must change in a downward direction as education rises. As Bumpass, Rindfuss, Palmore, Concepcion, and Choi (1982:243) aptly put it, however: "Educational differences in fertility may reflect anything from the acquisition of new ideas, opportunities or aspirations to the filtering of certain skills, attitudes and social positions by the selection and attrition processes. . . . It is unlikely that in many settings education represents a single dimension."

As noted, Graff identified the task of conceptualizing education as the heart of the matter in reaching understanding of the education–fertility relationship. In looking at microeconomic, demographic-transition, and modernization "theories," he concluded that transition theory has probably yielded the weakest and loosest conceptualization. According to him (1979:119): "Education has meant all things and has played a wide variety of roles in the various formulations of demographic transition. It should not be surprising that complications are so often found." But the microeconomic and modernization approaches fare no better. Graff (*ibid.*) maintained that all these formulations are of little use in interpreting and explaining education–fertility relationships and that education should be viewed as more often contributing its influence on fertility less directly and less linearly, since it seems to operate and mediate through and with other factors, such as cultural and structural factors, as is the case with the other determinants of fertility.

Caldwell (1980) is in accord with the position taken by other scholars cited here that the principal impact of education on fertility is indirect, but his concern with this impact focused on the changes it brings in children rather than in their parents and on his model of family change and the reversal of intergenerational wealth flows, a conceptual framework described earlier in this discussion. In the view of Caldwell (*ibid.*:228), education makes children less productive and more costly to the family and introduces Western middle-class values. These changes in turn bring about changes in family economies "from a situation in which high fertility is worthwhile to one in which it is disastrous." For Caldwell, the key factor in the onset of fertility decline is the advent of mass education. He concluded (*ibid.*:249) that ". . . the evidence suggests that the most potent force for change is the breadth of education (the proportion of the community receiving some schooling) rather than the depth (the average duration of schooling among those who have attended school)."

The list of possible indirect effects of education on fertility is long, which is probably why the inverse relationship between the two is the most widely accepted generalization in the literature on the determinants of fertility. Holsinger and Kasarda (1976) compiled a list of the arguments that have been made for the indirect effects of education on fertility (see also Germain and Smock, 1974; McNamara, 1977; Cochrane, 1979, 1983; Jain, 1981). Some of these indirect effects are: Education facilitates acquisition of information on modern contraceptive methods and use; increases aspirations for upward mobility and accumulation of wealth, which reduces the desirability of large families; enhances a woman's prospects for obtaining outside employment, which competes with child-raising as a career (an argument shown to be subject to important qualifications); imparts and helps to inculcate a set of attitudes, values, and beliefs identified as the essence of "modernity," which motivates the practice of birth limitation (an argument also subject to a variety of qualifications); and delays age at marriage and thereby reduces the total possible number of a wife's childbearing years.

With regard to this last argument, it is true that most research findings indicate a strong correlation between rising levels of education and delay of age at marriage (see, for example, Cochrane, 1979, 1983; Rindfuss, Parnell, and Hirschman, 1983).[13] The premise that delaying age at marriage will lead to reduced fertility is pervasive in the literature, as indicated in a number of reviews (Population Information Program, 1979; P. C. Smith, 1983; Mason, 1984). But as Ware (1978:56) pointed out: ". . . it has yet to be demonstrated that the later age at marriage of the more highly educated is associated with lower lifetime fertility levels. . . . Available evidence for West Africa strongly suggests that, once started, educated women do in fact bear children at a more rapid pace than the illiterate." In a similar vein, an analysis of survey results from nine Asian and eight Latin American and Caribbean countries that participated in the World Fertility Survey showed that women who marry late tend to bear children more rapidly in the early years of marriage[14]: "This allows them to catch up with women who married earlier; their completed fertility is only slightly lower than that of women who married at younger ages."

The problems of and requirements for causal analysis in fertility research were considered at some length earlier in this book. Here, it may be noted that identifying and documenting the direction of causality among the variables that affect the education–fertility relationship is probably a more formidable task than in other areas of this field because of the sheer number of variables through which education may influence fertility indirectly. It seems clear that there are many ways in which education may influence fertility behavior through economic, psychological, sociocultural, and institutional factors, only some of which have been mentioned in this discussion. As in the case of other population–development relationships (including those considered in this and the previous chapter), an appropriate conceptual framework and a methodological approach for untangling the lines of causation have yet to be adequately formulated and tested (Todaro, 1980). Jones and Potter (1978:11) emphasized the magnitude of the task when they said: "The development of education . . . is inextricably intertwined with the evolution of the population, the economy and the society, and the interactions are so many and so complex that it is beyond the researcher's or planner's competence to disentangle them completely." As Graff (1979:124) said: "Principal problems lie in the empirical analyses that find education . . . correlating both positively and negatively with fertility, the definitions of variables and the comparability of data . . . and especially in the conceptualization and expectations of the educational factor itself." He concluded that there are no systematic formulations as yet within which to place the "patterns of reversals, inconsistencies, and irregularities."

Consider as one example of the variability that characterizes the education–fertility relationship the question of the number of years of schooling necessary for a decline in fertility to take place. Urzua (1978) concluded from a review of Latin American data that although a certain level of schooling appears to be critical for accelerating (not starting) fertility decline, this level varies not only from country to country but also from region to region within a country, as well as from urban to rural areas. Consequently, the formulation of educational policies that are fertility-sensitive, a task that will be considered presently, requires more finely honed surveys and location-specific studies to assess the impact of formal education on fertility in particular cases.

Turning now to the effects of fertility on education, it seems evident that population growth creates greater strains in education than in almost any other development sector, particularly because the age distribution in LDCs generates very high proportions of school-age persons in a population. Assuming "standard" rather than "rapid" fertility declines for population projections in the Third World, "the number of school-age children would almost double . . . by the year 2000" (International Bank for Reconstruction and Development, 1984:77). Even assuming "rapid" fertility declines, the number would still increase by 50% by the year 2000.

As indicated at the beginning of this section, the financial investment by the LDCs in education over the past several decades has increased massively, although the expenditures vary widely by country and region. Over a 20-year projection period, beginning in 1975, the contribution of population growth to the increase in recurrent costs of primary education was estimated to be on the order of 50–70%, and higher if capital costs are added (Jones, 1975). For a 10-year period, in LDCs making strong efforts to expand the proportion of the school-age population covered by the education system, the contribution of population growth to the increase in educational costs was estimated to be on the order of 30–50% (Jones, 1976; Jones and Potter, 1978). As would be expected and as these projections indicate, the contribution of population growth to the rise in educational costs tends to become proportionately greater the longer the time period considered.

Current high fertility virtually ensures that more children will enter school in the future. The single most important factor in increasing educational costs is the absolute increase in the number of students, but associated factors, such as an increase in the number of teachers and their rising wages, as well as extra facilities, also elevate costs. Acknowledging that there are reasons other than rapid population growth that help to account for low enrollment rates, the frequently poor quality of education, and the high frequency of dropouts, reasons that may be found in poverty and related problems, population growth must be accounted a critical factor in the limited supply of educational resources and facilities. It is unfortunate that the huge effort to expand educational coverage in response to population growth has for the most part been at the expense of improvement in quality and that the prospects for upgrading quality are dim. As Schultz (1985:1) notes: "School expenditures in some low and middle income countries have recently not increased as rapidly as enrollment; this growing gap in public expenditures per pupil between poorer and richer countries is a worrisome trend that suggests a deterioration in the 'quality' of schooling may be occurring in the low income countries." On the basis of an analysis of data for 89 countries in the period 1960–1980, Schultz (*ibid.*:59) concludes: "Clearly at the secondary level, and probably also at the primary level, rapid population growth has depressed levels of expenditure per child of school age. This has occurred by increasing class size and lowering teacher salaries, but not by restricting notably enrollments."

Given the widespread documentation of an inverse relationship between education and fertility, it seems tempting to view education as a critical policy measure in attempts to reduce fertility. Since the reasons for this inverse relationship and the directions of causation are not well understood, however, and there are still no explanations for what Graff called the "patterns of reversals, inconsistencies, and irregularities," there is no clear rationale as yet for promoting a policy of expanded education primarily as a means of fertility reduction (Cassen, 1976; De

Tray, 1976; Todaro, 1980). Acknowledging that quite substantial research is still needed for further exploration of the relationship between education and fertility, Cochrane (1979) drew a few policy conclusions from her comprehensive review, qualifying them as fairly tentative: First, although education cannot be expected automatically to reduce fertility in all circumstances, there is tentative evidence that over time, education will ultimately reduce fertility. Second, increasing female education will be more likely to reduce fertility than will increasing education of males. Third, education is more likely to reduce fertility in urban than in rural areas.

In view of the uncertainty, and the evidence (limited though it may be) that education influences decisions on family size through a wide variety of indirect channels, it is possible, as a number of writers have noted, that an alternative policy to affect these indirect channels would slow population growth more effectively than would a policy aimed at expanding education primarily for this purpose. De Tray (1976), for example, mentioned as examples of such alternative policies that might reduce family size more effectively and quickly than adult education policies those that directly influence a wife's wages, a couple's contraceptive behavior, and the early health and nutrition of children. Todaro (1980) said that until better and more convincing evidence that expansion of educational opportunities for women will lead to fertility reduction is available, the rationale for such a policy is simply not compelling. In the meantime, he suggested (*ibid.*:209) placing "more emphasis on the provision of increased rural as well as urban job opportunities for women, both educated and uneducated, as the principal economic mechanism for raising standards of living and lowering fertility."

The position taken by De Tray and by Todaro—namely, that alternative policy options must be considered because no clear and compelling rationale can be found for expanding education as a means of reducing fertility—is carried somewhat further by other writers. They opt for a focus on general broad-based economic development as the most effective way of reducing fertility, since such a strategy in any case encompasses most of the indirect factors by which education influences fertility. Holsinger and Kasarda (1976:179), for example, suggested that ". . . since these factors are interwoven in the social and economic structure of a society, we expect that in the long run outlays for fertility control might bring greater returns if they were invested in general economic development of which education is an important feature." This suggestion may have merit if education is indeed an important feature of development strategies, but as indicated earlier, general economic development is not by itself the most effective road to fertility reduction. Top priorities must be accorded to education, to health, and to the other objectives of broad-based development if both poverty and fertility are to be reduced.

Of course, most writers who express reservations about recommending policy measures for the expansion of education as a strategy for slowing population growth on the grounds of an inadequate rationale are quick to note that the expansion of educational opportunities for women is a significant and valuable goal for reasons of equity and has its own justification. In any case, for a variety of compelling reasons, the improvement of educational opportunities for women hardly needs the rationale of fertility reduction. Birdsall (1977:87) pointed out that "better educated women will be more productive workers, better parents, and better-informed citizens; however, where male/female student ratios indicate that women suffer some schooling disadvantage, fertility effects provide additional justification for rectifying the imbalance." Education reform in the direction of broad access to educational and occupational opportunities for the poor majority, both male and female, indeed has its own justification, but to the extent that mass education becomes fully available, it will eventually help to produce greater aggregate-level declines in fertility.

CONCLUDING OBSERVATIONS

The sectoral reviews in this and the preceding chapter provide graphic illustrations of the complex nature of the interrelationships between fertility and important sectors of development. Building an adequate knowledge base for understanding the determinants and consequences of population growth has been substantially constrained by the limitations of the conceptual approaches that have dominated the field, as described in Chapters 4 and 5, but understanding has also been impeded by the sheer complexity of the task involved in untangling the lines of causation as they operate in these relationships. Further consideration of the links between population growth and development factors and perspectives and of conceptual and methodological approaches to the study of fertility change is undertaken, along with other issues, in Chapter 8.

NOTES

[1]For further elaboration of the adverse effects of development on women, see Germain (1976–1977), Youssef (1976), Safilios-Rothschild (1982), and Arizpe (1982). Buvinic and Youssef (1978) called attention to the plight of female heads of household, who are in a

particularly disadvantaged position as compared both with the female population in general and with the population of men who are household heads in particular, and who are totally ignored in development planning. They noted (*ibid.*:ii) that "most studies suggest that explanatory factors for female family headship should be sought in both internal and international migration; mechanization of agriculture; the development of agribusiness and urbanization; overpopulation; lower class marginality; and the emergence of a class system of labor—all of which are integral parts/consequences of rapid economic transformation." The increase of female-headed households has become a significant trend in many LDCs: The average percentage of potential household heads who are women is 22% for sub-Saharan Africa, 20% for Central America and the Caribbean, 16% for North Africa and the Middle East, and 15% for South America (*ibid.*:i). Safilios-Rothschild (1985a) observed that the higher the proportion of female-headed households, the greater is women's access to paid employment. "It seems," she says (*ibid.*:24–25), "that structural factors that question the basic premise of the sex stratification system relating to women's economic dependence on men help enhance women's access to paid employment."

[2]The international assistance agencies are increasingly becoming aware of the need for systematic efforts to integrate women and girls into development programs and projects, as expressed in their policy and program papers, if the objectives of broad-based development are to be achieved. See, for example, United States Agency for International Development (1982). This policy paper, it is stated (*ibid.*:1), "is meant to provide the policy framework for each sector and for the Agency as a whole in its efforts to incorporate women into the total development process." (The sectors are agricultural development, employment and income generation, human resource and institutional development, energy and natural resource conservation, and water and health.) As indicated in this discussion with regard to other development issues, it remains to be seen whether this rhetoric will be converted into practice.

[3]For further elaboration of this conceptualization, see Oppong (1982, 1983) and Oppong and Church (1981). The variety and diversity emphasized by Whyte and by Oppong are exemplified in a collection of essays in Matthiasson (1974) about women in a wide array of cultural settings around the world.

[4]In a similar vein, Fried and Settergren (1985) set out to examine changes in the United States population between 1965 and 1975 in the differential impact of children on wives' and husbands' allocation of time among work in the home and the labor market and in leisure activities. They concluded (*ibid.*:20): "These data offer little encouragement to those who maintain that fundamental social change has been taking place and bringing about more egalitarian relations between men and women. The entry of women into the labor force in ever greater proportions may have expanded the roles performed by wives and mothers but it does not appear to have reduced the time they spend in responding to the increased demands for home work as represented by children. The differences in these responses by women and men are as great in 1975 as they were in 1965."

[5]One dramatic indicator of the low status of women in Bangladesh is that the life expectancy of men exceeds that of women by 2 years. In the DCs, women live longer than men, on average by more than 6 years. With the exception of India and Bangladesh, female life expectancy in Asian countries exceeds that of males by 3–6 years (International Bank for Reconstruction and Development, 1980a). On sex differentials in mortality in Bangladesh, see D'Souza and Chen (1980).

[6]Staudt (1980) contended that women may be the largest landless class in the world and that this circumstance has important long-term implications for women's productivity, their enforced dependency on men, and overall development goals.

[7]On the basis of their analysis of the results of studies conducted by the International

Labor Organization in seven LDCs, Anker and Hein (1985:37) suggested that minimizing role incompatibility would help to increase women's status and influence in the work force and that this effort in turn should contribute to fertility reduction. They concluded: "Rather than thinking of increasing the incompatibility between motherhood and employment in the hope of reducing fertility rates (which would have the effect of accentuating sexual inequalities in the labour market and perpetuating the low status of women), efforts should be made to decrease this incompatibility so that women can have the opportunity to voluntarily take up jobs on an equal footing with men."

[8]For a discussion of the principal problems of determining causal direction in the relationship between fertility and female employment with reference to United States data, see Cramer (1980).

[9]Optimism about the role of education in development was not easily dispelled. Consider the opening paragraph in the compendium of Coleman (1965a:3) on education and development: " 'Education is the key that unlocks the door to modernization.' Statements like this recent one are gaining acceptance as truisms by many nation builders, policy planners, and scholars interested in the modernization process. Once regarded as an essentially conservative, culture-preserving, culture-transmitting institution, the educational system now tends to be viewed as the master determinant of all aspects of change."

[10]In a study in Karnataka, India, that addressed the questions of why so many children start school and why they leave after a short time, Caldwell, Reddy, and Caldwell (1985:41) found that the "majority of children are withdrawn for two interrelated reasons: because the cost, whether direct or in labor forgone, is felt to be prohibitive or because the investment in education is perceived to have failed." In their conclusion, they stated (ibid.:48): ". . . there is still, as in much of the rest of the Third World, tremendous capriciousness about educational chances. Our family histories reveal that children stayed at school or did not do so largely because a brother's leaving school or the hiring of a laborer or the division of the household and its property meant that there was or was not a demand at a given point for their work."

[11]In a more recent review of the literature on the relationship between education and fertility by Cochrane (1983), the conclusions are essentially consistent with her 1979 monograph.

[12]It would be difficult to find in the literature a more forceful claim for the role of mother's education in reducing infant and child mortality than the report of Caldwell (1979:408) on Nigeria: ". . . maternal education is the single most significant determinant of these marked differences in child mortality. These are also affected by a range of other socioeconomic factors, but no other factor has the impact of maternal education and in their totality they do not even come close to explaining the effect of maternal education." See also Cochrane et al. (1980).

[13]Gille (1985:289) reported that a United Nations study of World Fertility Survey data in 22 LDCs found consistent positive effects of education on age at marriage with one exception, but he qualified this finding as follows: "It seems, however, that improvement in primary education as such will not have much effect on girls' age at marriage; only raising of the attainment level to secondary education may have such an effect and usually only if improved employment opportunities outside the home are made available at the same time."

[14]Reported in Digest (1981:25) from Caldwell, McDonald, and Ruzicka (1980). See also De Tray (1977).

Conclusions

A great deal of work has been done over the past two decades on the determinants of population growth, but far less on its consequences. As this discussion has shown, however, the resulting knowledge base yields only a very broad understanding of why, how, and when fertility changes occur. It is evident that there is no generally accepted theoretical framework for explaining the conditions, correlates, causes, and consequences of population change in the developing world. This lack accounts to a great extent for the inadequacy of the data base (United Nations Secretariat, 1984). In their comprehensive review of the state of knowledge about population–development relationships in the less-developed countries (LDCs), which includes mortality and migration as well as fertility, Miro and Potter (1980:147) concluded: "It seems clear . . . that the present state of knowledge on the determinants and consequences of demographic behaviour is somewhat uneven: there remain several important areas where no central paradigm has emerged and several different views or schools of thought are in competition with one another. Perhaps the three most important unresolved questions are with regard to the determinants of fertility, the consequences of internal migration, and the consequences of alternative trends in fertility." In the conclusions to their large-scale study on the determinants of fertility in the developing world, Bulatao and Lee (1983a) acknowledge that there is no dominant theory or paradigm in the field and provide (1983b), as indicated in Chapter 5, a description of how fertility responds to modernization, which they qualify as speculative and "far from being an established view" (ibid.:785).

A number of priorities for research in key areas of the determinants of fertility have been indicated in the sectoral reviews in Chapters 6 and 7, and the matter of consequences will be considered again shortly. Among the most notable agendas for research on the determinants of fertility in the LDCs are those prepared by Miro and Potter (1980) and by a committee for a program of research awards sponsored by the Population Council (1981). The most detailed agenda specifying priorities for research on the determinants of fertility is that provided by the National

Academy of Sciences—National Research Council Panel on Fertility Determinants (Bulatao and Lee, 1983a).

INTERRELATIONSHIPS: POPULATION GROWTH AND DEVELOPMENT

The various explanations of why the results of fertility research are subject to such uncertainties have been considered at various levels earlier and need not be repeated here. Suffice it to say that even though there has emerged a limited consensus on the linkage of at least a few development sectors to fertility reduction (reviewed in Chapters 6 and 7), not only do variations in the status and employment of women and in access to natural resources, education, and health and nutrition services have implications for fertility levels, and not only do fertility levels have implications for each of these development sectors, but also these sectors, including fertility itself, are key determinants of each other, and all affect and are affected by income levels. Together, they constitute what has been called the "seamless web of interrelations" (International Bank for Reconstruction and Development, 1980a:69; United Nations Secretariat, 1984:89). As Jones (1982:2) has observed: "Part of the problem is that the interactions are so many and varied that the only way they could be fully understood would be through the construction of a massive econometric model in which population trends were integrated as endogenous factors influencing and in turn influenced by socio-economic development, with extended chains of causation, appropriate feedback loops, 'spin-off' effects, and lag effects." Attempts to develop such models have been of questionable value (see, for example, Arthur and McNicoll, 1975).

The discussion of the effects of population growth on economic development in Chapter 5 and the sectoral reviews in Chapters 6 and 7 revealed that the consequences of rapid population growth for the various sectors on which development efforts are focused are still far from understood. In a discussion of these consequences, McNicoll (1984) suggested that the available knowledge base may be so limited because consequences have received much less research attention than determinants. The reasons for this disparity are as follows: Population growth is not exclusively a demographic subject, since it spills over into a number of other fields concerned with understanding social, economic, and environmental change; modern theoretical developments in both demography and economic-growth theory gave scant attention to considerations of absolute size of population and product; and it was casually assumed by many that early efforts to model economic–demographic relationships had definitively demonstrated the negative effects of rapid population growth for realizing development objectives. Although McNicoll does identify a number of important political, economic, and social organizational consequences, he enters the following qualification (*ibid.*:222): "Evidence for the most part is qualitative; assertions backed merely by argument and casual illustration abound. In part this situation reflects narrowness of the research base."[1]

In the World Bank's seventh annual report on development issues (International Bank for Reconstruction and Development, 1984), the focus is on population change and its links with development, and the consequences of rapid population growth receive substantial attention. A major conclusion of the report is that rapid population growth does slow development. In a review of the report, Lee (1985:130), after indicating his belief that most scholars, though not all, would agree with this conclusion, stated: "No really new evidence has been brought forward, and although the old evidence has been very skillfully marshalled, there is nothing here to convince the previously skeptical." Similarly, Leibenstein (1985:136), also reviewing the report, observed that many scholars think it "obvious" that the consequences of population growth are negative and stated: "It comes as a surprise to those outside the fields of economics and population that there are very few hard data and very few good studies directly measuring economic consequences of population growth. . . . While I agree with the conclusion [of the report], I am not sure about the evidence."

World Bank staff (International Bank for Reconstruction and Development, 1984) introduced their own qualifications, namely, that not all the interrelationships between population and development are fully understood (surely a safe enough claim) and that the implications of rapid population growth vary considerably depending on the economic, cultural, institutional, and demographic differences among LDCs. They also observe wistfully (*ibid.*:105), "The complexity of the subject makes it tempting to be agnostic about the consequences of rapid population growth." Nevertheless, as indicated, they state flatly that the evidence overwhelmingly points to the conclusion that rapid population growth slows development.

A number of writers have identified a wide range of adverse consequences, some more convincing than others. A substantial list can be compiled, even on a selective basis. The World Bank's own list (*ibid.*) includes a series of macroeconomic effects, whereby population growth can negatively affect economic growth through its influence on savings per person, on the amount of capital invested per person, and on the efficiency with which the economy operates; constraints on agricultural production due, for example, to increasing shortages of land and water; environmental damage, such as deforestation and desertification; and increase in economic disparities between developed countries (DCs) and LDCs. Robert S. McNamara (1984) grouped the consequences of population growth into two broad categories: effects on national economic growth and political stability and effects on the international system. In the first category, the effects include rising numbers of entrants into the labor force, expanding urban populations, pressure on food supplies, ecological degradation, and increasing numbers of people living in absolute poverty, all of which, according to McNamara, can be viewed by governments as threats to social stability and orderly change. Rapid population growth is seen as generating more pervasive regulation of social life in countries in which demographic pressures build to extremes and there are increasing coercive government intrusions into individual reproductive decision making. In the second category, at the level of the international economy, differences in population growth between the DCs and LDCs will contribute significantly to maintaining and even widening the income gap between rich and poor countries well into the next century.

There are other lists, some of which overlap with the above lists and also consider such matters as the effects of the dependency burden, needs in health, nutrition, and housing, and quality vs. quantity with regard to human capital development (see, for example, Jones, 1982; Benedick, 1984; G. Zeidenstein, 1984; Population Crisis Committee, 1985). There are few scholars so unsophisticated as to maintain that rapid population growth is necessarily the principal cause of problems in these areas, any more than they would maintain that widespread poverty is caused by rapid population growth, but many do claim that these problems are certainly exacerbated by such growth, and it is likely that it can exert a relatively complex and subtle influence at a series of levels.

The nature of this complexity and subtlety is conveyed quite effectively by McNicoll (1984). Despite his qualification as cited above and his frequent reminders about the paucity of empirical evidence, he does conclude (ibid.:212): "On balance there is little doubt that rapid population growth is a serious burden on efforts to generate sustained increase in per capita product." In addition to effects on the economy, McNicoll examines effects on social and political organization and suggests that rapid population growth may induce changes in the organization of the family, local community, and forms of government administration; may evoke new responses in a country's administrative and political systems;

and may, over time, bring about substantial shifts in international relations. Finally, he goes on to examine the effects on individual experience and on income distribution.

In another kind of categorization, Demeny (1982) identified four overlapping and interrelated concerns that in his view reflect the perceived consequences of rapid population growth. These concerns focus on shifts in relative demographic size among nations, international economic and political stability, humanitarian and welfare issues, and narrowing options with respect to long-term social development, including the option of population growth itself. These concerns give impetus to increasing attention to population policy formation in both national and international contexts.

The uncertainty regarding the consequences of rapid population growth is due largely to the dearth of definitive empirical evidence in this area, but it has also been fueled by the argument exemplified in the work of Julian Simon, discussed in Chapter 5, that rapid population growth in the LDCs will help rather than hinder their development by contributing to greater economic innovation, increased investment, and more efficient use of natural and human resources. This argument has been instrumental in generating what has been called "the new policy debate," or "new population debate," at the heart of which is the question of whether rapid population growth helps or hinders economic development (Population Crisis Committee, 1985). The argument is based in part on the expectation that the LDCs will follow the same path as did the DCs to economic modernization and thus to low fertility. Clearly, the modernization model and one of its offspring, the demographic-transition theory, both considered extensively earlier in this discussion, continue to retain validity for some economists and demographers.[2]

Simon is by no means alone in departing from the orthodox position that rapid population growth is a development problem.[3] As McNicoll (1984:178) has observed, "In the last decade a revisionist stream of thought has emerged that seems to cast doubt on the previous orthodoxy: rapid population growth, according to scholars of this persuasion, is often a neutral and can even be a positive factor in development." One version of this revisionist approach is described by its proponents as "supply-side demography." According to this view (Wattenberg and Zinsmeister, 1985), the crucial determinant, apparently, is whether those of the next generation are born into societies economically and politically organized to take advantage of their productive potential.

A review and assessment of the voluminous literature that has been generated regarding the nature of the consequences of rapid population growth for economic development could easily be the subject of a separate book. All that can be done further here is to discuss briefly a report on this topic issued in 1986 by the National Academy of Sciences (NAS) that was prepared by the National Research Council's Working Group on Population Growth and Economic Development (National Research Council, 1986). Also to be considered briefly are a number of responses to this NAS report that were published after its appearance.

First, however, mention should be made of a contribution to the "debate" that appeared a year earlier in the form of two views, by King and Kelley (1985), of the effects of population growth on economic development. In the conclusion to his statement, King identifies a series of "first principles," about which he believes there is a consensus. Among these principles are that for many LDCs, food supply remains a serious problem and (*ibid.*:10) "the main worry about rapid population growth is that it aggravates problems caused by poverty, such as malnutrition, illiteracy, and underemployment"; that development programs that reduce poverty contribute to solving population problems; and that population programs aimed at reducing fertility levels complement rather than compete with these development efforts. Kelley (*ibid.*:19) says his statement is "a revisionist interpretation" that "de-emphasizes some of the 'traditional' hypothesized direct influences of population, and assigns population the role of an accomplice in contrast to the leading role of villain (or hero) in the development story." Kelley accords much emphasis to his perspective as being "revisionist" because it presumably debunks the alarmist assessments that overstated the antinatalist case and places population growth "in a balanced perspective whereby the causes, and not the symptoms, of poverty are addressed." As indicated above, there are few scholars so unsophisticated as to consider population growth the principal cause of poverty and related problems. Kelley is apparently lumping with the group of doomsayers who gave us such images as "the population bomb" and "standing room only" those scholars who have espoused the moderate orthodox stance (of which King's statement is a good example) that rapid population growth is a development problem. Unless he is attacking the moderate orthodox position, one that has been legitimized, in the words of Demeny (1986:486), as part of "the long-standing intellectual tradition" of demography, as well as the position of the extreme Malthusians, is there need of revisionism? Population growth may not be *the* villain of the piece, but there is widespread agreement, whatever varying emphases there may be, that is is *one* of the villains in the cast.

The NAS report (National Research Council, 1986) was prepared by a panel of nine scholars, most of whom are economists. The report focuses almost exclusively on economic factors and emphasizes in particular (*ibid.*:7) "variables that are closely related to levels of per capita income, which is a widely recognized indicator of economic welfare," although it is recognized "that per capita income is not identical to well-being." It is a curious document, in part because it essentially limits the population and development dialogue to the orientation of neoclassic economics wherein per capita income once again becomes the principal indicator of development. The report is organized around nine questions about the effect of slower population growth on economic welfare and development, including resources and the environment; increase in supply of capital per worker, productivity, and per capita income; decrease in innovation; and improvement in human capital. Additional questions consider issues of employment and income inequality and ask whether a couple's fertility behavior imposes costs on society at large.

The report provides a variety of possible answers to these questions, but on the whole, they tend to be in the direction of finding that the impact of population growth has often been exaggerated and that, in a number of the areas under consideration, slower population growth is not likely to make much difference. In view of this tendency in their assessment of the effects of population growth, it is surprising that the authors sum up their work as follows (*ibid.*:90): "On balance, we reach the qualitative conclusion that slower population growth would be beneficial to economic development for most developing countries."

A review symposium on the NAS report, to which four economists contributed, offers enough variety in response to provide something for everyone (Daly, 1986; Kelley, 1986; Potter, 1986; Simon, 1986). Kelley (1986:564) is quite content with the report and regards it as revisionist because "it retreats very substantially from many previous assessments which concluded that population growth exerted a strong negative impact on development." In his view (*ibid.*:566), "The revisionist assessment of the impact of population on development is based on a realistic and tenable formulation of the development process in which feedbacks are taken into account. . . ." He goes on to say (*ibid.*:567) that "prospects for development are not precluded by rapid population growth, but they are enhanced by slower growth rates. Neither alarmism nor total complacency about population growth can be supported by the current evidence."

Simon (1986:577) lauds the report because he believes that it reaches a number of well-founded judgments that erode "the conventional wisdom that population growth is an unmitigated destructive force," but this is overshadowed by his concern that the conclusion supports and enhances the interests and activities of the NAS study's sponsors, such as the United States Agency for International Development, the Rockefeller Foundation, and the Hewlett Foundation. Simon (*ibid.*:574) contends not only that "there are grounds for concern that the funding sources influenced the conclusion," but also that it was "imprudent to have people . . . serve on the Working Group . . . whose very jobs in such organizations as the World Bank and the Population Council[4] depend upon the proposition that the world faces a population 'problem.'" Simon concludes his review with a lament that despite the soundness of the findings, the report has communicated the wrong conclusion.

Potter (1986) is troubled not only by the extent to which the NAS report abstracts from the macroeconomic context of the interrelationships between population and development but also by its lack of historical perspective. The possible future role of the LDCs in the global economy is not considered, nor is there any reference to the depredations introduced by the debt crisis in the Third World. Potter (*ibid.*:579) remarks that "to issue a report in the mid-1980s that does not take note of the changing balance of economic and demographic forces in the developing world is to pass over one of the more important phenomena that such a document might have addressed."

Also concerned about the abstract nature of the discussion, Daly (1986:584) perceived the major failing of the report to be "the common neoclassical inability or unwillingness to separate scale problems from allocation problems, and the consequent tendency to treat issues of scale and carrying capacity as nothing but questions of improving allocation by better definition of property rights. Population, of all issues, is intimately tied to scale and carrying capacity, and far too much is left out by questions that make for us a world that is indifferent to scale, a world in which only allocation problems exist."

Another publication in 1986, by the American Assembly of Columbia University (Menken, 1986), following a conference on the choices facing the United States with regard to international population policy, also addresses the NAS report. After reviewing the findings of the NAS report, Menken (*ibid.*:24) concluded: "The new studies undertaken by the National Academy of Sciences were directed explicitly to the economic consequences of population growth. They can add little to our thinking about some of the questions . . . concerning other societal effects of rapid versus slower increase in numbers." In reporting on the discussions held at the American Assembly conference, Wulf and Klitsch (1986:184) state that "Ansley Coale perhaps best summarized the majority viewpoint when he criticized the NAS report for being 'too dedicated to the economists' paradigm.' There are human values, he argued, that don't necessarily fit into the schemes erected in the study of economics." In contrast to the findings of the NAS report, the participants in the American Assembly conference, as reflected in their final report, took the position that population growth is an important impediment to development in the Third World. In presenting their rationale for a United States Government role in reducing high fertility, they stated (Menken, 1986:231): "First, high fertility, over the long term, has negative effects on social and economic circumstances, such as those relating to education, health, and income, and on natural resources and the environment. Second, involuntary high fertility may infringe upon a person's human right to choose his or her family size."

The most trenchant criticism of the NAS report is perhaps that of Demeny (1986:486–487), who says: "It is distinctive chiefly in pronouncing the near irrelevance of rapid population growth to anything really important in development and development policy. . . . The report asks its questions in such a way as to foreordain its conclusions. Its fundamental perspective is a narrow marginalism, fit perhaps for analyzing questions of day-to-day economics but wholly inappropriate for looking at the long-term impact of population growth in human affairs." As will be indicated presently, the outlook for international donor assistance for population activities is problematic at present. The message of the NAS report and of other proponents of the "revisionist" approach—that population growth has no important negative consequences for economic development and may even have some positive effects—can only have an unfavorable impact on donor support, whether for family planning and related programs, information and education activities, or research and analysis for population policy formulation in relation to development planning.

To the extent that the NAS report is taken seriously by LDC planners and policy-makers, it could only obfuscate efforts to incorporate population policy analysis into national development planning. Its findings regarding the role of population growth, despite its concluding statement, are at variance with the widespread concern of the LDCs with the negative consequences of population growth for development, as expressed in the principal documents adopted by the International Conference on Population in Mexico City (Documents, 1984b) and in a statement on population stabilization by world leaders (Documents, 1985c). Moreover, government support for population policy apparently should be limited to family planning programs. In the view of the Working Group (National Research Council, 1986:91), for most problems "a fundamental solution . . . lies in better policies outside the population arena." Potter (1986:578) states it well: "None of the mechanisms by which population growth is posited to impede economic development stands up as a secure justification for government interventions to bring down the birth rate. Either the effect is judged to be relatively unimportant . . . or there is a better or more direct way to deal with the problem." It may also be noted that the NAS report's reliance on per capita income as the principal indicator of development is clearly at variance with the priority now accorded to the "growth with equity" approach in the development literature.

If the participants in the "new population debate" are taken to be those who hold the extreme positions—at one end the doomsayers who evoke apocalyptic images and at the other those who contend that people are the most precious resource so that population growth is the solution rather than the problem—then there is no hope that a debate embracing such differences of opinion can ever be resolved. Even if these extremes are omitted from consideration, however, there are still substantial differences of opinion and judgment among scholars in the field regarding the nature of the consequences of population growth for economic and social development, as this discussion has shown. These differences are not likely to be resolved by continuing to resort to the "assertions backed merely by argument and casual illustration" that McNicoll (1984:222) attributes in part to the "narrowness of the research base." The members of the Working Group themselves (National Research Council, 1986:6) qualified their findings by noting the paucity of "adequate studies of the effects of slower population growth in developed countries and fewer still on the effects in developing countries." They go on to say: "Consequently, there is much less certainty than we would like about the specific quantifiable effects of different rates of population growth on . . . the numerous . . . questions that are addressed in the following chapters," and subsequently note that further research is needed.

If continued credence is to be accorded the mainstream view that population growth is detrimental to development, there is an urgent need for careful and focused empirical research and analysis on the nature of the relationships between population growth and social and economic development, given the increments of population still in store for the world and the gains in broad-based development that have yet to be attained in the Third World.[5] Calls for such research, on both determinants and consequences, have been cited at a number of points in this discussion. Consideration of the tasks for theory and research, focused primarily on determinants, is undertaken later in this concluding chapter.

EQUITY AND POPULATION GROWTH

The nature of the available evidence regarding the aggregate relationships between population growth and economic development is
such, then, that no definitive claim can be made as to whether the
former either inhibits or promotes the latter. Since so many other variables are associated with both birthrates and rates of economic growth,
it is not likely that adequate knowledge for making definitive claims will
be available in the near term, as urgently as this knowledge may be
needed. As indicated early on and at many points in this discussion,
however, there has been a fundamental shift in development perspectives from a virtually exclusive focus on economic growth, which has
had a long history, to an increasing emphasis, beginning in the 1970s,
on improving equity in distribution and consumption along with economic growth. This emphasis on equity has brought with it expanding
awareness that the most appropriate development policies are those that
will have a maximum impact on the quality of life of the hundreds of
millions of people in the LDCs existing at or near subsistence levels by
giving them adequate access to education, health care, and nutrition, a
share in income growth, productive employment, and participation in
shaping their own future, rather than the limited impact achieved by
policies oriented to growth in average per capita income.

In this discussion, the concept of "basic needs" has been employed
to exemplify the current orientation to promotion of broad-based development, together with economic growth, as the way to achieve greater
equity and the reduction of poverty. The objective is what is important,
not the slogan "basic needs." As Haq (1981:ix) put it: "What needs to be
protected is the objective, not the word. Emphasis on basic needs must
be seen as a pragmatic response to the urgent problem of world poverty;
as the ultimate objective of economic development, it should shape
national planning for investment, production, and consumption." This
orientation to broad-based development offers an enhanced potential
for the design of development policies that can be fertility-sensitive. As
indicated earlier in this discussion, development policies that seek to
promote equity and reduce poverty and population policies aimed at
reducing fertility go hand in hand. All the dimensions of broad-based
development considered in this discussion—which include employment, education, the status of women, health and nutrition, the
distribution of assets (particularly income and land), and greater popular participation and community-level action—largely coincide with the

factors generally considered to constitute the important determinants of fertility. All the available evidence seems to point toward the proposition that fertility would decline, in the long run, were broad-based development to be implemented, concurrent with economic growth, to bring improved well-being to the poor majorities in the LDCs, which decades of economic growth by itself have failed to do. To the extent that a large proportion of the population could share in the benefits of development, they would also experience fertility decline that would eventually produce a greater aggregate-level fertility decline.

In the short run, however, there is an imperative need to move ahead in evaluating and improving policy measures that can be undertaken for the specific purpose of reducing fertility, which include family planning programs, their incorporation into other development programs, the use of incentives, and the assessment of a variety of interventions that may have more immediate fertility-reducing effects. To the extent that these measures can be effective, they will in turn help to make easier the attainment of broad-based development objectives.

Concern with the implementation of broad-based development strategies for the realization of the objectives of greater equity and reduction of poverty pervades the recent writings of development economists (see, for example, Ranis, West, Leiserson, and Taft, 1984; Seligson, 1984c), just as the idea that the attainment of these objectives is conducive to fertility reduction is central to the statements issued by such international agencies as the World Bank (International Bank for Reconstruction and Development, 1984; Clausen, 1984b) and the United Nations Fund for Population Activities (Salas, 1985). The connections between equity and fertility reduction were repeatedly emphasized in the declarations and manifestos associated with the International Conference on Population in Mexico City. As Wulf and Willson (1984:229) stated: "In numerous formal declarations to the plenary session, and during the drafting committee sessions, delegates made reference to the complex and mutually reinforcing links between efforts to spur development and those to reduce population growth." Of the 22 statements in the "Mexico City Declaration on Population and Development," 12 are explicitly concerned with equity and population problems, and of the 88 "Recommendations" adopted by the conference, 21 are concerned with one or another basic human need (Documents, 1984b).

As noted in Chapter 4, marked fertility declines have already occurred in a number of countries in which, contrary to the conditions specified by demographic-transition theory, populations are mainly poor and rural and at least some efforts have been made in the direction of broad-based development. Clausen (1984b:18) observed that the dramatic fertility declines in the 1960s in South Korea, Singapore, and Hong Kong conformed to demographic-transition theory since they were industrializing economies, but that subsequent declines in the LDCs came "with a different kind of development: education, health, the alleviation of poverty, improved opportunities for women, and government effort to assure widespread access to family planning services." He cited Sri Lanka, Thailand, and Turkey as countries with fertility declines in which income gains and social services were relatively more evenly distributed. Freedman (1979) was cited earlier, with regard to fertility declines in Sri Lanka, Kerala (India), and China, as identifying other changes these countries had in common, namely, reduced mortality, high levels of education of both boys and girls, provision of welfare programs, and improved communication and transportation facilities, all of which may have directly influenced the perceived needs and benefits of children. Jones (1982) refers to other instances, in Asia, of dramatic fertility declines occurring among poor rural populations, namely, Chiangmai in northern Thailand along with a substantial decline in Thailand as a whole, Bali in Indonesia, and North Vietnam. In an in-depth study of the state of Kerala in India, Zachariah (1983) found that the principal determinants of Kerala's fertility decline were widespread improvements in health and education and an effective family planning program, a conclusion with which Nag (1984b) is in essential accord. In an assessment of development and population policies on fertility in India during the 1970s, Jain (1985) found that improvements in female literacy and education, decrease in infant mortality, and increased use of contraception were the most important conditions conducive to lowering fertility. As cited in Chapter 4, Cutright (1983), in a study of 83 LDCs, found that indicators of education, health, and family planning program effort have a significant independent effect on fertility.

Although none of these examples documents that improvements in the well-being of the poor are a necessary and sufficient condition for fertility decline, at least they demonstrate that high levels of income, urbanization, and industrialization are not necessary conditions either. In each of the analyses considered here, improvements in health and education, together with effective family planning programs, are prominently associated with fertility declines, and these are among the key areas in broad-based development strategies. Consistent with these findings, as indicated in Chapter 5, Cutright and Hargens (1984), on the basis of their analysis of data from 20 LDCs in Latin America, found that according to their measures of threshold levels, if such threshold levels in literacy and life expectancy (in their view the most important indicators of social development) are surpassed, fertility will decline from traditional high levels.

In Chapter 3, political and other constraints on the implementation of broad-based development strategies were considered, and it was concluded that restructuring political and economic power relationships and mobilizing popular participation and community-level action programs are prerequisites for realizing the objectives of broad-based development. Changing the distribution of productive wealth and thus the distribution of economic power, and increasing the participation of the poor in decision making and thus enabling them to exercise political power, are formidable tasks, but they do not necessarily require revolution. The discussion pointed to incremental approaches that could be adopted by reformist alliances to achieve equity and reduction of poverty in an orderly manner. Streeten *et al.* (1981) observe that indexes of inequality and measures of poverty are lower in socialist than in capitalist countries and that revolutionary land reforms and public ownership of all means of production make it easier to pursue a basic-needs strategy. But they also point to the fact that a number of non-socialist countries have been successful in satisfying basic needs, indicating that socialism is not a prerequisite for doing so. Actually, they list a wide variety of political regimes that have been effective in implementing broad-based development, including Japan, Israel, Costa Rica, South Korea, Singapore, China, Yugoslavia, and Sri Lanka.

If fertility declines are to be accelerated in the substantial number of LDCs that have not experienced them thus far, structural change will have to occur if equity is to be achieved. Writing more than a decade ago about the problems of welfare and population in India, Cassen (1975:65–66) remarked that although in the short run only family planning programs are likely to reduce fertility significantly, in the long run much depends on bringing education and improved health to the poor majority, and to do this it would be necessary to raise the incomes of the poor. He went on to say: "The basic scarcity of resources and the social and economic structure of village life severely hinder this evolution, if they do not altogether prevent it. Without the transformation of that structure, expectations of rapid fertility decline in India are not realistic." Similarly, considering the issue of whether family planning programs can suffice to lower fertility, Gille (1985:279–280) observed that "this is not only a theoretically important question but carries policy implications as well. If, for instance, it is true that high fertility is deeply embedded in the economic or social structure, then family planning provision by itself is unlikely to bring about a fertility reduction without structural changes."

DONOR ASSISTANCE: DIRECTIONS AND DIMENSIONS

As noted in the discussion of foreign aid, the rhetoric of both bilateral and multilateral donors is replete with the conviction that the focus of international assistance must shift to the poorest countries and to the poorest people in those countries. The World Bank's International Development Association (IDA), which provides concessional assistance to low-income countries, is a notable example of an attempt to match the rhetoric in practice, but as A. W. Clausen (1985b), the bank's president until 1986, reported, the IDA is now severely underfunded. As indicated earlier, he identified an alarming trend in which donor governments are reallocating their funds for aid to serve their own national security purposes rather than Third World development objectives and, despite the rhetoric, to provide funding for the middle-income countries, in which they have greater commercial or political interests, rather than for the poorest countries.

As Streeten and other advocates of broad-based development programs have emphasized, substantial increases in international assistance are essential to the effective implementation of such programs. Nevertheless, the international flow of resources is being reduced rather than expanded. Faaland (1982:19) posed the question of whether the DCs will ever be willing to give the LDCs a transfer of resources that will be commensurate with needs: "At a time when economic systems are functioning badly, and when affluence is assailed by inflation, high interest rates, unemployment and little or no economic growth, there is little inclination for any country to think of the needs of other nations." This retrenchment on the part of the DCs has occurred at a time when the absolute income gap between the DCs and the LDCs, which has grown dramatically over the past 30 years, is greater than ever (Seligson, 1984c) and "will not decrease significantly because the initial difference in per capita income is, for many developing countries, so large" (International Bank for Reconstruction and Development, 1984:100).[6]

The demands by the LDCs for a new international economic order (NIEO) that would result in wealth transfers from DCs to LDCs was in large part a response to the gap. Calls by the LDCs for an NIEO are still heard in international forums, as in two held in July 1985—the conference on the United Nations Decade for Women (*New York Times*,

1985b) and the meeting of the Organization of African Unity (May, 1985). But the cohesive stance taken by the LDCs in the late 1970s and early 1980s, always maintained at considerable cost because of the substantial differences among groups of LDCs, has now frayed to some extent. Finkle and Crane (1985) said that the LDCs find it increasingly advantageous to pursue bilateral or regional approaches to gain economic concessions from the DCs, rather than to follow the global strategy associated with the NIEO. Nevertheless, such economic concessions from the DCs are hard to come by, and the debt crisis that afflicts the LDCs, considered in some detail in Chapter 3, remains acute. As indicated, the financial drains to which the LDCs are subjected by debt service and interest payments have brought economic growth, let alone broad-based development, largely to a halt.

These changes on the part of both DCs and LDCs in the arena of international relations do not bode well for a "North–South dialogue" or, in turn, for the future of international assistance for the poor countries. And the income gap between the DCs and LDCs is matched within many LDCs by a growing internal gap between their own rich and poor citizens (Seligson, 1984a). If the interests of international and intranational equity are to be served, there is clearly need for better understanding on the part of both DCs and LDCs of the realities of global interdependence and for reaching a consensus that international and national reforms are essentially complementary and both need to be pursued. But the prospects for such a consensus at this time seem dim indeed.[7]

International assistance for development began in the late 1940s and began to be targeted for population programs only in the late 1950s. Funding for population work was minimal until 1970.[8] In 1971, the net total of assistance for population activities from governmental, multilateral, and private donors was $168.5 million; by 1980, this increased to slightly less than $520 million (Mauldin, 1983). In 1984, this total had decreased to about $490 million (Salas, 1985). Despite the substantial increase in population assistance since the early 1970s, the current level represents no more than about 2% of the total official development assistance provided by the DCs (Herz, 1984). The United States, through its Agency for International Development (USAID), has always been the single largest source of population assistance. By the end of 1983, it had provided more than $2 billion in technical assistance and commodities to the LDCs (Sinding, 1984). The United Nations Fund for Population Activities (UNFPA), which has been the largest multilateral assistance agency in the population field since its inception in the late 1960s, has provided over $1 billion (which includes $336 million received from the USAID) in assistance to 130 countries (ibid.). Over a period of 14 years, the World Bank, through IDA credits and loans, has committed $355 million for population projects, of which $255 million had been disbursed by the end of 1983 (International Bank for Reconstruction and Development, 1984). The bank's total lending for population, health, and nutrition projects during the past 15 years has been about $700 million, a tiny fraction of its total lending program (Documents, 1985b).

In the 1970s, many LDC population programs were initiated and funded largely by external donors, but it is now the rule, rather than the exception, that LDCs initiate their own population programs (Sinding, 1984), and many LDC governments now help pay for programs that only a few years ago were supported by international assistance (International Bank for Reconstruction and Development, 1984).[9] Nevertheless, future funding is a big question. The budgets of the USAID and other donors have essentially reached a plateau, but requests for assistance are on the increase, both to initiate programs in regions such as Africa and to support the external resource needs of ongoing programs in many of the more populous countries, particularly in Asia (Sinding, 1984).[10] To ensure a rapid fertility decline by the year 2000 in those LDCs that have not yet experienced such declines, particularly in South Asia, the Middle East and North Africa, and sub-Saharan Africa, the World Bank estimates that foreign and domestic population assistance together would have to reach an annual total of $7.6 billion (in 1980 dollars) by the year 2000. Assuming that the current proportion of spending for family planning programs provided by foreign aid, which is about 25% of the total, remains about the same, the current level of foreign population assistance would have to quadruple to an annual level of $2 billion (in 1980 dollars) by the year 2000 (International Bank for Reconstruction and Development, 1984). In 1980, total expenditures for population and family planning programs in the Third World, from *both* foreign *and* domestic sources, were estimated to have been $2.6 billion (Bulatao, 1985). The great bulk of population assistance comes from a handful of wealthy industrial nations, a group that has become increasingly heterogeneous but is still small (Ness, Alhambra, and Pressman, 1984).[11]

About two thirds of international population assistance is allocated to family planning and related programs (International Bank for Reconstruction and Development, 1984). Although a certain amount of the balance, in the case of the UNFPA, for example, goes for information and education activities, about 25% is spent on the utilization of population data and research for policy formulation in relation to development planning (United Nations Fund for Population Activities, 1985). Clausen (1984b) reported that the World Bank was exploring opportunities to support research on the consequences of population growth, on social and economic factors that influence population growth, and on more effective service delivery. Ness *et al.* (1984) state that from the beginning of international population assistance, a large portion of the total funds went directly to family planning programs in Asia, but that in Latin America, the funds went first to basic data collection and only subsequently to family planning programs, while in Africa, a substantial proportion of current assistance goes to basic data collection and policy research. They explain this pattern as due largely to Asia's having a far greater administrative absorptive capacity than had the other regions and state that as this capacity is developed in Africa, more funds are likely to go to family planning programs.[12]

In examining the effects of international population assistance in Asia, Ness *et al.* (*ibid.*) make the important observation that there is no simple relationship between the volume, or scale, of aid flows and either national family planning program performance or fertility decline, and they use the cases of Malaysia, Indonesia, the Philippines, and Thailand to illustrate this proposition. Internal political and administrative conditions in the countries themselves have been more decisive than has foreign assistance in shaping family planning program activity or the programs' impact on fertility. To cite just one of their examples, Malaysia has received large loans, including loans for population work, from the World Bank, but the Malaysians have been unwilling to use the population funds because political issues, primarily racial or communal, are paramount, although it is never admitted that they are. Malaysia's rulers are Malay, but there is a large Chinese minority of about 40%, so that the regime is not eager to see a decline in Malay fertility. Thus, the explosive and delicate balance between Malays and Chinese has been a more important factor in determining the course of population planning than has the availability of World Bank funds. Consistent with this situation, Malaysia has recently reversed its long-standing policy of seeking to reduce population growth and has announced its intention of achieving a population of 70 million (almost five times the current population). Even if the present growth rate of 2.0% is maintained, the objective of 70 million would not be reached until well into the 21st century. The explanation given for the new policy by Malaysia's Prime Minister was that Malaysia needs a larger domestic market if it is going to industrialize, and a large domestic market is particularly important in a protectionist international environment (Documents, 1983). No reference was made, of course, to ethnic issues. According to C. Hirschman (1986:161): "These statements [about the new policy], combined with the highly charged issue of ethnic balance in Malaysian society, have led many Malaysians to believe the new population policy is primarily directed at an increase in the Malay population. Although this association is officially denied by the government, there is far greater demographic potential for growth in the Malay population, given its younger age structure and currently higher fertility levels."[13]

The analysis by Ness *et al.* (1984:29) shows that international population assistance in Asia has had some impact on policy decisions to reduce fertility, but even this for the most part has been highly indirect. They go on to conclude: "Foreign assistance can help countries to do what they are willing and able to do themselves. It cannot create policies by itself; it cannot create programs, nor can it make them more or less efficient than they are by virtue of the environment in which they operate."

TASKS FOR THEORY AND RESEARCH

This chapter opened with the observation that there is no generally accepted theoretical framework for explaining the interrelationships between population growth and development factors. Even though definitive answers are not likely to be within reach in the near future, theoretical work that seeks to identify possible chains of links between cause and effect through which a particular developmental change or intervention is or is not conducive to reducing fertility is a worthy objective to strive for in the interest of gaining greater precision in this field. The key question that has been asked repeatedly in this discussion is: Within the array of the most prominent candidates considered to be the determinants of fertility, what are the particular combinations of fundamental variables at specific levels that constitute the necessary and sufficient conditions to precipitate a fertility decline? There are no wholly adequate answers from the existing conceptual models. To date, conceptualization about the relationships between development and fertility consists essentially of accounting schemes, frameworks for specifying what a theory must contain, rather than constituting a theory as such. As Hawthorn (1970) has said, to be able to verify or falsify the putative relationships, values have to be attached to the variables in a framework. Only then could a testable and potentially explanatory theory be formulated.

The formulation of such an explanatory theory is not likely to be achieved in the near future. In the words of Burch (1980:19): "A truly general theory of human fertility behaviour must be quite general indeed, applicable not just to contemporary developed or developing societies, or historical full-fledged agricultural societies, but to all human societies past, present, and by implication, future." These are awesome requirements. Robinson and Harbison (1980) specify the areas that a cohesive theory must embrace, as indicated in Chapter 5, and propose (*ibid.*:229) a theoretical framework that "suggests no fixed relationship among economic, social and psychological factors in the fertility decision, only that all are present and that a unified theory must take all into account."

The lack of a dominant theory need not lead, however, to the depressing conclusion that social science research cannot move further in generating a knowledge base that will have greater explanatory power regarding population change. At this point, the task to be undertaken is that of developing appropriate middle-range theories that will facilitate asking the right questions to be addressed in empirical research on both the determinants and consequences of population growth. One call for new research on the determinants of fertility (Population Council, 1981:315) stated that what is needed "are fresh attempts to elaborate empirically grounded theories of the social, economic, and decision processes that yield individual-level statistical associations. This effort in turn entails empirical investigation of how social, political, administrative, and cultural structures create fertility incentives or disincentives and otherwise impinge on reproductive behavior."

The review undertaken in this discussion of the mainstream approaches to the study of population change, namely, demographic-transition theory and microeconomic theory, shows that they are not capable of interpreting whatever aggregate relationships have been identified because they abstract from the fertility decision-making context and are removed from empirical reality. Conceptualization in this field needs to take into systematic account the sociocultural and institutional factors operative in the fertility decision-making context, factors that have been largely ignored in these mainstream approaches. As Ryder (1983:15) put it, "We . . . have consigned to residual neglect the institutional setting which always and everywhere conditions individual decisions and behaviour."

It should be made clear that there is no intention here of according sociocultural and structural (institutional) factors any arbitrary priority over economic factors. A principal theoretical issue is not whether economic, structural, or sociocultural variables are the most appropriate focus, but rather what are the conceptual requirements for specifying the priorities with regard to the kinds of data needed to get at explanations, by identifying, for particular situations, the combinations of variables that are conducive to sustaining high fertility and to precipitating fertility decline.

There is a clear need for methodological approaches that can exploit aggregative, household, and individual-level data (Casterline, 1985; S. Singh and Casterline, 1985). To meet theoretical requirements for generating explanatory power, all three levels need to be employed as units of analysis. Because of their limitations, cross-sectional surveys designed only to identify statistical relationships between fertility and its correlates cannot serve as research instruments for the study of the sociocultural and institutional contexts of fertility decision making. Moreover, causal directions are unclear in these aggregate-level findings. To the extent that they are country- and region-specific, however, surveys can help to provide a knowledge base for the design of "focused, in-depth, village-level studies" of the kind called for by Jones (1978:40) and others to document the role of sociocultural and institutional factors at community and household levels. Such an approach, although it may not serve the cause of generality, would yield closer approximations to reality. It might also serve generality if the design of such studies were oriented to a more or less common conceptual framework that could eventually enhance the value of comparative (cross-cultural) research. Chapman (1981:87) maintained that "results from microstudies reveal far more common ground and consequently a much greater ability to generalize than is commonly assumed." The work already done at the community and family levels by such researchers as Caldwell, Cain, and Arthur and McNicoll, to mention only a few of the scholars cited in this book, could provide a departure point for the conceptual framework.

What is needed, then, is an articulation of the cross-sectional survey and village-level approaches with an orientation to a common conceptual framework. Village-level studies, by themselves, are too likely to be anecdotal and idiosyncratic, but Potter (1983) suggests that one way of transcending these limitations would be to combine the two approaches.[14] If research were designed to collect national- and community-level data on relevant variables, on one hand, and individual- and household-level data, on the other, the findings could have substantial application potential that would be of importance for policy recommendations. Potter noted that such a combined approach would of course require considerable conceptual and experimental effort as well as methodological innovation.

As has been noted at several points in these pages, the relationships between demographic and development variables vary not only among countries but also among different socioeconomic, occupational, and cultural groups within countries. As Demeny (1985a:2) has stated: "Considerations of national policy . . . must primarily draw on assessments of the demographic situation in the country in question: in such assessments, too, a closer look invariably reveals further diversity. It is also likely to show that changes in various subpopulations often move over time in directions concealed by average trends." A combined research approach of the kind proposed could focus on how changes in incomes and welfare affect reproductive behavior among different groups in the population—groups based on social class, rural or urban residence, kinship, occupation, and ethnicity or religion. With these problems in mind, research could be designed to test ongoing or projected innovative and experimental development program interventions to determine their demographic impact. More finely honed survey approaches together with focused village-level studies could contribute to the identification and explanation of group differentials in fertility behavior.[15]

COORDINATION OF POPULATION POLICY ANALYSIS AND DEVELOPMENT PLANNING

As this book has shown, much has yet to be done before research and analysis reaches a level of specificity that can be operationally useful for comprehensive development planning and policy formulation. Nevertheless, enough has been accomplished to provide the basis for systematic, if limited, assessment of the fertility impacts of development policy and to affirm that the coordination of population and development policies is feasible and desirable. Such coordination will not come about by itself, but will require systematic organizational arrangements for its facilitation. For the most part, decisions about what research on population problems is to be undertaken have rested largely with individual social scientists pursuing their own disciplinary interests, and relatively little attention has been given to the needs of development planners and policy-makers.[16] In undertaking research at national, community, household, and individual levels and to ensure that it has policy relevance, there is a need to bring to planners and policy-makers an understanding of what is already known that is of policy relevance, to engage them with researchers in a common effort to identify the key questions that are researchable and need to be answered, and to provide policy-makers with continuing consultation, based on the best available knowledge, of what options may be open to them, together with the anticipated effects, as they engage in the decision-making process (O. G. Simmons and Saunders, 1975).

Moreover, if program actions that emerge from collaboration among researchers, planners, and policy-makers are to be effective, systematic attention will have to be given to local-level economic, social, and administrative arrangements that prevail in a particular society, arrangements that are frequently ignored. McNicoll (1983:23) pointed out that "these arrangements make up a large part of the proper arena for policy design and are basic to determining policy effect" because (ibid.:10) "population policy as a national programmatic activity also typically seeks to work through local administration in some measure." It should also be noted that decisions about population policy issues may not always be based on the technical knowledge researchers may make available to planners and policy-makers, but rather may be based on paramount political concerns. The shift from an antinatalist to a pronatalist orientation in Malaysian population policy is a case in point.

A number of types of organizational arrangements for coordinating planning and policy-making in development and population have been proposed, of which the most prominent, as called for by the World Population Plan of Action (WPPA), is the establishment of a population policy and development planning unit "at a high level of the national administrative structure" (World Population Conference, 1975:179).[17] In the decade spanned by the Bucharest conference in 1974 and the International Conference on Population (ICP) in Mexico City in 1984, about 40 LDCs issued explicit population policy statements, some in separate declarations, some as part of long-term development plans (Population Information Program, 1984b). A number of recommendations presented by the ICP focus on implementation of population policies in development planning (ibid.; Documents, 1984b), and analysis and research for population policy formulation and development planning have been accorded high priority by the UNFPA (United Nations Fund for Population Activities, 1985; Salas, 1985).[18]

The Fifth Population Inquiry among Governments, conducted by the United Nations Population Division in 1983, asked, among other matters, whether there is a unit within a government's planning organization charged with the responsibility of taking into account population variables as part of the social and economic planning process. Of the 81 governments of LDCs that replied to this question, 62 reported that they have established such units (United Nations Population Division, 1983). According to Heisel and Benbow (1984:12), the population issue referred to most frequently in the Fifth Inquiry (and explicitly identified by just slightly more than 40% of all countries that responded) "was the need for discussion of the relationship between population and social and economic development or the closely related matter of how best to integrate population policies into social and economic development policies." The experience of population policy analysis units in the Third World is obviously still too recent and limited to provide any basis for assessment of performance. Moreover, it is likely that the role, location, and potential effectiveness of each of these units will be affected differentially by country variations in political, economic, and sociocultural characteristics, their current demographic situations, likely demographic trends, official perceptions of population as a priority issue, and perceptions of available policy options, as well as by their organizational arrangements, priorities, and strategies for development planning (Baron, 1980).[19]

In general terms, the principal tasks of a population policy unit are to generate, organize, and analyze knowledge about population variables as they relate to other development variables and, in collaboration with planning and policy agencies, to use that knowledge to forecast future trends and conditions helpful in formulating alternative development policy and program actions (Jones, Saunders, and Simmons, 1978). Stated another way, the task is at least threefold: to demonstrate the effect of population variables on development goals; to assess the population effects, direct and indirect, of current and proposed development policies and programs; and to identify, design, and test the potential effectiveness and feasibility—leaving for subsequent consideration the question of acceptability—of alternative policy options that can facilitate the realization of development goals (O. G. Simmons and Saunders, 1975). These are formidable tasks, beset with many conceptual and methodological difficulties.

In concluding this discussion, it is instructive to point to a series of imposing constraints with which population policy analysts and researchers will have to cope in working with development planners and policy-makers. Advocates of the coordination of development and of demographic policies often tend to view the problems posed by population growth and distribution as of central importance to development planning efforts and to the implementation of development goals, but it would be unrealistic as well as unreasonable to assume that this view is shared widely by planners and policy-makers. Population policy objectives are not ends in themselves, but are intermediate to the ultimate objectives of development. From the point of view of planners and policy-makers, these latter objectives are of much greater importance as they try, on a relatively short-term basis, to work out the design and implementation of development projects, depending on their particular priorities, in such sectors as employment and income generation, agricultural productivity, health and education, industrialization, an array of needs in infrastructure, and so on. The fact that population factors are not at the top of the hierarchy of objectives requires that population policy analysts view demographic policies as instrumental, along with other kinds of policy measures, in achieving the goals of development plans and that they sort out, in working with planners, what may be in a particular case the effect of alternative development policies on fertility as well as the anticipated effect of incorporating measures to induce fertility reduction in development policies and programs.

Differences in time frames constitute a second major constraint. Most development plans encompass, at most, a 5-year period, but virtually all the policy measures related to the development sectors considered relevant to population growth are not likely to have desired fertility effects for three to four times that time span. In the near term, even if populations increase by 10–15% over a 5-year period, the effects of this growth are swamped by the pressures on planners and policy-makers engendered by the short-run targets they set for their development efforts. Given this asymmetry in time frames, population analysts will have to complement the 5-year orientations of planners with a vision of what the situation is likely to be a decade or two hence with respect to the needs of a substantially larger population even if this vision cannot be presented with any great degree of precision.

Although population policy analysts may be persuasive in gaining the attention and collaboration of development planners, it is safe to say that lack of access to budget allocation authority is a limitation that will have to be lived with for the foreseeable future. As has been indicated (Baron, 1980:14), population policy analysts can have data analysis, research, and advisory functions, but in advocating their particular perspectives on national development planning, "they cannot exercise the traditionally most effective bureaucratic lever: access to or control over budgetary resources."

As though these limitations were not enough, it must be noted that there are serious constraints imposed on the situation within which development planning is itself carried out that will have to be taken into account. Depending on the country, development planners may or may not be powerful arbiters of major development issues, but whoever the arbiters may be, their power is constrained by a variety of political and bureaucratic considerations.

The coordination of development and of population policies is a complex and formidable task. It can be made easier by organizational arrangements that can foster a mutual learning process, to help planners see the relevance of demographic variables for their problems and to help researchers understand better the constraints under which they and planners must operate. What is still lacking is the broad base of empirical research and theoretical sophistication needed for detailed policy analysis in the wide range of economic, sociocultural, and institutional settings that prevail in the developing world. Only when the knowledge base that can be generated by such research is available will analysts concerned with population policy be able to demonstrate to the makers of development policy not only that demographic variables are critical to the development process but also that their course can be altered without adversely affecting the other goals of development.

NOTES

[1] In one explanation of why the research base is so narrow (Documents, 1985a:565), it is stated that for many years there has been "a broad consensus of informed opinion" that rapid population growth constituted a major impediment to economic development in the Third World so that "in recent years, as they considered the relevant main issues well settled, most sponsors of social science research, including US government agencies, assigned low priority to research on the economic consequences of population change."

[2] See, for example, Schubnell (1984:7), who, as editor of a symposium on population policies in Asia, pointed to the "dilemma [that] everybody is using the notion of the demographic transition or, more generally, the road of modernization. In nearly all the papers submitted to the Symposium . . . modernization is claimed as a remedy for solving the severe problems of today etc., but we do not have a reliable theory of this phenomenon."

[3] It is the writings of Simon, as Finkle and Crane (1985) noted, that gave new intellectual legitimacy and ammunition to critics of LDC population programs, a criticism that surfaced prominently in the policy statement adopted by the United States delegation to the International Conference on Population held in Mexico City in August 1984. This statement, according to the *Population and Development Review* (Documents, 1984a:575), "marks the most notable conceptual and philosophical departure from previous US population policy statements." The statement claimed (*ibid.*:576) that "the relationship between population growth and economic development is not necessarily a negative one. . . . Indeed, in the economic history of many nations, population growth has been an essential element in economic progress." The United States position that population growth need not adversely affect economic development received virtually no support from the other delegations (Finkle and Crane, 1985; Wulf and Willson, 1984). As Demeny (1985b:101) reported, "The virtually unanimous answer to this question [whether population growth has deleterious consequences for development] given at Mexico City was affirmative." It is beyond the scope of this book to consider the domestic politics that led to the adoption by the Reagan administration of the United States position as an attempt to mollify the demands of the New Right coalition when the 1984 presidential election was in the offing. Both Finkle and Crane (1985) and Wulf and Willson (1984) provide informed, detailed analyses.

[4] It should be noted that the Working Group did not include anyone affiliated with the Population Council.

[5] A broadening of the research base regarding the consequences of rapid population growth for economic and social development at national and subnational levels, and among the diverse groups within countries, should enable empirically oriented scholars to discuss their disagreements on the basis of more objective knowledge than is at

present available for the "debate." Presumably, they could then come closer to a consensus that could facilitate formulation of appropriate policies to influence population growth. Even if such consensus were to be achieved by virtue of documenting what in fact are the consequences of rapid growth, however, there could still be, as McNicoll (1984) points out, substantial disagreement on the valuation of these consequences. The issues involve, among others, choice of welfare criteria, judgments of distributional equity, and considerations of options to be kept open vs. those to be foreclosed. As McNicoll (*ibid.*:229) put it, "Differences in value assumptions can concern anything from details of individual preferences to fundamental ethical premises."

[6]Rapid population growth in the LDCs during the last 20 years has been a prominent factor in increasing the income gap. In an assessment of the income gap from a demographic perspective, Demeny (1981:308) concluded: ". . . material progress in the South is so hindered by current demographic patterns and prospective demographic developments that in the foreseeable future a further widening of the North–South income gap is highly probable."

[7]In this connection, consider the following comments of Heilbroner (1982:236): ". . . population prospects are not so promising that there is any chance of perceptibly narrowing, much less closing, the gap between the levels of material well-being in the developed and underdeveloped worlds. . . . What is the economic challenge posed by this state of things? It is to devise a policy that will minimize the disruptive consequences of this irremediable condition. . . . to encourage the rapid increase of outputs that are both within the productive capability of the less developed lands, and also able to give the masses satisfactions unattainable from material production . . . in the form of social services and collective consumption."

[8]For an account of international assistance for population programs and an analysis of its impact, see Warwick (1982).

[9]According to Warwick (1982:67), "International donors have influenced almost every stage of population policy in the developing countries, from the incipient sense that there is a population problem to be solved to concrete strategies for implementing family planning programs."

[10]Bulatao (1985:44) concluded: "The trend in international donor support for population activities is not encouraging, but whether the trend will continue over the next decade is not known. Expenditures by developing-country governments will probably rise. . . . In the least developed areas, government and foreign donor funding of population programs will continue to be essential. . . . Should subsequent funding fall short of requirements, possibilities for running programs more cheaply and more efficiently will receive increasing attention." On the rising demand for assistance, see also Herz (1984).

[11]Although the UNFPA received contributions from 100 countries in 1985, 95% of the total funds received came from 12 Organisation for Economic Co-operation and Development countries (Population Crisis Committee, 1986). The largest donor has always been the United States, but in 1985, the United States withheld part of its contribution because the UNFPA was providing assistance to China's family planning program, which allegedly used "coercive abortion," a charge denied by both the UNFPA and the government of China (Documents, 1986). In 1986, the United States withheld its entire contribution, and when the UNFPA held its annual pledging conference in November 1986 for 1987 contributions, the United States did not participate. At the time of this writing (mid-1988), it was still unclear whether the United States would resume its contribution, in the amount of $25 million, to the UNFPA even for the Fiscal Year 1989.

[12]Nortman (1985:28) has noted that the experience of China, and to some extent that of India, shows that foreign donor assistance is not a necessary condition for fertility

decline. She added: "Neither is it a sufficient condition as indicated by continuing high fertility in Botswana, Ecuador, Haiti, and Honduras, countries which have received well above average per capita UNFPA family planning assistance. The mixed record suggests that when the absorptive capacity is favorable, foreign assistance can have a catalytic effect on contraceptive use."

[13]In an analogous situation in another region, nationalistic and ethnic issues have prompted the Russians to try to reverse their declining birthrate. The Slavic republics of the Soviet Union, of which Russia is one, have crude birthrates of 16.0–17.7, while rates in the Central Asian republics vary between 24.4 and 38.7. In the Transcaucasion republics, birthrates vary between 18.0 and 26.2 (Schmemann, 1985).

[14]Other advocates of combining macro- and microlevel approaches to the study of fertility change are Hobcraft (1985) and Caldwell (1985). Caldwell (ibid.:51) argues: "There is now a strong case for applying more resources to the study of the causes of fertility decline, and for establishing the best mix of survey and other approaches for attempting this more difficult task. The studies may be more limited, and very much subnational, but they may be of value both for the construction of a theory of fertility change and to policy-makers predicting trends and evaluating the likely effects of different policy options."

[15]By way of illustration, consider the findings of T. H. Hull and V. J. Hull (1977), based mainly on an intensive study of an Indonesian village in central Java (but including data from a national census and a sample survey as well). Contrary to the usual finding of a negative correlation between fertility and class or socioeconomic status, which they say (ibid.:43) "has virtually acquired the force of a socio-demographic law," they found a positive relationship, associated with differences in patterns of marital disruption, postpartum abstinence, and fecundity. They go on to say (ibid.:57): ". . . changes [in fertility] occur at quite different rates and at different periods for people in different economic groups. The relation between class and fertility . . . is very much a function of the stage of socio-cultural change which is being examined. This has the important implication for both demographers and policy-makers that any hypotheses or expectations about the relations of economic status and family size must be firmly grounded in an understanding of the social structure of the society in question rather than the a priori acceptance of a presumed socio-demographic law."

[16]There are in the literature a number of suggested agendas for policy analysis and research on population and development issues. These agendas are usually presented with the important qualification that policy research priorities must ultimately be identified at individual country and intracountry regional levels by local researchers in conjunction with their own development planners and policy-makers. See, for example, Demeny (1974), World Population Conference (1975), McNicoll (1978), International Labor Organization (1979), Miro and Potter (1980), Committee for International Cooperation in National Research in Demography (1981), and Documents (1984b).

[17]A variety of proposals for integrating population policy analysis into development planning have appeared in the literature, both before and after the WPPA call in 1974. See, for example, Saunders and Hardee (1972), Stamper (1973, 1984), Robinson (1975), O. G. Simmons and Saunders (1975), Bilsborrow (1976), Stycos (1977), Todaro (1977b), Snodgrass (1978), Baron (1980), Jones (1982), O. G. Simmons (1984b), Pante (1985), Urzua (1985), and Mundigo (1986).

[18]Rafael Salas (1982:245), the late Executive Director of the UNFPA, observed that "population programmes are not thought of as substitutes for development programmes. . . . However, the emphasis given to population in national development strategies is often

too weak compared with that given to other economic and social variables. This is unfortunate, because the integration of population programmes with development strategies is possible only if population is treated as a sector just like any other sector in the planning process."

[19]In this connection, a statement by staff of the United Nations Population Division on the integration of population and development policies provides a realistic qualification with regard to the degree of integration to be sought. They concluded (United Nations Population Division, 1984:148) that "it is . . . clear that governments are more likely to make an active effort to integrate population and development policies chiefly in those areas of high priority immediately facing the country. . . . a more limited integration of those specific aspects of the population and development issue which attract the highest concern and thus the highest level of committment by the government may be the most effective."

References

Adams, Patricia (1987). All in the name of aid. *Sierra, 72,* 45–50.

Adelman, I. (1979). Redistribution before growth: A strategy for developing countries. In Institute of Social Studies, *Development of Societies: The Next Twenty-Five Years* (pp. 160–176). The Hague: Martinus Nijhoff.

Ahluwalia, Montek S., and Chenery, Hollis (1974). The economic framework. In Hollis B. Chenery, Montek S. Ahluwalia, C. L. G. Bell, John H. Duloy, and Richard Jolly, *Redistribution with Growth* (pp. 38–51). London: Oxford University Press (for the World Bank and the Institute of Development Studies).

Ahooja-Patel, Krishna (1977). Another development for women. In Marc Nerfin (ed.), *Another Development: Approaches and Strategies* (pp. 66–89). Uppsala: Dag Hammarskjöld Foundation.

Ahooja-Patel, Krishna (1982). Another development with women. *Development Dialogue,* 1-2, 17–28.

Alba, Francisco, and Potter, Joseph E. (1986). Population and development in Mexico since 1940: An interpretation. *Population and Development Review, 12,* 47–75.

Allman, J. (ed.) (1978). *Women's Status and Fertility in the Muslim World.* New York: Praeger.

American Association for the Advancement of Science (1974). *Culture and Population Change.* Washington, D.C.: American Association for the Advancement of Science.

Anderson, Barbara A. (1986). Regional and cultural factors in the decline of marital fertility in Western Europe. In Ansley J. Coale and Susan Cotts Watkins (eds.), *The Decline of Fertility in Europe* (pp. 293–313). Princeton, New Jersey: Princeton University Press.

Anker, Richard, and Hein, Catherine (1984). Fertility and employment in the Third World. *Populi, 12,* 29–37.

Anker, Richard, Buvinic, Mayra, and Youssef, Nadia H. (eds.) (1982). *Women's Roles and Population Trends in the Third World.* London: Croom Helm.

Apter, D. E. (1976). Charters, cartels, and multinationals—some colonial and imperial questions. In D. E. Apter and L. W. Goodman (eds.), *The Multinational Corporation and Social Change* (pp. 1–39). New York: Praeger.

Apthorpe, Raymond (1976). Peasants and planistrators in Eastern Africa 1960–1970. In David C. Pitt (ed.), *Development from Below: Anthropologists and Development Situations* (pp. 21–55). Paris: Mouton.

Apthorpe, Raymond (1979). The burden of land reform: An Asian model land reform re-analysed. In Institute of Social Studies, *Development of Societies: The Next Twenty-Five Years* (pp. 103–119). The Hague: Martinus Nijhoff.

Arizpe, Lourdes (1982). Women and development in Latin America and the Caribbean: Lessons from the Seventies and hopes for the future. *Development Dialogue,* 1-2, 74–84.

Arthur, W. Brian, and McNicoll, Geoffrey (1975). Large-scale simulation models in population and development: What use to planners? *Population and Development Review, 1,* 251–265.

Arthur, W. Brian, and McNicoll, Geoffrey (1978). An analytical survey of population and development in Bangladesh. *Population and Development Review, 4*, 23–80.

Austin, James E., and Levinson, F. James (1974). Population and nutrition: A case for integration. *Milbank Memorial Fund Quarterly*, pp. 169–184.

Baer, Werner (1974). The World Bank Group and the process of socio-economic development in the Third World. *World Development, 2*, 1–10.

Balasubramanian, K. (1977). Socio-cultural factors influencing fertility in India. In Lado Ruzicka (ed.), *The Economic and Social Supports for High Fertility* (pp. 119–134). Canberra: Australian National University.

Barlow, Robin (1979). Health and economic development: A theoretical and empirical review. In Ismail Sirageldin (ed.), *Research in Human Capital and Development: A Research Annual*, Vol. 1 (pp. 45–75). Greenwich, Connecticut: JAI Press.

Barnes, Douglas F., and Allen, Julia C. (1981). Deforestation and social forestry in developing countries. *Resources*, No. 66, 7.

Baron, Barnett F. (ed.) (1980). *Population Policy and Development Planning Units in Asia.* Bangkok, Thailand: Population Council Regional Office for South and East Asia.

Barr, Terry N. (1981). The world food situation and global grain prospects. *Science, 214*, 1087–1095.

Bauer, P. T. (1976). *Dissent on Development.* Cambridge, Massachusetts: Harvard University Press.

Bauer, P. T. (1981). *Equality, the Third World, and Economic Delusion.* Cambridge, Massachusetts: Harvard University Press.

Becker, Gary S. (1960). An economic analysis of fertility. In National Bureau of Economic Research, *Demographic and Economic Change in Developed Countries* (pp. 209–231). Princeton, New Jersey: Princeton University Press.

Beenstock, Michael (1980). *Health, Migration, and Development.* Farnborough, England: Gower.

Bell, C. L. G. (1974). The political framework. In Hollis B. Chenery, Montek S. Ahluwalia, C. L. G. Bell, John H. Duloy, and Richard Jolly, *Redistribution with Growth* (pp. 52–72). London: Oxford University Press (for the World Bank and the Institute of Development Studies).

Bell, C. L. G., and Duloy, John H. (1974). Rural target groups. In Hollis B. Chenery, Montek S. Ahluwalia, C. L. G. Bell, John H. Duloy, and Richard Jolly, *Redistribution with Growth* (pp. 113–135). London: Oxford University Press (for the World Bank and the Institute of Development Studies).

Bell, David E. (1980). Introduction. *Social Science and Medicine, 14C*, 63–65.

Bell, David E. (1986). Population policy: Choices for the United States. In Jane Menken (ed.), *World Population and U.S. Policy: The Choices Ahead* (pp. 207–228). New York: W. W. Norton (for the American Assembly).

Benedick, Richard E. (1984). World population growth and economic development. *World Affairs Journal, 3*, 1–7.

Berg, Alan (1973). *The Nutrition Factor: Its Role in National Development.* Washington, D.C.: Brookings Institution.

Bergsten, Fred C., Horst, Thomas, and Moran, Theodore H. (1978). *American Multinationals and American Interests.* Washington, D.C.: Brookings Institution.

Bernstein, Henry (1971). Modernization theory and the sociological study of development. *Journal of Development Studies, 7*, 141–160.

Bernstein, Henry (1979). Sociology of underdevelopment vs. sociology of development? In Henry Lehmann (ed.), *Development Theory: Four Critical Case Studies* (pp. 77–106). London: Frank Cass.

Berry, Leonard, and Kates, Robert W. (eds.) (1980). *Making the Most of the Least: Alternative Ways to Development.* New York: Holmes and Meier.

Berry, R. Albert, and Cline, William R. (1979). *Agrarian Structure and Productivity in Developing Countries.* Baltimore: Johns Hopkins University Press.

Biddle, Wayne (1983). U.S. leads in sale of arms abroad. *New York Times,* May 14, A1.

Bilsborrow, Richard E. (1976). *Population in Development Planning: Background and Bibliography.* Chapel Hill: University of North Carolina.

Birdsall, Nancy (1977). Analytical approaches to the relationship of population growth and development. *Population and Development Review, 3,* 63–102.

Birdsall, Nancy (1980). Population and poverty in the developing world. *World Bank Staff Working Papers No. 404.* Washington, D.C.: World Bank.

Birdsall, Nancy (ed.) (1985). The effects of family planning programs on fertility in the developing world. *World Bank Staff Working Papers No. 677.* Washington, D.C.: World Bank.

Bissell, Richard E. (1983). Political origins of the new international economic order. In W. Scott Thompson (ed.), *The Third World: Premises of U.S. Policy* (pp. 223–238). San Francisco: ICS Press.

Blaug, Mark (1979). The quality of population in developing countries, with particular reference to education and training. In Philip M. Hauser (ed.), *World Population and Development: Challenges and Prospects* (pp. 361–402). Syracuse, New York: Syracuse University Press.

Bongaarts, John (1978). A framework for analyzing the proximate determinants of fertility. *Population and Development Review, 4,* 105–132.

Bongaarts, John (1979). Malnutrition and fecundity: A summary of evidence. *Center for Policy Studies Working Papers No. 51.* New York: Population Council.

Bongaarts, John (1982). The fertility-inhibiting effects of the intermediate fertility variables. *Studies in Family Planning, 13,* 179–189.

Bongaarts, John (1983). The proximate determinants of natural marital fertility. In Rodolfo A. Bulatao and Ronald D. Lee (eds.), *Determinants of Fertility in Developing Countries,* Vol. 1 (pp. 103–138). New York: Academic Press.

Bongaarts, John (1986). The transition in reproductive behavior in the Third World. In Jane Menken (ed.), *World Population and U.S. Policy: The Choices Ahead* (pp. 105–132). New York: W. W. Norton.

Bongaarts, John, and Menken, Jane (1983). The supply of children: A critical essay. In Rodolfo A. Bulatao and Ronald D. Lee (eds.), *Determinants of Fertility in Developing Countries,* Vol. 1 (pp. 27–60). New York: Academic Press.

Bongaarts, John, and Potter, Robert G. (1983). *Fertility, Biology, and Behavior: An Analysis of the Proximate Determinants.* New York: Academic Press.

Borlaug, Norman E., Anderson, R. Glenn, and Sprague, Ernest W. (1982). Food and population: The unequal equation. *IDRC Reports, 10,* 22–23.

Boserup, Ester (1965). *The Conditions of Agricultural Growth.* London: Allen and Unwin.

Boserup, Ester (1970). *Women's Role in Economic Development.* New York: St. Martin's.

Boserup, Ester (1981). *Population and Technological Change: A Study of Long-Term Trends.* Chicago: University of Chicago Press.

Boserup, Ester (1984). Technical change and human fertility in rural areas of developing countries. In Wayne A. Schutjer and C. Shannon Stokes (eds.), *Rural Development and Human Fertility* (pp. 23–33). New York: Macmillan.

Boulding, Elise (1983). Measures of women's work in the Third World: Problems and suggestions. In Mayra Buvinic, Margaret A. Lycette and William Paul McGreevey (eds.), *Women and Poverty in the Third World* (pp. 286–299). Baltimore: Johns Hopkins University Press.

Boulier, Bryan L. (1982). Income redistribution and fertility decline: A sceptical view. *Population and Development Review, 8*(Supplement), 159–173.

Brady, Nyle C. (1982). Chemistry and world food supplies. *Science, 218,* 847–853.

Brookfield, Harold (1975). *Interdependent Development.* Pittsburgh: University of Pittsburgh Press.

Brown, Peter G. (1977). *Some Relationships between Food, Population and International Justice.* Hastings, New York: Institute of Society, Ethics and the Life Sciences.

Bulatao, Rodolfo A. (1983). A framework for the study of fertility determinants. In Rodolfo A. Bulatao and Ronald D. Lee (eds.), *Determinants of Fertility in Developing Countries* (Vol. 1, pp. 1–26). New York: Academic Press.

Bulatao, Rodolfo A. (1985). Expenditures on population programs in developing regions: Current levels and future requirements. *World Bank Staff Working Papers No. 679,* Population and Development Series No. 4. Washington, D.C.: World Bank.

Bulatao, Rodolfo A., and Lee, Ronald D. (eds.) (1983a). *Determinants of Fertility in Developing Countries,* Vols. 1 and 2. New York: Academic Press.

Bulatao, Rodolfo A., and Lee, Ronald D. (1983b). An overview of fertility determinants in developing countries. In Rodolfo A. Bulatao and Ronald D. Lee (eds.), *Determinants of Fertility in Developing Countries,* Vol. 2 (pp. 757–787). New York: Academic Press.

Bumpass, Larry, Rindfuss, Ronald R., Palmore, James A., Concepcion, Mercedes, and Choi, Byoung Mohk (1982). Intermediate variables and educational differentials in fertility in Korea and the Philippines. *Demography, 19,* 241–260.

Burch, Thomas K. (1975). Theories of fertility decline as guides to policy: Some preliminary thoughts. *Social Forces, 54,* 126–138.

Burch, Thomas K. (1979). Household and family demography: A bibliographic essay. *Population Index, 45,* 173–194.

Burch, Thomas K. (1980). Decision-making theories in demography: An introduction. In Thomas K. Burch (ed.), *Demographic Behavior: Interdisciplinary Perspectives on Decision-Making* (pp. 1–22). Boulder, Colorado: Westview.

Butz, William P., and Habicht, Jean-Pierre (1976). The effects of nutrition and health on fertility: Hypotheses, evidence, and interventions. In Ronald G. Ridker (ed.), *Population and Development: The Search for Selective Interventions* (pp. 210–238). Baltimore: Johns Hopkins University Press.

Buvinic, Mayra (1983). Women's issues in Third World poverty: A policy analysis. In Mayra Buvinic, Margaret A. Lycette, and William Paul McGreevey (eds.), *Women and Poverty in the Third World* (pp. 14–31). Baltimore: Johns Hopkins University Press.

Buvinic, Mayra, and Youssef, Nadia H. (1978). *Women-Headed Households: The Ignored Factor in Development Planning.* Washington. D.C.: International Center for Research on Women.

Cain, Mead (1977). The economic activities of children in a village in Bangladesh. *Population and Development Review, 3,* 201–227.

Cain, Mead (1981). Risk and insurance: Perspectives on fertility and agrarian change in India and Bangladesh. *Population and Development Review, 7,* 435–474.

Cain, Mead (1982). Perspectives on family and fertility in developing countries. *Population Studies, 36,* 159–175.

Cain, Mead (1983). Fertility as an adjustment to risk. *Population and Development Review, 9,* 688–702.

Cain, Mead (1984). Women's status and fertility in developing countries: Son preference and economic security. *Center for Policy Studies Working Papers No. 110.* New York: Population Council.

Cain, Mead (1985). On the relationship between landholding and fertility. *Population Studies, 39,* 5–15.

Cain, Mead (1986a). Risk and fertility: Reply to Robinson. *Population Studies, 40,* 299–304.

Cain, Mead (1986b). Landholding and fertility: A rejoinder. *Population Studies, 40,* 313–317.

Cain, Mead (1986c). The consequences of reproductive failure: Dependence, mobility, and mortality among the elderly of rural South Asia. *Population Studies, 40,* 375–388.

Cain, Mead, and Lieberman, Samuel S. (1982). Development policy and the prospects for fertility decline in Bangladesh. *Center for Policy Studies Working Papers No. 91.* New York: Population Council.

Cain, Mead, Khanam, Syeda Rokeya, and Nahar, Shamsun (1979). Class, patriarchy, and women's work in Bangladesh. *Population and Development Review, 5,* 405–438.

Caldwell, John C. (1976). Toward a restatement of demographic transition theory. *Population and Development Review, 2,* 321–366.

Caldwell, John C. (1978). A theory of fertility: From high plateau to destabilization. *Population and Development Review, 4,* 553–578.

Caldwell, John C. (1979). Education as a factor in mortality decline: An examination of Nigerian data. *Population Studies, 33,* 395–413.

Caldwell, John C. (1980). Mass education as a determinant of the timing of fertility decline. *Population and Development Review, 6,* 225–255.

Caldwell, John C. (1982). *Theory of Fertility Decline.* New York: Academic Press.

Caldwell, John C. (1985). Strengths and limitations of the survey approach for measuring and understanding fertility change: Alternative possibilities. In John Cleland and John Hobcraft (eds.), *Reproductive Change in Developing Countries: Insights from the World Fertility Survey* (pp. 45–63). New York: Oxford University Press.

Caldwell, John C. (1986). Routes to low mortality in poor countries. *Population and Development Review, 12,* 171–220.

Caldwell, John C. (undated). The failure of theories of social and economic change to explain demographic change: Puzzles of modernization or Westernization (unpublished paper).

Caldwell, John C., and Caldwell, Pat (1978). The achieved small family: Early fertility transition in an African city. *Studies in Family Planning, 9,* 2–18.

Caldwell, John C., McDonald, P. F., and Ruzicka, L. T. (1980). Interrelationships between nuptiality and fertility: The evidence from the World Fertility Survey (paper presented at the World Fertility Survey Conference, London, July 7–11).

Caldwell, John C., Reddy, P. H., and Caldwell, Pat (1985). Educational transition in rural south India. *Population and Development Review, 11,* 29–51.

Calloway, Doris Howes (1980). Functional consequences of malnutrition (unpublished paper). Berkeley: Department of Nutritional Sciences, University of California.

Cardoso, Fernando Henrique (1977). Towards another development. In Marc Nerfin (ed.), *Another Development: Approaches and Strategies* (pp. 21–39). Uppsala: Dag Hammarskjöld Foundation.

Cardoso, Fernando Henrique (1979). The originality of the copy: The Economic Commission for Latin America and the idea of development. In Albert O. Hirschman (ed.), *Toward a New Strategy for Development* (pp. 53–72). New York: Pergamon.

Cardoso, Fernando Henrique, and Faletto, Enzo (1979). *Dependency and Development in Latin America.* Berkeley: University of California Press (English translation of the original edition published in 1971).

Carnoy, Martin (1980). Can education alone solve the problem of unemployment? In John Simmons (ed.), *The Education Dilemma: Policy Issues for Developing Countries in the 1980s* (pp. 153–163). Oxford: Pergamon.

Cassel, John (1971). Health consequences of population density and crowding. In National

Academy of Sciences, *Rapid Population Growth: Consequences and Policy Implications* (pp. 462–478). Baltimore: Johns Hopkins University Press.

Cassen, Robert H. (1975). Welfare and population: Notes on rural India since 1960. *Population and Development Review*, 1, 31–70.

Cassen, Robert H. (1976). Population and development: A survey. *World Development*, 4, 785–830.

Cassen, Robert H. (1978a). Basic needs: An appraisal. In International Union for the Scientific Study of Population, *Conference on "Economic and Demographic Change: Issues for the 1980's" Helsinki 1978* (pp. 3.3.2). Liege: IUSSP.

Cassen, Robert H. (1978b). *India: Population, Economy, Society*. New York: Holmes and Meier.

Cassen, Robert H. (1978c). Health. In Robert H. Cassen and Margaret Wolfson (eds.), *Planning for Growing Populations* (pp. 79–102). Paris: Organisation for Economic Co-operation and Development.

Casterline, John B. (1985). The macro determinants of fertility lessons from the WFS experience (unpublished paper). Providence, Rhode Island: Population Studies and Training Center, Brown University.

Castro, Alfonso Peter, Hakansson, N. Thomas, and Brokensha, David (1981). Indicators of rural inequality. *World Development;* 9, 401–427.

Chapman, Murray (1981). Policy implications of circulation: Some answers from the grass roots. In G. W. Jones and H. V. Richter (eds.), *Population Mobility and Development: Southeast Asia and the Pacific* (pp. 71–87), Development Studies Centre Monograph No. 27. Canberra: Australian National University.

Charlton, Sue Ellen M. (1984). *Women in Third World Development*. Boulder, Colorado: Westview.

Chaudhury, R. H. (1978). Female status and fertility behaviour in a metropolitan urban area of Bangladesh. *Population Studies, 32*, 261–273.

Chen, Lincoln C. (1983). Child survival: Levels, trends, and determinants. In Rodolfo A. Bulatao and Ronald D. Lee (eds.), *Determinants of Fertility in Developing Countries*, Vol. 1 (pp. 199–232). New York: Academic Press.

Chenery, Hollis B. (1979). *Structural Change and Development Policy*. New York: Oxford University Press (for the World Bank).

Chenery, Hollis B., and Duloy, John H. (1974). Research directions. In Hollis B. Chenery, Montek S. Ahluwalia, C. L. G. Bell, John H. Duloy, and Richard Jolly, *Redistribution with Growth* (pp. 245–249). London: Oxford University Press (for the World Bank and the Institute of Development Studies).

Chenery, Hollis B., Ahluwalia, Montek S., Bell, C. L. G., Duloy, John H., and Jolly, Richard (1974). *Redistribution with Growth*. London: Oxford University Press (for the World Bank and the Institute of Development Studies).

Chilcote, Ronald H. (1984). *Theories of Development and Underdevelopment*. Boulder, Colorado: Westview.

Chirot, Daniel (1985). The rise of the West. *American Sociological Review*, 50, 181–195.

Choi, E. Kwan, and Hicks, W. Whitney (1984). Agricultural mechanization policy and human fertility. In Wayne A. Schutjer and C. Shannon Stokes (eds.), *Rural Development and Human Fertility* (pp. 252–268). New York: Macmillan.

Clark, Colin (1967). *Population Growth and Land Use*. London/New York: Macmillan/St. Martin's Press.

Clausen, A. W. (1984a). *International Trade and Global Economic Growth: The Critical Relationship*. Washington, D.C.: World Bank.

Clausen, A. W. (1984b). *Population Growth and Economic and Social Development*. Washington, D.C.: World Bank.

Clausen, A. W. (1985a). *Address to the Board of Governors, Seoul, Korea, October 8, 1985.* Washington, D.C.: World Bank.

Clausen, A. W. (1985b). *Poverty in the Developing Countries 1985.* Washington, D.C.: World Bank.

Clawson, Marion (1981). Entering the twenty-first century—the Global 2000 Report to the President. *Resources,* No. 66, 19–21.

Cleland, John (1985). Marital fertility decline in developing countries: Theories and the evidence. In John Cleland and John Hobcraft (eds.), *Reproductive Change in Developing Countries: Insights from the World Fertility Survey* (pp. 223–252). New York: Oxford University Press.

Cleland, John, and Hobcraft, John (eds.) (1985). *Reproductive Change in Developing Countries: Insights from the World Fertility Survey.* New York: Oxford University Press.

Coale, Ansley J. (1975). The demographic transition. In United Nations, *The Population Debate: Dimensions and Perspectives,* Vol. 1 (pp. 347–355). New York: United Nations.

Coale, Ansley J. (ed.) (1976). *Economic Factors in Population Growth.* New York: John Wiley.

Coale, Ansley J. (1978). Population growth and economic development: The case of Mexico. *Foreign Affairs, 56,* 415–429.

Coale, Ansley J. (1978–1979). Reply. *Foreign Affairs, 57,* 410–411.

Coale, Ansley J., and Watkins, Susan Cotts (eds.) (1986). *The Decline of Fertility in Europe.* Princeton, New Jersey: Princeton University Press.

Coale, Ansley J., Anderson, Barbara A., and Härm, Erna (1979). *Human Fertility in Russia Since the Nineteenth Century.* Princeton, New Jersey: Princeton University Press.

Cochrane, Susan H. (1979). *Fertility and Education: What Do We Really Know?* World Bank Staff Occasional Paper. Baltimore: Johns Hopkins University Press.

Cochrane, Susan H. (1983). Effects of education and urbanization on fertility. In Rodolfo A. Bulatao and Ronald D. Lee (eds.), *Determinants of Fertility in Developing Countries,* Vol. 2 (pp. 587–626). New York: Academic Press.

Cochrane, Susan H., O'Hara, Donald J., and Leslie, Joanne (1980). The relationship between education and health (unpublished paper). Washington, D.C.: World Bank.

Coleman, James S. (1965a). Introduction: Education and political development. In James S. Coleman (ed.), *Education and Political Development* (pp. 3–32). Princeton, New Jersey: Princeton University Press.

Coleman, James S. (1965b). Introduction to part III: The education of modern elites in developing countries. In James S. Coleman (ed.), *Education and Political Development* (pp. 353–371). Princeton, New Jersey: Princeton University Press.

Coleman, James S. (1965c). Introduction to part IV: Educational planning and political development. In James S. Coleman (ed.), *Education and Political Development* (pp. 521–540). Princeton, New Jersey: Princeton University Press.

Coles, Robert (1986a). *The Moral Life of Children.* Boston: Atlantic Monthly Press.

Coles, Robert (1986b). *The Political Life of Children.* Boston: Atlantic Monthly Press.

Committee for International Cooperation in National Research in Demography (1981). *A New Approach to Cooperative Research in the Population Field: Population Variables in the Planning Process.* Paris: CICRED.

Conde, Julien (1978). Rapid population growth in developing countries. In Robert H. Cassen and Margaret Wolfson (eds.), *Planning for Growing Populations* (pp. 26–48). Paris: Organisation for Economic Co-operation and Development.

Cool, John C. (1979). Landlessness and rural poverty in Asia: The circular trap (unpublished paper). New York: Ford Foundation.

Cooper, Richard N. (1979). Developed country reactions to calls for a new international economic order. In Albert O. Hirschman (ed.), *Toward a New Strategy for Development* (pp. 243–274). New York: Pergamon.

Council on Environmental Quality and United States Department of State (1980). *The Global 2000 Report to the President*, Vols. 1 and 2. Washington, D.C.: U.S. Government Printing Office.

Cowgill, George L. (1975). On causes and consequences of ancient and modern population changes. *American Anthropologist, 77*, 505–525.

Cramer, James C. (1980). Fertility and female employment: Problems of causal direction. *American Sociological Review, 45*, 167–190.

Crane, Barbara, and Finkle, Jason L. (1981). Organizational impediments to development assistance: The World Bank's population program. *World Politics, 33*, 516–553.

Cutright, Phillips (1983). The ingredients of recent fertility decline in developing countries. *International Family Planning Perspectives, 9*, 101–109.

Cutright, Phillips (1986). Review of Donald J. Hernandez, *Success or Failure? Family Planning Programs in the Third World. International Family Planning Perspectives, 12*, 105–106.

Cutright, Phillips, and Hargens, Lowell (1984). The threshold hypothesis: Evidence from less developed Latin American countries, 1950 to 1980. *Demography, 21*, 459–473.

Daly, Herman E. (1986). Review of National Research Council, *Population Growth and Economic Development: Policy Questions. Population and Development Review, 12*, 582–585.

Davidson, Maria (1977). Female work status and fertility in Latin America. In Stanley Kupinsky (ed.), *The Fertility of Working Women: A Synthesis of International Research* (pp. 342–354). New York: Praeger.

Davis, Kingsley (1963). The theory of change and response in modern demographic history. *Population Index, 30*, 345–366.

Davis, Kingsley (1973). Zero population growth: The goal and the means. *Daedalus, 102*, 15–30.

Davis, Kingsley, and Blake, Judith (1956). Social structure and fertility: An analytic framework. *Economic Development and Cultural Change, 4*, 211–235.

Dell, Sidney (1978). Basic needs or comprehensive development. *CEPAL Review*, pp. 7–33 (United Nations E.78.II.G.3.).

Demeny, Paul (1974). Population and development: An agenda for policy-oriented research. In Ford Foundation, *Social Science Research on Population and Development* (pp. 51–63). New York: Ford Foundation.

Demeny, Paul (1981). The North–South income gap: A demographic perspective. *Population and Development Review, 7*, 297–310.

Demeny, Paul (1982). Population policies. In Just Faaland (ed.), *Population and the World Economy in the 21st Century* (pp. 206–228). Oxford: Blackwell.

Demeny, Paul (1984). A perspective on long-term population growth. *Population and Development Review, 10*, 103–126.

Demeny, Paul (1985a). The world demographic situation. *Center for Policy Studies Working Papers No. 121*. New York: Population Council.

Demeny, Paul (1985b). Bucharest, Mexico City, and beyond. *Population and Development Review, 11*, 99–106.

Demeny, Paul (1986). Population and the invisible hand. *Demography, 23*, 473–487.

De Tray, Denis N. (1976). Population growth and educational policies: An economic perspective. In Ronald G. Ridker (ed.), *Population and Development: The Search for Selective Interventions* (pp. 182–209). Baltimore: Johns Hopkins University Press (for Resources for the Future).

De Tray, Denis N. (1977). Age of marriage and fertility: A policy review. *Pakistan Development Review, 16*, 89–100.

Digest (1981). *International Family Planning Perspectives, 7*, 24–26.

Dixon, Ruth B. (1976). The roles of rural women: Female seclusion, economic production, and reproductive choice. In Ronald G. Ridker (ed.), *Population and Development: The Search for Selective Interventions* (pp. 290–321). Baltimore: Johns Hopkins University Press.

Dixon, Ruth B. (1978). *Rural Women at Work: Strategies for Development in South Asia.* Baltimore: Johns Hopkins University Press (for Resources for the Future).

Dixon, Ruth B. (1983). Rural women: Working toward recognition. *Contemporary Sociology, 12,* 495–497.

Dixon, Ruth B. (1985). New jobs needed for rural women. *Populi, 12,* 16–28.

Documents (1982). Answer to Malthus? Julian Simon interviewed by William Buckley. *Population and Development Review, 8,* 205–218.

Documents (1983). Population and the size of the domestic market: A Malaysian view. *Population and Development Review, 9,* 389–391.

Documents (1984a). US policy statement for the international conference on population. *Population and Development Review, 10,* 574–579.

Documents (1984b). Mexico City declaration on population and development, and recommendations for the further implementation of the world population plan of action. *Populi, 11,* 46–70.

Documents (1985a). Population growth as a critical North–South issue: A debate. *Population and Development Review, 11,* 565–572.

Documents (1985b). The World Bank on environment and development. *Population and Development Review, 11,* 795–796.

Documents (1985c). A statement on population stabilization by world leaders. *Population and Development Review, 11,* 787–788.

Documents (1986). USAID/UNFPA discord over support for China's family planning program. *Population and Development Review, 12,* 159–163.

Dodd, Nicholas (1986). Review of Donald J. Hernandez, *Success or Failure? Family Planning Programs in the Third World. Populi, 13,* 69–70.

Dorfman, Ariel (1984). Bread and burnt rice: Culture and economic survival in Latin America. *Grassroots Development, 8,* 3–25.

Dos Santos, Theotonio (1976). The crisis of development theory and the problem of dependence in Latin America. In Henry Bernstein (ed.), *Underdevelopment and Development: The Third World Today* (pp. 57–80). Harmondsworth, England: Penguin Books.

Dreyer, O. (1976). *Cultural Changes in Developing Countries.* Moscow: Progress Publishers.

D'Souza, Stan, and Chen, Lincoln C. (1980). Sex differentials in mortality in rural Bangladesh. *Population and Development Review, 6,* 257–270.

Dyson, Tim, and Murphy, Mike (1985). The onset of fertility transition. *Population and Development Review, 11,* 399–440.

Easterlin, Richard A. (1969). Towards a socioeconomic theory of fertility: A survey of recent research on economic factors in American fertility. In S. J. Behrman, L. Corsa, and R. Freedman (eds.), *Fertility and Family Planning: A World View* (pp. 127–156). Ann Arbor: University of Michigan Press.

Easterlin, Richard A. (1971). Does human fertility adjust to the environment? *American Economic Review, 61,* 399–407.

Easterlin, Richard A. (1975). An economic framework for fertility analysis. *Studies in Family Planning, 6,* 54–63.

Easterlin, Richard A. (1976). Population change and farm settlement in the northern United States. *Journal of Economic History, 36,* 45–75.

Easterlin, Richard A. (1978). The economics and sociology of fertility: A synthesis. In Charles Tilly (ed.), *Historical Studies of Changing Fertility* (pp. 57–133). Princeton, New Jersey: Princeton University Press.

Easterlin, Richard A. (1983). Modernization and fertility: A critical essay. In Rodolfo A.

Bulatao and Ronald D. Lee (eds.), *Determinants of Fertility in Developing Countries*, Vol. 2 (pp. 562–586). New York: Academic Press.

Easterlin, Richard A., and Crimmins, Eileen M. (1985). *The Fertility Revolution: A Supply–Demand Analysis*. Chicago: University of Chicago Press.

Easterlin, Richard A., Pollak, Robert A., and Wachter, Michael L. (1980). Toward a more general economic model of fertility determination: Endogenous preferences and natural fertility. In Richard A. Easterlin (ed.), *Population and Economic Change in Developing Countries* (pp. 81–135). Chicago: University of Chicago Press.

Edmonston, Barry, and Martorell, Reynaldo (1984). Mortality and nutrition: A review of selected micro-level relationships (unpublished paper). Ithaca, New York: International Population Program and Division of Nutritional Sciences, Cornell University.

Edsall, Thomas Byrne (1984). *The New Politics of Inequality*. New York: W. W. Norton.

Edwards, Edgar O., and Todaro, Michael P. (1974). Education, society and development: Some main themes and suggested strategies for international assistance. *World Development*, 2, 25–30.

Eisenstadt, S. N. (1966). *Modernization: Protest and Change*. Englewood Cliffs, New Jersey: Prentice-Hall.

Enloe, C. H. (1980). Least development and political development: Some Asian experiences. In Leonard Berry and Robert W. Kates (eds.), *Making the Most of the Least: Alternative Ways to Development* (pp. 39–46). New York: Holmes and Meier.

Faaland, Just (1982). Overview. In Just Faaland (ed.), *Population and the World Economy in the 21st Century* (pp. 1–22). Oxford: Blackwell.

Fawcett, J. T., and Bornstein, M. F. (1973). Modernization, individual modernity, and fertility. In J. T. Fawcett (ed.), *Psychological Perspectives on Population* (pp. 106–131). New York: Basic Books.

Fei, John C. H., and Ranis, Gustav (1984). Task orientation and technology change: A suggested approach. In Gustav Ranis, Robert L. West, Mark W. Leiserson, and Cynthia Taft Morris (eds.), *Comparative Development Perspectives* (pp. 1–16). Boulder, Colorado: Westview.

Fields, Gary S. (1980). *Poverty, Inequality, and Development*. Cambridge, England: Cambridge University Press.

Finkle, Jason L., and Crane, Barbara B. (1985). Ideology and politics at Mexico City: The United States at the 1984 international conference on population. *Population and Development Review*, 11, 1–25.

Flegg, A. T. (1979). The role of inequality of income in the determination of birth rates. *Population Studies*, 33, 457–477.

Ford Foundation (1982). *The Search for a New Economic Order*. New York: Ford Foundation.

Ford, R. B. (1980). Least development: Questions in search of answers. In Leonard Berry and Robert W. Kates (eds.), *Making the Most of the Least: Alternative Ways to Development* (pp. 3–9). New York: Holmes and Meier.

Frank, Andre Gunder (1969). *Latin America: Underdevelopment or Revolution*. New York: Monthly Review Press.

Frank, Andre Gunder (1980). *Crisis: In the World Economy*. New York: Holmes and Meier.

Frank, Odile (1985). The demand for fertility control in sub-Saharan Africa. *Center for Policy Studies Working Papers No. 117*. New York: Population Council.

Freedman, Ronald (1979). Theories of fertility decline: A reappraisal. In Philip M. Hauser (ed.), *World Population and Development: Challenges and Prospects* (pp. 63–79). Syracuse, New York: Syracuse University Press.

Freedman, Ronald (1986). Policy options after the demographic transition: The case of Taiwan. *Population and Development Review*, 12, 77–116.

French, Howard (1986). Speakers at U.N. cite needs of Third World. *New York Times,* September 23, A13.

Fried, Ellen Shapiro, and Settergren, Susan (1985). The more things change. . . (unpublished paper). Research Triangle Park, North Carolina: Research Triangle Institute.

Furtado, Celso (1977). *Economic Development of Latin America: Historical Background and Contemporary Problems.* Cambridge, England: Cambridge University Press.

Garcia-Bouza, Jorge (1980). *A Basic-Needs Analytical Bibliography.* Paris: Organisation for Economic Co-operation and Development.

Gereffi, Gary (1985). Review of Charles P. Kindleberger, *Multinational Excursions. Contemporary Sociology, 14,* 728–730.

Germain, Adrienne (1975). Status and roles of women as factors in fertility behavior: A policy analysis. *Studies in Family Planning, 6,* 192–200.

Germain, Adrienne (1976–1977). Poor rural women: A policy perspective. *Journal of International Affairs, 30,* 1–20.

Germain, Adrienne, and Smock, Audrey (1974). The status of Ghanaian and Kenyan women: Implications for fertility behavior (unpublished paper). New York: Ford Foundation.

Ghai, D. P., and Alfthan, T. (1977). On the principles of quantifying and satisfying basic needs. In International Labour Office, *The Basic Needs Approach to Development* (pp. 19–59). Geneva: International Labour Office.

Giele, Janet Zollinger (1977). Introduction: Comparative perspectives on women. In Janet Zollinger Giele and Audrey C. Smock (eds.), *Women: Roles and Status in Eight Countries* (pp. 3–31). New York: John Wiley.

Gilland, Bernard (1983). Considerations on world population and food supply. *Population and Development Review, 9,* 203–211.

Gille, Halvor (1985). Policy implications. In John Cleland and John Hobcraft (eds.), *Reproductive Change in Developing Countries: Insights from the World Fertility Survey* (pp. 273–295). New York: Oxford University Press.

Gish, Oscar (1983). Health with equity. *People, 10,* 3–5.

Goldberg, David (1975). Socioeconomic theory and differential fertility: The case of the LDCs. *Social Forces, 54,* 84–106.

Goldstein, Sidney (1972). The influence of labor force participation and education on fertility in Thailand. *Population Studies, 26,* 419–436.

Goldthorpe, J. E. (1984). *The Sociology of the Third World.* Cambridge, England: Cambridge University Press.

Goulet, Denis (1971). *The Cruel Choice: A New Concept in the Theory of Development.* New York: Atheneum.

Goulet, Denis (1979). Development as liberation: Policy lessons from case studies. *World Development, 7,* 555–566.

Graff, Harvey J. (1979). Literacy, education, and fertility, past and present: A critical review. *Population and Development Review, 5,* 105–140.

Grant, James P. (1977). Foreword. In International Labour Office, *Employment, Growth and Basic Needs: A One-World Problem* (pp. v–xi). New York: Praeger.

Gray, Ronald (1983). The impact of health and nutrition on natural fertility. In Rodolfo A. Bulatao and Ronald D. Lee (eds.), *Determinants of Fertility in Developing Countries,* Vol. 1 (pp. 139–162). New York: Academic Press.

Green, Reginald H. (1977). Income distribution and the eradication of poverty in Tanzania. In Irving Louis Horowitz (ed.), *Equity, Income, and Policy: Comparative Studies of Three Worlds of Development* (pp. 212–272). New York: Praeger.

Greenhalgh, Susan (1985). Sexual stratification: The other side of "growth with equity" in East Asia. *Population and Development Review, 11,* 265–314.

Griffin, Keith (1969). *Underdevelopment in Spanish America: An Interpretation.* Cambridge, Massachusetts: MIT Press.

Griffin, Keith (1978). *International Inequality and National Poverty.* New York: Holmes and Meier.

Griffin, Keith (1981). Economic development in a changing world. *World Development, 9,* 221–226.

Griffin, Keith, and Khan, Azizur Rahman (1978). Poverty in the Third World: Ugly facts and fancy models. *World Development, 6,* 295–304.

Grosse, Robert N., and Harkavy, Oscar (1980). The role of health in development. *Social Science and Medicine, 14C,* 165–169.

Gunatilleke, Godfrey (1984). Working paper on strategies for meeting basic socio-economic needs in the context of achieving the goals of population policies and programmes. In Economic and Social Commission for Asia and the Pacific, *Third Asian and Pacific Population Conference: Selected Papers* (pp. 253–266), Asian Population Studies Series No. 58. Bangkok: Economic and Social Commission for Asia and the Pacific.

Gurak, Douglas T., and Kritz, Mary M. (1982). Female employment and fertility in the Dominican Republic: A dynamic perspective. *American Sociological Review, 47,* 810–818.

Haq, Mahbub ul (1976). *The Poverty Curtain: Choices for the Third World.* New York: Columbia University Press.

Haq, Mahbub ul (1981). Foreword. In Paul Streeten with Shahid Javed Burki, Mahbub ul Haq, Norman Hicks, and Frances Stewart, *First Things First: Meeting Basic Human Needs in the Developing Countries* (pp. vii–x). New York: Oxford University Press (for the World Bank).

Hauser, Philip M. (1979). Introduction and overview. In Philip M. Hauser (ed.), *World Population and Development: Challenges and Prospects* (pp. 1–62). Syracuse, New York: Syracuse University Press.

Hawthorn, Geoffrey (1970). *The Sociology of Fertility.* London: Collier-Macmillan.

Hawthorn, Geoffrey (1978). Introduction. *Journal of Development Studies, 14,* 1–21.

Hawthorn, Geoffrey (1981). Review of Richard A. Easterlin (ed.), *Population and Economic Change in Developing Countries. Population and Development Review, 7,* 702–703.

Heilbroner, Robert (1982). Population growth and policies: Discussion. In Just Faaland (ed.), *Population and the World Economy in the 21st Century* (pp. 234–238). Oxford, England: Blackwell.

Hein, Catherine (1982). Factory employment, marriage and fertility: The case of Mauritian women. *World Employment Programme Working Papers No. 118.* Geneva: International Labour Office (WEP 2-21/WP.118).

Heisel, Donald, and Benbow, Carolyn (1984). The fifth inquiry: A summary. *Populi, 11,* 4–12.

Henriot, Peter J. (1976). *Population and Ecology: An Overview.* Washington, D.C.: Center of Concern.

Hernandez, Donald J. (1984). *Success or Failure? Family Planning Programs in the Third World.* Westport, Connecticut: Greenwood.

Hernandez, Donald J. (1985). Fertility reduction policies and poverty in Third World countries: Ethical issues. *Studies in Family Planning, 16,* 76–87.

Herz, Barbara K. (1984). Official development assistance for population activities: A review. *World Bank Staff Working Papers No. 688,* Population and Development Series No. 13. Washington, D.C.: World Bank.

Hicks, Norman L. (1984). Is there a tradeoff between growth and basic needs? In Mitchell

A. Seligson (ed.), *The Gap between Rich and Poor* (pp. 338–347). Boulder, Colorado: Westview.

Hicks, Norman L., and Streeten, Paul (1979). Indicators of development: The search for a basic needs yardstick. *World Development*, 7, 567–580.

Higgins, Benjamin (1977). Economic development and cultural change: Seamless web or patchwork quilt? In Manning Nash (ed.), *Essays on Economic Development and Cultural Change in Honor of Bert F. Hoselitz* (pp. 99–122). Chicago: University of Chicago Press.

Hirschman, Albert O. (1967). *Development Projects Observed*. Washington, D.C.: Brookings Institution.

Hirschman, Albert O. (ed.) (1979). *Toward a New Strategy for Development*. New York: Pergamon.

Hirschman, Charles (1986). The recent rise in Malay fertility: A new trend or a temporary lull in a fertility transition? *Demography*, 23, 161–184.

Hjort, Howard (1982). Will food output be sufficient? *New York Times*, February 14, 14.

Hobcraft, John (1985). Family-building patterns. In John Cleland and John Hobcraft (eds.), *Reproductive Change in Developing Countries: Insights from the World Fertility Survey* (pp. 64–86). New York: Oxford University Press.

Hollerbach, Paula E. (1982). Fertility decision-making processes: A critical essay. *Center for Policy Studies Working Papers No. 90*. New York: Population Council.

Hollnsteiner, Mary Racelis (1979). Mobilizing the rural poor through community organization. *Philippine Studies*, 27, 387–416.

Holsinger, Donald B., and Kasarda, John D. (1976). Education and human fertility: Sociological perspectives. In Ronald G. Ridker (ed.), *Population and Development: The Search for Selective Interventions* (pp. 154–181). Baltimore: Johns Hopkins University Press.

Hough, Richard L. (1982). *Economic Assistance and Security: Rethinking US Policy*. Washington, D.C.: National Defense University Press.

Hull, Terence H. (1983). Cultural influences on fertility decision styles. In Rodolfo A. Bulatao and Ronald D. Lee (eds.), *Determinants of Fertility in Developing Countries*, Vol 2 (pp. 381–414). New York: Academic Press.

Hull, Terence H., and Hull, Valerie J. (1977). The relation of economic class and fertility: An analysis of some Indonesian data. *Population Studies*, 31, 43–57.

Hull, Valerie J. (1977). Fertility, women's work, and economic class: A case study from Southeast Asia. In Stanley Kupinsky (ed.), *The Fertility of Working Women: A Synthesis of International Research* (pp. 35–80). New York: Praeger.

Hulse, Joseph H. (1982). Food science and nutrition: The gulf between rich and poor. *Science*, 216, 1291–1294.

Huston, Perdita (1979). *Third World Women Speak Out: Interviews in Six Countries on Change, Development, and Basic Needs*. New York: Praeger.

Hutton, Caroline, and Cohen, Robin (1975). African peasants and resistance to change: A reconsideration of sociological approaches. In Ival Oxaal, Tony Barnett, and David Booth (eds.), *Beyond the Sociology of Development: Economy and Society in Latin America and Africa* (pp. 105–130). London: Routledge and Kegan Paul.

Ilchman, Warren F. (1975). Population knowledge and fertility policies. In Warren F. Ilchman (ed.), *Policy Sciences and Population* (pp. 15–63). Lexington, Massachusetts: D. C. Heath.

Ilchman, Warren F., and Uphoff, Norman T. (1975). Beyond the economics of labor-intensive development: Politics and administration. *Ekistics*, 237, 88–101.

Immerwahr, George E. (1977). Socio-economic: How much economic and how much "socio"? In Lado Ruzicka (ed.), *The Economic and Social Supports for High Fertility* (pp. 187–201). Canberra: Australian National University.

Inkeles, Alex, and Smith, David H. (1974). *Becoming Modern: Individual Change in Six Developing Countries.* Cambridge, Massachusetts: Harvard University Press.

Inter-American Foundation (1985). *Annual Report 1985.* Rosslyn, Virginia: Inter-American Foundation.

International Bank for Reconstruction and Development (1975). *The Assault on World Poverty: Problems of Rural Development, Education and Health.* Baltimore: Johns Hopkins University Press (for the World Bank).

International Bank for Reconstruction and Development (1980a). *World Development Report 1980.* Washington, D.C.: World Bank.

International Bank for Reconstruction and Development (1980b). *Health Sector Policy Paper.* Washington, D.C.: World Bank.

International Bank for Reconstruction and Development (1981a). *The McNamara Years at the World Bank.* Baltimore: Johns Hopkins University Press.

International Bank for Reconstruction and Development (1981b). *World Development Report 1981.* New York: Oxford University Press (for the World Bank).

International Bank for Reconstruction and Development (1982). *World Development Report 1982.* New York: Oxford University Press (for the World Bank).

International Bank for Reconstruction and Development (1984). *World Development Report 1984.* New York: Oxford University Press (for the World Bank).

International Bank for Reconstruction and Development (1985). *World Development Report 1985.* New York: Oxford University Press (for the World Bank).

International Bank for Reconstruction and Development (1986). *World Development Report 1986.* New York: Oxford University Press (for the World Bank).

International Labour Office (1977). *Employment, Growth and Basic Needs: A One-World Problem.* New York: Praeger (for the Overseas Development Council in cooperation with the International Labour Office).

International Labor Organization (1979). *Population and Development: A Progress Report on ILO Research.* Geneva: International Labour Office.

Jain, Anrudh K. (1981). The effect of female education on fertility: A simple explanation. *Demography, 18,* 577–595.

Jain, Anrudh K. (1985). The impact of development and population policies on fertility in India. *Studies in Family Planning, 16,* 181–198.

Jain, Anrudh K., and Nag, Moni (1985). Female primary education and fertility reduction in India. *Center for Policy Studies Working Papers No. 114.* New York: Population Council.

Jenney, E. Ross, and Simmons, Ozzie G. (1954). Human relations and technical assistance in public health. *Scientific Monthly, 78,* 365–371.

Johnson, D. Gale (1976). Food for the future: A perspective. *Population and Development Review, 2,* 1–20.

Johnson, Nan E. (1984). Rural development and the value of children: Implications for human fertility. In Wayne A. Schutjer and C. Shannon Stokes (eds.), *Rural Development and Human Fertility* (pp. 172–194). New York: Macmillan.

Jolly, Richard (1974). International dimensions. In Hollis B. Chenery, Montek S. Ahluwalia, C. L. G. Bell, John H. Duloy, and Richard Jolly, *Redistribution with Growth* (pp. 158–180). London: Oxford University Press (for the World Bank and the Institute of Development Studies).

Jones, Gavin W. (1975). Educational planning and population growth. In Warren C. Robinson (ed.), *Population and Development Planning* (pp. 69–94). New York: Population Council.

Jones, Gavin W. (1976). The influence of demographic variables on development via their impact on education. In Ansley J. Coale (ed.), *Economic Factors in Population Growth* (pp. 553–580). New York: John Wiley.

Jones, Gavin W. (1977). Economic and social supports for high fertility: Conceptual framework. In Lado Ruzicka (ed.), *The Economic and Social Supports for High Fertility* (pp. 3–47). Canberra: Australian National University.

Jones, Gavin W. (1978). Social science research on population and development in South-East and East Asia. Appendix 3 to Carmen A. Miro and Joseph E. Potter, *Population Policy: Research Priorities in the Developing World.* London: Frances Pinter, 1980 (reproduced from El Colegio de Mexico edition, Mexico City, 1978).

Jones, Gavin W. (1982). Review of the integration of population and development policies and programs in Asia. *Development Studies Centre Occasional Paper No. 30.* Canberra: Australian National University.

Jones, Gavin W., and Potter, Joseph E. (1978). The economic consequences of population change (unpublished paper prepared for the International Review Group of Social Science Research on Population and Development).

Jones, Gavin W., Saunders, Lyle, and Simmons, Ozzie G. (1978). Population and development planning: Policy analysis in the Philippines (unpublished paper). New York: Ford Foundation.

Joseph, Stephen C., and Russell, Sharon Stanton (1980). Is primary care the wave of the future? *Social Science and Medicine, 14C,* 137–144.

Kahl, Joseph A. (1976). *Modernization, Exploitation and Dependency in Latin America.* New Brunswick, New Jersey: Transaction Books.

Kelley, Allen C. (1986). Review of National Research Council, *Population Growth and Economic Development: Policy Questions. Population and Development Review, 12,* 563–568.

Keyfitz, Nathan (1976). World resources and the world middle class. *Scientific American, 235,* 28–35.

Keyfitz, Nathan (1981). The limits of population forecasting. *Population and Development Review, 7,* 579–593.

Keyfitz, Nathan (1985). An East Javanese village in 1953 and 1985. *Population and Development Review, 11,* 695–719.

Khan, A. R. (1977). Basic needs targets: An illustrative exercise in identification and quantification. In International Labour Office, *The Basic Needs Approach to Development* (pp. 72–95). Geneva: International Labour Office.

King, Timothy, and Kelley, Allen C. (1985). The new population debate: Two views on population growth and economic development. *Population Trends and Public Policy No. 7.* Washington, D.C.: Population Reference Bureau.

King, Timothy, with Cuca, Roberto, Gulhati, Ravi, Hossain, Monowar, Stern, Ernest, Visaria, Pravin, Zachariah, K. C., and Zafros, Gregory (1974). *Population Policies and Economic Development.* Baltimore: Johns Hopkins University Press (for the World Bank).

Kirk, Dudley (1971). A new demographic transition? In National Academy of Sciences, *Rapid Population Growth: Consequences and Policy Implications* (pp. 123–147). Baltimore: Johns Hopkins University Press.

Knodel, John, and van de Walle, Etienne (1979). Lessons from the past: Policy implications of historical fertility studies. *Population and Development Review, 5,* 217–245.

Knowles, John H. (1980). Health, population and development. *Social Science and Medicine, 14C,* 67–70.

Kocher, James E. (1973). *Rural Development, Income Distribution, and Fertility Decline.* New York: Population Council.

Kocher, James E. (1984). Income distribution and fertility. In Wayne A. Schutjer and C.

Shannon Stokes (eds.), *Rural Development and Human Fertility* (pp. 216–234). New York: Macmillan.

Korten, David C. (1980). Community organization and rural development: A learning process approach. *Public Administration Review*, 480–511.

Kristof, Nicholas D. (1985). The Third World: Back to the farm. *New York Times*, July 28, 3:1.

Krueger, Anne O. (1986). Aid in the development process. *World Bank Research Observer, 1*, 57–78.

Kunstadter, Peter (1979). Demographic transition theory: Requiescat in pace? *Family Planning Perspectives, 11*, 71–72.

Kupinsky, Stanley (1977a). The fertility of working women in the United States: Historical trends and theoretical perspectives. In Stanley Kupinsky (ed.), *The Fertility of Working Women: A Synthesis of International Research* (pp. 188–249). New York: Praeger.

Kupinsky, Stanley (1977b). Overview and policy implications. In Stanley Kupinsky (ed.), *The Fertility of Working Women: A Synthesis of International Research* (pp. 369–380). New York: Praeger.

Lall, Sanjaya, and Streeten, Paul (1977). *Foreign Investment: Transnationals and Developing Countries*. London: Macmillan.

Lee, Ronald D. (1985). Review of International Bank for Reconstruction and Development, *World Development Report 1984*. *Population and Development Review, 11*, 127–130.

Leff, Nathaniel H. (1983). Beyond the new international economic order. In W. Scott Thomspon (ed.), *The Third World: Premises of U.S. Policy* (pp. 239–266). San Francisco: ICS Press.

Lehmann, David (ed.) (1979). *Development Theory: Four Critical Studies*. London: Frank Cass.

Leibenstein, Harvey (1985). Review of International Bank for Reconstruction and Development, *World Development Report 1984*. *Population and Development Review, 11*, 135–137.

Leonard, Ann (undated). The white revolution. *Cycle*. New York: Ford Foundation.

Levine, David (1986). Review of Ansley J. Coale and Susan Cotts Watkins (eds.), *The Decline of Fertility in Europe*. *Population and Development Review, 12*, 335–340.

LeVine, Robert A., and Scrimshaw, Susan C. M. (1983). Effects of culture on fertility: Anthropological contributions. In Rodolfo A. Bulatao and Ronald D. Lee (eds.), *Determinants of Fertility in Developing Countries*, Vol. 2 (pp. 666–695). New York: Academic Press.

Lipton, Michael (1977). *Why Poor People Stay Poor: A Study of Urban Bias in World Development*. Cambridge, Massachusetts: Harvard University Press.

Lipton, Michael (1983). Demography and poverty. *World Bank Staff Working Papers No. 623*. Washington, D.C.: World Bank.

Lipton, Michael (1984). Urban bias and inequality. In Mitchell A. Seligson (ed.), *The Gap between Rich and Poor* (pp. 89–94). Boulder, Colorado: Westview.

MacKellar, F. Landis, and Vining, Daniel R. (1985). Natural resource scarcity: A global survey (unpublished paper). Philadelphia: Department of Regional Science, University of Pennsylvania.

Magdoff, Harry (1976). The multinational corporation and development—a contradiction? In D. E. Apter and L. W. Goodman (eds.), *The Multinational Corporation and Social Change* (pp. 200–222). New York: Praeger.

Mandelbaum, David (1974). *Human Fertility in India*. Berkeley: University of California Press.

Mansour, Fawzy (1979). Third World revolt and self-reliant auto-centered strategy of development. In Albert O. Hirschman (ed.), *Toward a New Strategy of Development* (pp. 198–239). New York: Pergamon.

Marshall, John F., Morris, Susan, and Polgar, Steven (1972). Culture and natality: A preliminary classified bibliography. *Current Anthropology, 13,* 268–277.

Mason, Karen Oppenheim (1984). The status of women, fertility, and mortality: A review of interrelationships. *Population Studies Center Research Reports No. 84–85.* Ann Arbor: University of Michigan.

Mason, Karen Oppenheim, and Palan, V. T. (1981). Female employment and fertility in peninsular Malaysia: The maternal role incompatibility hypothesis reconsidered. *Demography, 18,* 549–575.

Matras, Judah (1973). *Populations and Societies.* Englewood Cliffs, New Jersey: Prentice-Hall.

Matthiasson, Carolyn J. (ed.) (1974). *Many Sisters: Women in Cross-Cultural Perspective.* New York: Free Press.

Mauldin, W. Parker (1983). Population programs and fertility regulation. In Rodolfo A. Bulatao and Ronald D. Lee (eds.), *Determinants of Fertility in Developing Countries,* Vol. 2 (pp. 267–294). New York: Academic Press.

Mauldin, W. Parker, and Lapham, Robert J. (1985). Measuring family planning program effort in LDCs: 1972 and 1982. In Nancy Birdsall (ed.), *The Effects of Family Planning Programs on Fertility in the Developing World, World Bank Staff Working Papers No. 677,* (pp. 1–39). Washington, D.C.: World Bank.

Mauldin, W. Parker, and Segal, Sheldon J. (1986). *Prevalence of Contraceptive Use in Developing Countries.* New York: Rockefeller Foundation.

May, Clifford D. (1985). Africans declare an economic crisis. *New York Times,* July 21.

McClelland, David C. (1977). The psychological causes and consequences of modernization. In Manning Nash (ed.), *Essays on Economic Development and Cultural Change in Honor of Bert F. Hoselitz* (pp. 43–66). Chicago: University of Chicago Press.

McGreevey, William P., and Birdsall, Nancy (1974). *The Policy Relevance of Recent Social Research on Fertility,* Occasional Monograph Series No. 2. Washington, D.C.: Interdisciplinary Communications Program, Smithsonian Institution.

McNamara, Robert S. (1977). Possible interventions to reduce fertility. *Population and Development Review, 3,* 163–176.

McNamara, Robert S. (1984). Time bomb or myth: The population problem. *Foreign Affairs, 62,* 1107–1131.

McNicoll, Geoffrey (1975). Community-level population policy: An exploration. *Population and Development Review, 1,* 1–21.

McNicoll, Geoffrey (1977). Population and development: Outlines for a structuralist approach. *Center for Policy Studies Working Papers No. 15.* New York: Population Council.

McNicoll, Geoffrey (1978). On fertility policy research. *Population and Development Review, 4,* 681–693.

McNicoll, Geoffrey (1979). Technology and the social regulation of fertility. *Center for Policy Studies Working Papers No. 46.* New York: Population Council.

McNicoll, Geoffrey (1980). Institutional determinants of fertility change. *Population and Development Review, 6,* 441–462.

McNicoll, Geoffrey (1983). Notes on the local context of demographic change. *Center for Policy Studies Working Papers No. 98.* New York: Population Council.

McNicoll, Geoffrey (1984). Consequences of rapid population growth: An overview and assessment. *Population and Development Review, 10,* 177–240.

Mead, Margaret (1976). A comment on the role of women in agriculture. In Irene Tinker and Michele Bo Bramsen (eds.), *Women and World Development* (pp. 9–11). Washington, D.C.: Overseas Development Council.

Meadows, Donella H., Meadows, Dennis L., Randers, Jorgen, and Behrens, William H. (1972). *Limits to Growth.* New York: Universe Books (for Potomac Associates).

Mellor, John W. (1975). An employment oriented strategy of development. In Raymond E. Dumett and Lawrence J. Brainard (eds.), *Problems of Rural Development* (pp. 131–139). Leiden: E. J. Brill.

Mellor, John W. (1976). *The New Economics of Growth*. Ithaca, New York: Cornell University Press.

Mellor, John W. (1978). *Three Issues of Development Strategy—Food, Population, Trade*. Washington, D.C.: International Food Policy Research Institute.

Menken, Jane (ed.) (1986). *World Population and U.S. Policy: The Choices Ahead*. New York: W. W. Norton (for the American Assembly).

Menken, Jane, Watkins, Susan Cotts, and Trussell, James (1980). Nutrition, health, and fertility (unpublished report prepared for the Ford Foundation, New York).

Mernissi, Fatima (1976). The Moslem world: Women excluded from development. In Irene Tinker and Michele Bo Bramsen (eds.), *Women and World Development* (pp. 35–44). Washington, D.C.: Overseas Development Council.

Merrick, Thomas W. (1978). Fertility and land availability in Brazil. *Demography, 15,* 321–336.

Merrick, Thomas W. (1985). Recent fertility declines in Brazil, Colombia, and Mexico. *World Bank Staff Working Papers No. 692.* Washington, D.C.: World Bank.

Miller, K. A., and Inkeles, A. (1974). Modernity and acceptance of family limitation in four developing countries. *Journal of Social Issues, 30,* 167–188.

Miller, Ralph M. (1974). The meaning of development and its educational implications. In F. Champion Ward (ed.), *Education and Development Reconsidered: The Bellagio Conference Papers* (pp. 83–93). New York: Praeger.

Minhas, B. S. (1979). The current development debate. In Albert O. Hirschman (ed.), *Toward a New Strategy for Development* (pp. 75–96). New York: Pergamon.

Miro, Carmen A., and Potter, Joseph E. (1980). *Population Policy: Research Priorities in the Developing World*. London: Frances Pinter.

Mondot-Bernard, Jacqueline (1978). Planning food supplies for an expanding nation. In Robert Cassen and Margaret Wolfson (eds.), *Planning for Growing Populations* (pp. 49–78). Paris: Organisation for Economic Co-operation and Development.

Morawetz, David (1977). *Twenty-Five Years of Economic Development: 1950 to 1975*. Washington, D.C.: World Bank.

Morawetz, David (1978). Basic needs policies and population growth. *World Development, 6,* 1251–1259.

Morawetz, David (1984). The gap between rich and poor countries. In Mitchell A. Seligson (ed.), *The Gap betewen Rich and Poor: Contending Perspectives on the Political Economy of Development* (pp. 8–13). Boulder, Colorado: Westview.

Mosley, W. Henry (1983). Primary health care: Rhetoric and reality. *Populi, 10,* 41–53.

Mueller, Eva (1982). The allocation of women's time and its relation to fertility. In Richard Anker, Mayra Buvinic, and Nadia H. Youseff (eds.), *Women's Roles and Population Trends in the Third World* (pp. 55–86). London: Croom Helm.

Mueller, Eva (1983). Measuring women's poverty in developing countries. In Mayra Buvinic, Margaret A. Lycette, and William Paul McGreevey (eds.), *Women and Poverty in the Third World* (pp. 272–285). Baltimore: Johns Hopkins University Press.

Mueller, Eva (1985). Review of Gerry Rodgers, *Poverty and Population: Approaches and Evidence. Population and Development Review, 11,* 146–148.

Mundigo, Axel I. (1986). Seminar on the use of demographic knowledge for population policy formulation in Latin America. *International Union for the Scientific Study of Population Newsletter No. 27,* pp. 71–100.

Murdoch, William W. (1980). *The Poverty of Nations: The Political Economy of Hunger and Population*. Baltimore: Johns Hopkins University Press.

Myrdal, Gunnar (1970). *The Challenge of World Poverty: A World Anti-poverty Program in Outline*. New York: Pantheon Books.

Myrdal, Gunnar (1974). What is development? *Journal of Economic Issues, 8*, 84–87.

Nafziger, E. Wayne (1979). A critique of development economics in the U.S. In David Lehmann (ed.), *Development Theory: Four Critical Studies* (pp. 32–48). London: Frank Cass.

Nag, Moni (1980). How modernization can also increase fertility. *Current Anthropology, 21*, 571–587.

Nag, Moni (1981). Impact of social development and economic development on mortality: A comparative study of Kerala and West Bengal. *Center for Policy Studies Working Papers No. 78*. New York: Population Council.

Nag, Moni (1983). The impact of sociocultural factors on breastfeeding and sexual behavior. In Rodolfo A. Bulatao and Ronald D. Lee (eds.), *Determinants of Fertility in Developing Countries*, Vol. 1 (pp. 163–198). New York: Academic Press.

Nag, Moni (1984a). Some cultural factors affecting costs of fertility regulation. *Population Bulletin of the United Nations No. 17*, pp. 17–38. New York: United Nations (ST/ESA/SER.N/17).

Nag, Moni (1984b). Fertility differential in Kerala and West Bengal: Equity–fertility hypothesis as explanation. *Economic and Political Weekly, 19*, 33–41.

Nash, Manning (1977). Modernization: Cultural meanings—the widening gap between the intellectuals and the process. In Manning Nash (ed.), *Essays in Economic Development and Cultural Change in Honor of Bert F. Hoselitz* (pp. 16–28). Chicago: University of Chicago Press.

National Academy of Sciences (1971). *Rapid Population Growth: Consequences and Policy Implications*. Baltimore: Johns Hopkins Press (for the National Academy of Sciences).

National Research Council (1986). Working Group on Population Growth and Economic Development, Committee on Population, *Population Growth and Economic Development: Policy Questions*. Washington, D.C.: National Academy Press.

Nerfin, Marc (ed.) (1977). *Another Development: Approaches and Strategies*. Uppsala: Dag Hammarskjöld Foundation.

Ness, Gayl D., and Ando, Hirofumi (1984). *The Land Is Shrinking: Population Planning in Asia*. Baltimore: Johns Hopkins University Press.

Ness, Gayl D., Alhambra, Chris, and Pressman, Willa (1984). International assistance for fertility limitation in Asia (unpublished paper). Ann Arbor: Department of Sociology and Center for Population Planning, University of Michigan.

New York Times (1985a). Text of declaration at end of 7-nation economic conference, May 5, A16.

New York Times (1985b). U.S. delegate protests conference on women. July 28, A1.

New York Times (1986). Latin America's bold new partners. August 12, A24.

Nortman, Dorothy L. (1985). Family planning program funds: Sources, levels, and trends. *Center for Policy Studies Working Papers No. 113*. New York: Population Council.

Nossiter, Bernard D. (1983). U.N. chief says threat of nuclear war grows. *New York Times*, February 16, A6.

O'Brien, Donal Cruise (1979). Modernization, order, and the erosion of a democratic ideal. In David Lehmann (ed.), *Development Theory: Four Critical Studies* (pp. 49–76). London: Frank Cass.

O'Brien, Philip J. (1975). A critique of Latin American theories of development. In Ivar Oxaal, Tony Barnett, and David Booth (eds.), *Beyond the Sociology of Development: Economy and Society in Latin America and Africa* (pp. 7–27). London: Routledge and Kegan Paul.

Oechsli, Frank W., and Kirk, Dudley (1975). Modernization and the demographic transition in Latin America and the Caribbean. *Economic Development and Cultural Change, 23,* 391–419.

Ohlin, Goran (1978). Introduction: Some implications of rapid population growth for social and economic planning. In Robert Cassen and Margaret Wolfson (eds.), *Planning for Growing Populations* (pp. 11–25). Paris: Organisation for Economic Co-operation and Development.

Ohlin, Goran (1979). Development in retrospect. In Albert O. Hirschman (ed.), *Toward a New Strategy of Development* (pp. 125–143). New York: Pergamon.

Oppenheimer, Valerie Kincaide (1982). *Work and the Family: A Study in Social Demography.* New York: Academic Press.

Oppong, Christine (1980). A synopsis of seven roles and status of women: An outline of a conceptual and methodological approach. *World Employment Programme Research,* Working Paper No. 94. Geneva: International Labour Office.

Oppong, Christine (1982). Family structure and women's reproductive and productive roles: Some conceptual and methodological issues. In Richard Anker, Mayra Buvinic, and Nadia H. Youssef (eds.), *Women's Roles and Population Trends in the Third World* (pp. 133–150). London: Croom Helm.

Oppong, Christine (1983). Women's roles, opportunity costs, and fertility. In Rodolfo A. Bulatao and Ronald D. Lee (eds.), *Determinants of Fertility in Developing Countries,* Vol. 1 (pp. 547–589). New York: Academic Press.

Oppong, Christine, and Church, Katie (1981). A field guide to research on seven roles of women: Focussed biographies. *World Employment Programme Research,* Working Paper No. 106. Geneva: International Labour Office.

Overseas Development Council Communique (1974). Self-reliance and international reform. *World Development, 2,* 53–55.

Palmer, Ingrid (1977). Rural women and the basic-needs approach to development. *International Labour Review, 115,* 97–107.

Palmer, Ingrid (1979). The Nemow case: Case studies of the impact of large scale development projects on women. *International Programs Working Paper No. 7.* New York: Population Council.

Pante, Filologo (1985). Population and development planning integration: The case of the Philippines. *Philippine Population Journal, 1,* 94–105.

Papanek, Gustav F. (1968). Development theory and DAS experience. In Gustav F. Papanek (ed.), *Development Policy—Theory and Practice* (pp. 345–359). Cambridge, Massachusetts: Harvard University Press.

Pearson, Lester B., Boyle, Edward, Campos, Roberto de Oliveira, Dillon, C. Douglas, Guth, Wilfred, Lewis, W. Arthur, Marjolin, Robert E., and Okita, Saburo (1969). *Partners in Development: Report of the Commission on International Development.* New York: Praeger.

Perlman, Mark (1982). Review of Julian L. Simon, *The Ultimate Resource. Population Studies, 36,* 490–494.

Pfanner, David E. (1978). Multiple-cropping and labor in North Thailand: A microlevel case study in agricultural development and population (unpublished paper). New York: Ford Foundation.

Pharr, Susan J. (1977). Japan: Historical and contemporary perspectives. In Janet Z. Giele and Audrey C. Smock (eds.), *Women: Roles and Status in Eight Countries* (pp. 217–255). New York: John Wiley.

Pinstrup-Andersen, Per, and Kumar, Shubh (1984). Food policy, human nutrition, and fertility. In Wayne A. Schutjer and C. Shannon Stokes (eds.), *Rural Development and Human Fertility* (pp. 235–251). New York: Macmillan.

Pitt, David C. (ed.) (1976a). *Development from Below: Anthropologists and Development Situations*. Paris: Mouton.

Pitt, David C. (1976b). *The Social Dynamics of Development*. New York: Pergamon.

Polgar, Steven (1972). Population history and population policies from an anthropological perspective. *Current Anthropology, 13,* 203–211.

Population Council (1981). Research on the determinants of fertility: A note on priorities. *Population and Development Review, 7,* 311–324.

Population Crisis Committee (1985). Population growth and economic development. *Population,* No. 14.

Population Crisis Committee (1986). The United Nations Fund for Population Activities. *Population,* No. 17.

Population Information Program (1979). Age at marriage and fertility. *Population Reports, 7* (Special Topic Monograph).

Population Information Program (1982). Community-based health and family planning. *Population Reports, 10,* Series L, No. 3.

Population Information Program (1984a). Healthier mothers and children through family planning. *Population Reports, 12,* Series J, No. 27.

Population Information Program (1984b). Laws and policies affecting fertility: A decade of change. *Population Reports, 12* (entire issue).

Population Information Program (1985a). The impact of family planning programs on fertility. *Population Reports, 13,* Series J, No. 29.

Population Information Program (1985b). Fertility and family planning surveys. *Population Reports, 13,* Series M, No. 8.

Population Reference Bureau (1987). *World Population Data Sheet*. Washington, D.C.: Population Reference Bureau.

Portes, Alejandro, and Benton, Lauren (1984). Industrial development and labor absorption: A reinterpretation. *Population and Development Review, 10,* 589–611.

Potter, Joseph E. (1983). Effects of societal and community institutions on fertility. In Rodolfo A. Bulatao and Ronald D. Lee (eds.), *Determinants of Fertility in Developing Countries,* Vol. 2 (pp. 627–665). New York: Academic Press.

Potter, Joseph E. (1986). Review of National Research Council, *Population Growth and Economic Development: Policy Questions. Population and Development Review, 12,* 578–581.

Powers, Mary G. (1984). *Compiling Social Indicators on the Situation of Women,* Studies in Methods, Series F, No. 32. New York: United Nations.

Prebisch, Raul (1979). The neoclassical theories of economic liberalism. *CEPAL Review,* 167–188. New York: United Nations (E/CEPAL/1084).

Preston, Samuel H. (1975). Health programs and population growth. *Population and Development Review, 1,* 189–199.

Preston, Samuel H. (1978a). Mortality, morbidity, and development (unpublished paper). New York: Population Division, United Nations.

Preston, Samuel H. (ed.) (1978b). *The Effect of Infant and Child Mortality on Fertility*. New York: Academic Press.

Preston, Samuel H. (1982). Review of Julian L. Simon, *The Ultimate Resource. Population and Development Review, 8,* 174–177.

Ranis, Gustav (ed.) (1973). *The United States and the Developing Economies*. New York: W. W. Norton.

Ranis, Gustav (1976). The multinational corporation as an instrument of development. In D. E. Apter and L. W. Goodman (eds.), *The Multinational Corporation and Social Change* (pp. 96–117). New York: Praeger.

Ranis, Gustav (1977). Development theory at three-quarters century. In Manning Nash (ed.), *Essays on Economic Development and Cultural Change in Honor of Bert F. Hoselitz* (pp. 16–28). Chicago: University of Chicago Press.

Ranis, Gustav (1978). Equity with growth in Taiwan: How "special" is the "special case"? *World Development, 6,* 397–409.

Ranis, Gustav (1981). Review of International Bank for Reconstruction and Development, *World Development Report 1980. Population and Development Review, 7,* 351–354.

Ranis, Gustav, West, Robert L., Leiserson, Mark W., and Taft, Cynthia (eds.) (1984) *Comparative Development Perspectives.* Boulder, Colorado: Westview.

Rao, D. C. (1974). Urban target groups. In Hollis B. Chenery, Montek S. Ahluwalia, C. L. G. Bell, John H. Duloy, and Richard Jolly, *Redistribution with Growth* (pp. 136–157). London: Oxford University Press (for the World Bank and the Institute of Development Studies).

Rao, D. C. (1978). Economic growth and equity in the Republic of Korea. *World Development, 6,* 383–396.

Repetto, Robert (1978). The interaction of fertility and the size distribution of income. *Journal of Development Studies, 14,* 22–39.

Repetto, Robert (1979). *Economic Equality and Fertility in Developing Countries.* Baltimore: Johns Hopkins University Press.

Repetto, Robert (1982). A reply. *Population and Development Review, 8*(Supplement), 174–178.

Repetto, Robert, and Holmes, Thomas (1983). The role of population in resource depletion in developing countries. *Population and Development Review, 9,* 609–632.

Reutlinger, Shlomo, and Selowsky, Marcelo (1976). *Malnutrition and Poverty: Magnitude and Policy Options.* World Bank Staff Occasional Paper No. 23. Baltimore: Johns Hopkins University Press (for the World Bank).

Rich, William (1973). *Smaller Families through Social and Economic Progress.* Washington, D.C.: Overseas Development Council.

Richards, Peter, and Gooneratne, Wilbert (1980). *Basic Needs, Poverty and Government Policies in Sri Lanka.* Geneva: International Labour Office.

Ridker, Ronald G. (1975). Natural resource adequacy and alternative demographic prospects. In United Nations, *The Population Debate: Dimensions and Perspectives,* Vol. II (pp. 34–40). New York: United Nations.

Ridker, Ronald G. (ed.) (1976). *Population and Development: The Search for Selective Interventions.* Baltimore: Johns Hopkins University Press.

Ridker, Ronald G., and Cecelski, Elizabeth W. (1979). Resources, environment, and population: The nature of future limits. *Population Bulletin, 34.* Washington, D.C.: Population Reference Bureau.

Ridker, Ronald G., and Watson, William D. (1979). *To Choose a Future: Resource and Environmental Problems of the U.S.: A Long-Term Global Outlook.* Baltimore: Johns Hopkins University Press (for Resources for the Future).

Rindfuss, R., Parnell, A., and Hirschman, C. (1983). The timing of entry into motherhood in Asia: A comparative perspective. *Population Studies, 37,* 253–272.

Robinson, Warren C. (ed.) (1975). *Population and Development Planning.* New York: Population Council.

Robinson, Warren C. (1980). Demographic issues in development planning in Asia, with special reference to agricultural change. In Barnett F. Baron (ed.), *Population Policy and Development Planning Units in Asia* (pp. 123–161). Bangkok, Thailand: Population Council Regional Office for South and East Asia.

Robinson, Warren C. (1986). High fertility as risk insurance. *Population Studies, 40,* 289–298.

Robinson, Warren C., and Harbison, Sarah F. (1980). Toward a unified theory of fertility. In Thomas K. Burch (ed.), *Demographic Behavior: Interdisciplinary Perspectives on Decision-Making* (pp. 201–235). Boulder, Colorado: Westview.

Rodgers, Gerry B. (1978). Demographic determinants of the distribution of income. *World Development, 6*, 305–318.

Rodgers, Gerry B. (1983). Population growth, inequality, and poverty. *International Labour Review, 122*, 443–460.

Rodgers, Gerry B. (1984). *Poverty and Population: Approaches and Evidence*. Geneva: International Labour Office.

Roemer, Michael (1981). Dependence and industrialization strategies. *World Development, 9*, 429–434.

Rosaldo, Michelle, and Lamphere, Louise (eds.) (1974). *Women, Culture, and Society*. Stanford, California: Stanford University Press.

Rostow, W. W. (1971). *The Stages of Economic Growth: A Non-Communist Manifesto*. Cambridge, England: Cambridge University Press.

Rothstein, Robert (1976). The political economy of redistribution and self-reliance. *World Development, 4*, 593–611.

Russell, Milton (1979). Energy in America's future: The choices before us. *Resources, 63*, 1–4.

Ryder, Norman B. (1983). Fertility and family structure. *Population Bulletin of the United Nations No. 15*, pp. 15–34. New York: United Nations.

Sadik, Nafis (1985). Muslim women today. *Populi, 12*, 36–51.

Safilios-Rothschild, Constantina (1977). The relationship between women's work and fertility: Some methodological and theoretical issues. In Stanley Kupinsky (ed.), *The Fertility of Working Women: A Synthesis of International Research* (pp. 355–368). New York: Praeger.

Safilios-Rothschild, Constantina (1978). The demographic consequences of the changing roles of men and women in the '80s. In International Union for the Scientific Study of Population, *Conference on "Economic and Demographic Change: Issues for the 1980's" Helsinki 1978* (pp. 4.1.2). Liege: IUSSP.

Safilios-Rothschild, Constantina (1982). The persistence of women's invisibility in agriculture: Theoretical and policy lessons from Lesotho and Sierra Leone. *Center for Policy Studies Working Papers No. 88*. New York: Population Council.

Safilios-Rothschild, Constantina (1985a). Socioeconomic development and the status of women in the Third World. *Center for Policy Studies Working Papers No. 112*. New York: Population Council.

Safilios-Rothschild, Constantina (1985b). The status of women and fertility in the Third World in the 1970–80 decade. *Center for Policy Studies Working Papers No. 118*. New York: Population Council.

Salas, Rafael (1982). Population growth and policies: Discussion. In Just Faaland (ed.), *Population and the World Economy in the 21st Century* (pp. 244–247). Oxford, England: Blackwell.

Salas, Rafael (1985). *Reflections on Population*. Elmsford, New York: Pergamon.

Salas, Rafael (1986). The state of world population 1986. *Populi, 13*, 5–14.

Saunders, Lyle (1978). Population and development: Prospects and problems (unpublished paper). New York: Ford Foundation.

Saunders, Lyle, and Hardee, J. Gilbert (1972). Rationale and suggestions for establishing a population unit: Malaysia (unpublished paper). New York: Ford Foundation.

Schmemann, Serge (1985). Russia wants a baby boom of its own. *New York Times*, July 28.

Schmidt, Wilson E. (1983). The role of private capital in developing the Third World. In W. Scott Thompson (ed.), *The Third World: Premises of U.S. Policy* (pp. 267–286). San Francisco: ICS Press.

Schneider, Keith (1986). Scientific advances lead to era of food surplus around the world. *New York Times*, September 9, C1.

Schubnell, Hermann (ed.) (1984). *Population Policies in Asian Countries: Contemporary Tar-*

gets, Measures, and Effects. Hong Kong: Centre of Asian Studies, University of Hong Kong.

Schultz, T. Paul (1976). Interrelationships between mortality and fertility. In Ronald G. Ridker (ed.), *Population and Development: The Search for Selective Interventions* (pp. 239–289). Baltimore: Johns Hopkins University Press.

Schultz, T. Paul (1985). School expenditures and enrollments, 1960–1980: The effects of income, prices and population growth (unpublished paper). New Haven, Connecticut: Department of Economics, Yale University.

Schumacher, E. F. (1975). *Small Is Beautiful: Economics as if People Mattered*. New York: Harper and Row.

Schutjer, Wayne A., and Stokes, C. Shannon (1982). Agricultural policies and human fertility: Some emerging conclusions. *Population Research and Policy Review, 1,* 225–244.

Schutjer, Wayne A., and Stokes, C. Shannon (eds.) (1984). *Rural Development and Human Fertility*. New York: Macmillan.

Schutjer, Wayne A., Stokes, C. Shannon, and Cornwell, Gretchen (1980). Relationships among land, tenancy, and fertility: A study of Philippine barrios. *Journal of Developing Areas, 15,* 83–96.

Schutjer, Wayne A., Stokes, C. Shannon, and Poindexter, John R. (1983). Farm size, land ownership, and fertility in rural Egypt. *Land Economics, 59,* 393–403.

Scrimshaw, Susan C. M. (1977). *Cultural Values and Behaviors Related to Population Change*. Hastings, New York: Institute of Society, Ethics and the Life Sciences.

Scrimshaw, Susan C. M. (1978). Infant mortality and behavior in the regulation of family size. *Population and Development Review, 4,* 383–403.

Seers, Dudley (1979a). The meaning of development, with a postscript. In David Lehmann (ed.), *Development Theory: Four Critical Studies* (pp. 9–30). London: Frank Cass.

Seers, Dudley (1979b). The congruence of Marxism and other neoclassical doctrines. In Albert O. Hirschman (ed.), *Toward a New Strategy for Development* (pp. 1–17). New York: Pergamon.

Seligson, Mitchell A. (1979). Public policies in conflict: Land reform and family planning in Costa Rica. *Comparative Politics, 12,* 49–62.

Seligson, Mitchell A. (1984a). The dual gaps: An overview of theory and research. In Mitchell A. Seligson (ed.), *The Gap between Rich and Poor: Contending Perspectives on the Political Economy of Development* (pp. 3–7). Boulder, Colorado: Westview.

Seligson, Mitchell A. (1984b). Inequality in a global perspective: Directions for further research. In Mitchell A. Seligson (ed.), *The Gap between Rich and Poor: Contending Perspectives on the Political Economy of Development* (pp. 397–408). Boulder, Colorado: Westview.

Seligson, Mitchell A. (ed.) (1984c). *The Gap between Rich and Poor: Contending Perspectives on the Political Economy of Development*. Boulder, Colorado: Westview.

Sewell, John W., with Gwatkin, Davidson R., Howe, James W., Kallab, Valeriana, Mathieson, John A., McLaughlin, Martin M., and Streeten, Paul (1980). *The United States and World Development: Agenda 1980*. New York: Praeger.

Shabecoff, Philip (1986). Ecologists press lending groups. *New York Times,* October 30, A1.

Sheehan, Glen, and Hopkins, Mike (1979). *Basic Needs Performance: An Analysis of Some International Data*. Geneva: International Labour Office.

Simmons, John (1980a). An overview of the policy issues in the 1980s. In John Simmons (ed.), *The Education Dilemma: Policy Issues for Developing Countries in the 1980s* (pp. 19–66). Oxford, England: Pergamon.

Simmons, John (1980b). Steps toward reform. In John Simmons (ed.), *The Education Dilemma: Policy Issues for Developing Countries in the 1980s* (pp. 235–250). Oxford, England: Pergamon.

Simmons, Ozzie G. (1958). *Social Status and Public Health,* Pamphlet 13. New York: Social Science Research Council.

Simmons, Ozzie G. (1982). Population and integrated programs. In Carann G. Turner (ed.), *Population Information: Politics and Policy* (pp. 32–50). New York: Association for Population/Family Planning Libraries and Information Centers—International.

Simmons, Ozzie G. (1983). *Development Perspectives and Population Change,* Papers of the East-West Population Institute, No. 85. Honolulu: East-West Center.

Simmons, Ozzie G. (1984a). Conclusions and policy implications. In Wayne A. Schutjer and C. Shannon Stokes (eds.), *Rural Development and Human Fertility* (pp. 291–308). New York: Macmillan.

Simmons, Ozzie G. (1984b). Population policy analysis and development planning. *Journal of Developing Areas, 18,* 433–448.

Simmons, Ozzie G., and Saunders, Lyle (1975). *The Present and Prospective State of Policy Approaches to Fertility,* Papers of the East-West Population Institute, No. 33. Honolulu: East-West Center.

Simon, Julian L. (1976). Income, wealth, and their distribution as policy tools in fertility control. In Ronald G. Ridker (ed.), *Population and Development: The Search for Selective Interventions* (pp. 36–76). Baltimore: Johns Hopkins University Press.

Simon, Julian L. (1977). *The Economics of Population Growth.* Princeton, New Jersey: Princeton University Press.

Simon, Julian L. (1981). *The Ultimate Resource.* Princeton, New Jersey: Princeton University Press.

Simon, Julian L. (1986). Review of National Research Council, *Population Growth and Economic Development: Policy Questions. Population and Development Review, 12,* 569–577.

Simon, Julian, and Kahn, Herman (eds.) (1984). *The Resourceful Earth: A Response to Global 2000.* New York: Blackwell.

Sinding, Steven W. (1984). From Bucharest to Mexico City: Evolution of the A.I.D. population program (unpublished paper). Washington, D.C.: Office of Population, AID.

Singer, Hans W. (1975). *The Strategy of International Development: Essays in the Economics of Backwardness.* White Plains, New York: International Arts and Sciences Press.

Singer, Hans W., and Ansari, Javed (1982). *Rich and Poor Countries.* London: George Allen and Unwin.

Singh, Ajit (1979). The "basic needs" approach to development vs. the new international economic order: The significance of Third World industrialization. *World Development, 7,* 585–606.

Singh, Susheela, and Casterline, John (1985). The socio-economic determinants of fertility. In John Cleland and John Hobcraft (eds.), *Reproductive Change in Developing Countries: Insights from the World Fertility Survey* (pp. 199–222). New York: Oxford University Press.

Sipes, Richard C. (1980). *Population Growth, Society, and Culture: An Inventory of Cross-Culturally Tested Causal Hypotheses.* New Haven, Connecticut: HRAF Press.

Sirageldin, Ismail, and Kantner, John F. (1982). Review of Julian L. Simon, *The Ultimate Resource. Population and Development Review, 8,* 169–173.

Smith, Peter C. (1983). The impact of age at marriage and proportions marrying on fertility. In Rodolfo A. Bulatao and Ronald D. Lee (eds.), *Determinants of Fertility in Developing Countries,* Vol. 2 (pp. 473–531). New York: Academic Press.

Smith, Richard A., and Powell, Rodney N. (1978). The emerging role of health in development. In Richard A. Smith (ed.), *Manpower and Primary Health Care: Guidelines for Improving/Expanding Health Services Coverage in Developing Countries* (pp. 1–16). Honolulu: University Press of Hawaii.

Smock, Audrey Chapman (1977a). Bangladesh: A struggle with tradition and poverty. In

Janet Z. Giele and Audrey C. Smock (eds.), *Women: Roles and Status in Eight Countries* (pp. 81–126). New York: John Wiley.

Smock, Audrey Chapman (1977b). Ghana: From autonomy to subordination. In Janet Z. Giele and Audrey C. Smock (eds.), *Women: Roles and Status in Eight Countries* (pp. 173–216). New York: John Wiley.

Smock, Audrey Chapman (1977c). Conclusion: Determinants of women's roles and status. In Janet Z. Giele and Audrey C. Smock (eds.), *Women: Roles and Status in Eight Countries* (pp. 385–421). New York: John Wiley.

Snodgrass, Donald R. (1978). The integration of population policy into development planning: A progress report (unpublished paper). Cambridge Massachusetts: Harvard Institute for International Development.

Spooner, Brian (ed.) (1972). *Population Growth: Anthropological Implications.* Cambridge, Massachusetts: MIT Press.

Stamper, B. Maxwell (1973). Population policy in development planning: A study of seventy less developed countries. *Reports on Population/Family Planning No. 13.* New York: Population Council.

Stamper, B. Maxwell (1984). Population policies and development. *Managing International Development, 1,* 61–83.

Standing, Guy (1978). *Labour Force Participation and Development.* Geneva: International Labour Office.

Standing, Guy (1983). Women's work activity and fertility. In Rodolfo A. Bulatao and Ronald D. Lee (eds.), *Determinants of Fertility in Developing Countries,* Vol. 1 (pp. 517–546). New York: Academic Press.

Staudt, Kathleen (1980). The landless majority. *People, 7,* 7–8.

Stavenhagen, Rodolfo (1975). *Social Classes in Agrarian Societies.* Garden City, New York: Anchor Books.

Stavenhagen, Rodolfo (1977). Basic needs, peasants and the strategy for rural development. In Marc Nerfin (ed.), *Another Development: Approaches and Strategies* (pp. 40–65). Uppsala: Dag Hammarskjöld Foundation.

Stokes, C. Shannon, and Hsieh, Yeu-Sheng (1983). Female employment and reproductive behavior in Taiwan, 1980. *Demography, 20,* 313–331.

Stokes, C. Shannon, and Schutjer, Wayne A. (1983). A cautionary note on public policies in conflict: Land reform and human fertility in rural Egypt. *Comparative Politics, 16,* 97–104.

Stokes, C. Shannon, and Schutjer, Wayne A. (1984). Access to land and fertility in developing countries. In Wayne A. Schutjer and C. Shannon Stokes (eds.), *Rural Development and Human Fertility* (pp. 195–215). New York: Macmillan.

Stokes, C. Shannon, Schutjer, Wayne A., and Bulatao, Rodolfo A. (1986). Is the relationship between landholding and fertility spurious? A response to Cain. *Population Studies, 40,* 305–311.

Stollnitz, George J. (1975). International mortality trends: Some main facts and implications. In United Nations, *The Population Debate: Dimensions and Perspectives,* Vol. 1 (pp. 220–236). New York: United Nations.

Streeten, Paul (1975). Industrialization in a unified development strategy. *World Development, 3,* 1–9.

Streeten, Paul (1979). Development ideas in historical perspective. In Albert O. Hirschman (ed.), *Toward a New Strategy for Development* (pp. 21–52). New York: Pergamon.

Streeten, Paul (1982). Approaches to a new international economic order. *World Development, 10,* 1–17.

Streeten, Paul, and Burki, Shahid Javed (1978). Basic needs: Some issues. *World Development, 6,* 411–421.

Streeten, Paul, with Burki, Shahid Javed, Haq, Mahbub ul, Hicks, Norman, and Stewart, Frances (1981). *First Things First: Meeting Basic Human Needs in the Developing Countries.* New York: Oxford University Press (for the World Bank).

Stromquist, Nelly (1984). Action–research: A new sociological approach in developing countries. *IDRC Reports, 12,* 24–25.

Stryker, Richard E. (1979). The World Bank and agricultural development: Food production and rural poverty. *World Development, 7,* 325–336.

Stycos, J. Mayone (1977). Population policy and development. *Population and Development Review, 3,* 103–112.

Szekely, Deborah (1985). The president's report. *Annual Report 1985.* Rosslyn, Virginia: Inter-American Foundation.

Szentes, Tamas (1977). The main theoretical questions of "underdevelopment." In Jozsef Nyilas (ed.), *Theory and Practice of Development in the Third World* (pp. 13–156). Budapest: A. W. Sijthoff/Akademiai Kiado.

Szentes, Tamas (1980). Least development in the context and theory of underdevelopment. In Leonard Berry and Robert W. Kates (ed.s), *Making the Most of the Least: Alternative Ways to Development* (pp. 25–37). New York: Holmes and Meier.

Tabah, Leon (1980). World population trends, a stocktaking. *Population and Development Review, 6,* 355–389.

Taeuber, Irene (1975). Ancient and emerging questions. In John F. Kantner and Lee McCaffrey (eds.), *Population and Development in Southeast Asia* (pp. 317–323). Lexington, Massachusetts: D. C. Heath.

Talbot, Lee M. (1986). Demographic factors in resource depletion and environmental degradation in East African rangeland. *Population and Development Review, 12,* 441–451.

Taylor, Carl E., Newman, Jeanne S., and Kelly, Narindar U. (1976). The child survival hypothesis. *Population Studies, 30,* 263–278.

Taylor, John G. (1979). *From Modernization to Modes of Production: A Critique of the Sociologies of Development and Underdevelopment.* London: Macmillan.

Taylor, Lance (1981). The costly arms trade. *New York Times,* December 22, A30.

Teitelbaum, Michael S. (1974). Population and development: Is a consensus possible? *Foreign Affairs, 52,* 742–760.

Teitelbaum, Michael S. (1975). Relevance of demographic transition theory for developing countries. *Science, 188,* 420–425.

Thompson, W. Scott (ed.) (1983). *The Third World: Premises of U.S. Policy.* San Francisco: ICS Press.

Timmer, C. Peter (1982). Review of Julian L. Simon, *The Ultimate Resource. Population and Development Review, 8,* 163–168.

Tinbergen, Jan (1975). Demographic development and the exhaustion of natural resources. *Population and Development Review, 1,* 23–32.

Tinker, Irene (1976). The adverse impact of development on women. In Irene Tinker and Michele Bo Bramsen (eds.), *Women and World Development* (pp. 22–34). Washington, D.C.: Overseas Development Council.

Tinker, Irene, and Bramsen, Michele Bo (1976). An overview of the major concerns of the seminar. In Irene Tinker and Michele Bo Bramsen (eds.), *Women and World Development* (pp. 141–146). Washington, D.C.: Overseas Development Council.

Todaro, Michael P. (1977a). *Economic Development in the Third World: An Introduction to Problems and Policies in a Global Perspective.* New York: Longman.

Todaro, Michael P. (1977b). Development policy and population growth: A framework for planners. *Population and Development Review, 3,* 23–43.

Todaro, Michael P. (1980). The influence of education on migration and fertility. In John

Simmons (ed.), *The Education Dilemma: Policy Issues for Developing Countries in the 1980s* (pp. 179–186). Oxford, England: Pergamon.

Todaro, Michael P., with Stilkind, Jerry (1981). *City Bias and Rural Neglect: The Dilemma of Urban Development.* New York: Population Council.

Torsten, Husen (1980). Foreword. In John Simmons (ed.), *The Education Dilemma: Policy Issues for Developing Countries in the 1980s* (pp. xiii–xiv). Oxford, England: Pergamon.

Turchi, Boone A. (1975). Microeconomic theories of fertility: A critique. *Social Forces, 54,* 107–125.

United Nations (1981a). *The Mapping of Interrelationships between Population and Development.* New York: United Nations (ST/ESA/SER.R/43).

United Nations (1981b). *The Work of the Task Force on Inter-relationships between Population and Development.* New York: United Nations (ESA/P/WP.76).

United Nations Fund for Population Activities (1978). *Population and Mutual Self-Reliance,* Population Profiles No. 12. New York: United Nations Fund for Population Activities.

United Nations Fund for Population Activities (1985). *UNFPA 1984.* New York: United Nations Fund for Population Activities.

United Nations Population Division (1983). Department of International Economic and Social Affairs, *Concise Report on the Fifth Inquiry among Governments: Monitoring of Government Perceptions and Policies on Demographic Trends and Levels in Relation to Development as of 1982.* New York: United Nations (E/CN.9/1984/3).

United Nations Population Division (1984). Integration of population and development policies: A comparison of the developing regions of the world. In Economic and Social Commission for Asia and the Pacific, *Third Asian and Pacific Population Conference (Colombo, September 1982)* (pp. 140–148). New York: United Nations.

United Nations Secretariat (1984). Population, resources, environment and development: Highlights of the issues in the context of the world population plan of action. In U.N. Department of International Economic and Social Affairs, *Population, Resources, Environment and Development* (pp. 63–95), Population Studies No. 90. New York: Department of International Economic and Social Affairs, United Nations (ST/ESA/SER. A/90).

United States Agency for International Development (1982). *Women in Development.* Washington, D.C.: USAID.

Uphoff, Norman T., and Ilchman, Warren F. (1972). Development in the perspective of political economy. In Norman T. Uphoff and Warren F. Ilchman (eds.), *The Political Economy of Development* (pp. 75–121). Berkeley: University of California Press.

Uri, Pierre (1976). *Development with Dependence.* New York: Praeger.

Urzua, Raul (1978). Social science research on population and development in Latin America. Appendix 11 to Carmen A. Miro and Joseph E. Potter, *Population Policy: Research Priorities in the Developing World.* London: Frances Pinter, 1980 (reproduced from El Colegio de Mexico edition, Mexico City, 1978).

Urzua, Raul (1985). The use of demographic knowledge for policies and planning in developing countries/problems and issues. *International Union for the Scientific Study of Population Newsletter No. 23-24,* pp. 99–120.

Valenzuela, J. Samuel, and Valenzuela, Arturo (1981). Modernization and dependence: Alternative perspectives in the study of Latin American development. In Jose J. Villamil (ed.), *Transnational Capitalism and National Development* (pp. 31–65). Atlantic Highlands, New Jersey: Humanities Press.

Van Den Bergh, G. Van Benthem (1979). The past and future of development studies. In Institute of Social Studies, *Development of Societies: The Next Twenty-Five Years* (pp. 46–50). The Hague: Martinus Nijhoff.

Van de Walle, Francine (1986). Infant mortality and the European demographic transition. In Ansley J. Coale and Susan Cotts Watkins (eds.), *The Decline of Fertility in Europe* (pp. 201–233). Princeton, New Jersey: Princeton University Press.

Vanek, Joann, Johnston, Robert, and Seltzer, William (1985). Improving statistics on women, *Populi, 12,* 57–66.

Vinovskis, Maris A. (1984). Historical perspectives on rural development and human fertility in nineteenth-century America. In Wayne A. Schutjer and C. Shannon Stokes (eds.), *Rural Development and Human Fertility* (pp. 77–96). New York: Macmillan.

Ward, F. Champion (1974). The age of innocence. In F. Champion Ward (ed.), *Education and Development Reconsidered: The Bellagio Conference Papers* (pp. xv–xxii). New York: Praeger.

Ware, Helen (1978). Population and development in Africa south of the Sahara. Appendix 7A to Carmen A. Miro and Joseph E. Potter, *Population Policy: Research Priorities in the Developing World.* London: Frances Pinter, 1980 (reproduced from El Colegio de Mexico edition, Mexico City, 1978).

Warren, Bill (1979). The postwar economic experience of the Third World. In Albert O. Hirschman (ed.), *Toward a New Strategy for Development* (pp. 144–168). New York: Pergamon.

Warwick, Donald P. (1982). *Bitter Pllls: Population Policies and Their Implementation in Eight Developing Countries.* Cambridge, England: Cambridge University Press.

Warwick, Donald P. (1986). Review of Donald J. Hernandez, *Success or Failure? Family Planning Programs in the Third World. Contemporary Sociology, 15,* 237–239.

Watkins, Susan Cotts (1986). Conclusions. In Ansley J. Coale and Susan Cotts Watkins (eds.), *The Decline of Fertility in Europe* (pp. 420–449). Princeton, New Jersey: Princeton University Press.

Watson, Walter, Rosenfield, Allan, Viravaidya, Mechai, and Chanawongse, Krasae (1979). Health, population, and nutrition: Interrelations, problems, and possible solutions. In Philip M. Hauser (ed.), *World Population and Development* (pp. 145–173). Syracuse, New York: Syracuse University Press.

Wattenberg, Ben J., and Zinsmeister, Karl (eds.) (1985). *Are World Population Trends a Problem?* Washington, D.C.: American Enterprise Institute.

Weeks, John (1975). Imbalance between the centre and the periphery and the "employment crisis" in Kenya. In Ivar Oxaal, Tony Barnett, and David Booth (eds.), *Beyond the Sociology of Development: Economy and Society in Latin America and Africa* (pp. 86–104). London: Routledge and Kegan Paul.

Weller, Robert H. (1984). The gainful employment of females and fertility with special reference to rural areas of developing countries. In Wayne A. Schutjer and C. Shannon Stokes (eds.), *Rural Development and Human Fertility* (pp. 151–171). New York: Macmillan.

WHO/UNICEF (1978). *Primary Health Care: Alma-Ata 1978.* Geneva: World Health Organization.

Whyte, Martin King (1978). *The Status of Women in Preindustrial Societies.* Princeton, New Jersey: Princeton University Press.

Wilczynski, J. (1976). *The Multinationals and East–West Relations: Towards Transideological Collaboration.* Boulder, Colorado: Westview.

Williams, Maurice J. (1981). The nature of the world food and population problem. In Richard G. Woods (ed.), *Future Dimensions of World Food and Population* (pp. 5–34). Boulder, Colorado: Westview.

Winikoff, Beverly, and Brown, George (1980). Nutrition, population and health: Theoretical and practical issues. *Social Science and Medicine, 14C,* 171–176.

Wolf, Margery (1985). *Revolution Postponed: Women in Contemporary China.* Stanford, California: Stanford University Press.

Wolfe, Marshall (1977). Preconditions and propositions for "another development." *CEPAL Review*, pp. 41–65 (United Nations E.77.II.G.5).

Wolfe, Marshall (1979). Reinventing development: Utopias devised by committees and seeds of change in the real world. *CEPAL Review*, pp. 7–39 (United Nations E.79.II.G.2).

Wong, Aline K. (1974). Women in China: Past and present. In Carolyn J. Matthiasson (ed.), *Many Sisters: Women in Cross-Cultural Perspective* (pp. 229–259). New York: Free Press.

Wood, Robert E. (1984). Development ledger. *Contemporary Sociology, 13,* 700–702.

World Bank (1983). *Report: News and Views from the World Bank.* Washington, D.C.: World Bank.

World Bank (1984). *The World Bank Annual Report 1984.* Washington, D.C.: World Bank.

World Bank (1985a). *The World Bank Annual Report 1985.* Washington, D.C.: World Bank.

World Bank (1985b). *The World Bank and International Finance Corporation.* Washington, D.C.: World Bank.

World Population Conference (1975). World population plan of action. *Population and Development Review, 1,* 163–181.

Worsley, Peter (1984). *The Three Worlds: Culture and World Development.* Chicago: University of Chicago Press.

Wortman, Sterling (1976). Food and agriculture. *Scientific American, 235,* 30–29.

Wray, Joe D. (1971). Population pressure on families: Family size and child spacing. In National Academy of Sciences, *Rapid Population Growth: Consequences and Policy Implications* (pp. 403–461). Baltimore: Johns Hopkins University Press (for the National Academy of Sciences).

Wulf, Deirdre, and Klitsch, Michael (1986). Population growth and economic development: Two new U.S. Perspectives. *Family Planning Perspectives, 18,* 181–184.

Wulf, Deirdre, and Willson, Peters D. (1984). Global politics in Mexico City. *Family Planning Perspectives, 16,* 228–232.

Youssef, Nadia H. (1974). *Women and Work in Developing Societies,* Population Monograph Series No. 15. Berkeley: University of California.

Youssef, Nadia H. (1976). Women in development: Urban life and labor. In Irene Tinker and Michele Bo Bramsen (eds.), *Women and World Development* (pp. 70–77). Washington, D.C.: Overseas Development Council.

Zachariah, K. C. (1983). Kerala: Solution or happenstance? *Populi, 10,* 3–15.

Zeidenstein, George (1984). The president's message. *The Population Council 1984 Annual Report,* pp. 4–9. New York: Population Council.

Zeidenstein, Sondra (1979). Introduction. *Studies in Family Planning, 10,* 309–312.

Index

Population growth (*Cont.*)
  constraints on agricultural production,
      208
  development policies and, 140–141
  differences in research attention to de-
      terminants and consequences of,
      206–207
  econometric models of interactions of
      development and, 206
  effects on development gains, 130–131
  effects on development of human cap-
      ital, 130, 208–209
  effects on economic disparities be-
      tween developed and less-devel-
      oped countries, 208
  effects on economic growth, 207–208
  effects on education, 130
  effects on international and political
      stability, 208, 209
  effects of labor-intensive methods on,
      155–156
  effects of resource policies and prac-
      tices on, 155–156
  inadequate data base for interre-
      lationships between development
      and, 205, 214
  income gap between developed and
      less-developed countries and,
      231nn6,7
  interelationships of development sec-
      tors and, 149
  knowledge base regarding effects of,
      230–231n5
  lack of dominant theory on interre-
      lationships between development
      and, 205
  lists of perceived consequences of,
      208–209
  middle-range theories on determi-
      nants and consequences of, 224
  momentum and, 107–108, 109
  "new population debate" and, 133
  polar views of effects of, 132
  poverty and, 106–108, 109, 114–115n7
  as principal cause of development
      problems, 208
  projections of, 108–109
  requirements for explanatory theory
      on development and, 223–224
  revisionist approaches to, 209–210
  selective interventions and, 140

Population growth (*Cont.*)
  short-run and long-run effects of, 132
  structural poverty and, 174–175
  technological progress and, 131–132
  See also Fertility; Fertility decline
Population policy analysis
  assessment of performance of, 227–
      228, 233n19
  constraints on coordination with de-
      velopment planning, 228–230
  differences in time frames of develop-
      ment planning and, 229
  implementation in development plan-
      ning, 227–228, 232n17
  as intermediate to development objec-
      tives, 228–229
  knowledge base required for, 229–230
  lack of access to budget allocation au-
      thority, 229
  local administrative arrangements for,
      226–227
  organizational arrangements for coor-
      dination with development plan-
      ning, 227–228
  principal tasks of, 228
  suggested research agendas for,
      232n16
  units established in less-developed
      country planning organizations,
      227–228
Population projections, global carrying
      capacity and, 174
Portes, Alejandro, and Benton, Lauren,
      112
Potter, Joseph E., 143, 212, 225
Poverty
  development policies and, 113
  explanations for persistence of, 50–51
  increases and decreases in the less-
      developed countries, 50
  incremental approaches to reduction
      of, 218
  lack of equity and, 42–43n12
  programs in less-developed countries
      to reduce, 51–52
  structural definition of, 50
Powers, Mary G., 181–182
Preston, Samuel H., 163, 164, 167–168
Primary health care
  basic-needs approach and, 172
  components of, 172

Women (*Cont.*)
  opportunity cost of children and, 186–187
  powerlessness in effecting policy changes, 179, 180
  representation in planning agencies, 179
  requirements for access to resources, 184, 186
  requirements for gender equality, 185–186
  role-incompatibility hypothesis and fertility, 187–188
  role incompatibility and status of, 203–204$n7$
  rural development and opportunities for nonagricultural employment of, 186
  socioeconomic indicators and access to resources, 189–190
World Bank, 75, 177$n2$, 207, 216
  assessments of, 83–84
  basic-needs approach and, 34–35
  "credit-worthiness" of less-developed countries and, 81–82
  growth with equity approach and, 41
  history of, 81

World Bank (*Cont.*)
  International Development Association and, 80, 82–83, 219
  International Finance Corporation and, 81, 89
  loans to middle-income and low-income countries, 81–82, 83
  member governments and, 83
  nature of lending operations, 81–82
  poverty-focused development perspectives and, 82–83, 89$n17$
  priorities in lending, 89$n17$
  sources of income, 81
World Fertility Survey, 137
World Health Organization/UNICEF, 172
World Population Plan of Action (WPPA), 227
World Population Conference (1974), 1, 140

Yugoslavia, 218

Zachariah, K. C., 217